D0500927

Better Homes and Gardens®

Eat Healthy, Lose Weight
Volume 1

Meredith® Consumer Marketing
Des Moines, Iowa

Better Homes and Gardens®
Eat Healthy, Lose Weight, Volume 1

Meredith Corporation Consumer Marketing
Vice President, Consumer Marketing: David Ball
Consumer Product Marketing Director: Kathi Prien
Consumer Product Marketing Manager: Amanda Werts
Business Manager: Todd Voss
Associate Director, Production: Douglas M. Johnston

Waterbury Publications, Inc.
Editorial Director: Lisa Kingsley
Associate Editor: Tricia Laning
Creative Director: Ken Carlson
Associate Design Director: Doug Samuelson
Contributing Editor: Lois White
Contributing Designer: Chad Jewell
Contributing Copy Editors: Terri Fredrickson,
    Gretchen Kauffman, Margaret Smith
Contributing Indexer: Elizabeth Parson

Better Homes and Gardens® **Magazine**
Editor in Chief: Gayle Goodson Butler
Deputy Editor, Food and Entertaining: Nancy Hopkins

Meredith Publishing Group
President: Jack Griffin
Executive Vice President: Andy Sareyan
Vice President, Manufacturing: Bruce Heston

Meredith Corporation
Chairman of the Board: William T. Kerr
President and Chief Executive Officer: Stephen M. Lacy

In Memoriam: E. T. Meredith III (1933–2003)

Copyright © 2009 by Meredith Corporation,
Des Moines, Iowa.
First Edition. All rights reserved.
Printed in the United States of America.
ISSN: 1949-2227
ISBN: 978-0-696-24407-0

All of us at Meredith® Consumer Marketing are dedicated
to providing you with the information and ideas you need
to create delicious foods. We welcome your comments and
suggestions. Write to us at: Meredith Consumer Marketing,
1716 Locust St., Des Moines, IA 50309-3023.

Pictured on the cover: Tortilla-Crusted Chicken, page 141

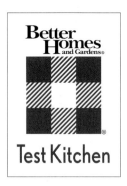

Test Kitchen

Our seal assures you that every
recipe in *Eat Healthy, Lose Weight,*
Volume 1 has been tested in the
Better Homes and Gardens® Test
Kitchen. This means that each recipe
is practical and reliable, and meets
our high standards of taste appeal.
We guarantee your satisfaction with
this book for as long as you own it.

CONTENTS

**Grain Pancakes with
Strawberry Sauce, Page 22**

**Lime-Marinated Flank Steak,
Page 117**

**Chocolate Cream Cheese Pie,
Page 240**

THIS IS "DIET" FOOD?

People always want to know which foods will help them drop weight quickly. Since there are no magic foods, the answer to all the dieters out there is to eat foods that offer the most nutrients and are the least processed. Do that and you'll automatically be eating fewer calories than if you ate high-calorie processed foods that fill you out but don't fill you up.

That simple guideline was used to create the more than 260 delicious recipes in *Eat Healthy, Lose Weight*. The goal was to develop recipes that include wholesome, basic ingredients, including whole grains, lean protein, nutrient-rich fruits and vegetables, and healthful fats. All of the recipes were developed and tested by registered dietitians in the Better Homes and Gardens® Test Kitchen to ensure that each one is delicious and satisfying. The finished dishes were so good that many of the taste testers couldn't believe these were "diet" foods.

As an added bonus, you'll find a shortcut dinner chapter for those times when you need a superfast meal. Although those recipes contain convenience foods, they use the best of the bunch, including frozen vegetable blends, vegetarian products, and spice blends.

And since many of you eat out and wish you could enjoy those same flavors at home, this book contains a chapter featuring restaurant entrées. Now you can re-create your favorite foods from some of the most popular chain restaurants in a version that's lower in calories, fat, and sodium. (Yes, the healthier versions still taste great!)

Why live on grapefruit and celery sticks while dieting when you could be eating BBQ Chicken Pizza and Blue Cheese Burgers? Welcome to *Eat Healthy, Lose Weight*—a dieter's best friend. Get cooking, lose weight, and feel great!

Chapter 1
Eat for Health

EAT FOR HEALTH.

Remember the grapefruit diet? How about the cabbage soup diet? These diets worked for a while because you were limited to eating only a few foods—which meant that your calories each day were extremely low. These diets also lacked important nutrients and left many people feeling tired and sick. Dieters did lose weight but quickly gained it back when they started eating regular food again.

As a dieter today, you don't want to live on grapefruit. You want to eat foods that are good for you but also lead to weight loss. You want to have energy and feel good even though you are dieting. In this book you'll find foods that let you lose weight and eat healthfully. When you've reached your goal and just want to maintain your weight, you'll find that this cookbook is perfect for everyday family meals. The recipes may be lower in calories and fat, but they aren't your typical diet foods. You'll find lots of pizzas, burgers, soups, pasta dishes, and desserts. A restaurant chapter even helps you re-create those favorite dishes at home—without all the calories and fat.

The Eat-Well Food Groups

Thinking back to your elementary school days, you may remember the four food groups poster hanging on the wall. Now those four food groups have been placed into a food pyramid. In addition to the four food groups of grains, dairy, fruits, and vegetables, the pyramid includes a new category for oils.

Although the pyramid includes the original food groups, the guidelines on what to eat within each group have changed. For instance, instead of a slice of white bread or a cup of regular pasta, guidelines

now recommend that you choose a hearty, whole grain bread and a cup of whole grain, high-fiber pasta. In this cookbook, the basic yet updated food groups are called the Eat Well Food Groups. Why? Because they remind you that not all foods are created equal. Some are better than others. When you are trying to lose or maintain your weight, choosing the best foods is even more important. If you only have a limited number of calories each day, you want to get the most nutrition you can out of those calories. The Eat Well Food Groups can help guide you to the best choices.

Great for Dieters!

You may have heard a lot about whole grains recently. The media are talking about them. Nutrition professionals are promoting them. And food companies are adding them to as many products as they can. Whole grains are high in fiber to help you feel full, making them perfect for dieters. They also have iron and B vitamins, as well as other important nutrients. Whole grains help to control blood glucose levels and reduce your risk of heart disease, among many other health benefits.

What exactly are whole grains? Basically they are grains that haven't been stripped of their outer coat. Still confused? A grain, such as wheat, has several layers to it. The outer layers have fiber and various nutrients that may be brown in color and rough in texture. Food manufacturers sometimes strip that layer off the grain, leaving only the inside layers, which are smooth in texture and lighter in color. You can see and taste the difference when you eat a slice of soft white bread versus a slice of 100% whole wheat bread. The whole wheat slice has a grainier texture and darker color. Examples of whole grains include whole wheat flour (and products made with it), oatmeal, brown rice, wild rice, quinoa (pronounced KEEN-wa), and popcorn.

Many people grew up on soft white bread and other refined grains, so they prefer those over whole grain varieties. As research continues to show the benefits of whole grains, manufacturers are working hard to include whole grains in products and also preserve some qualities of the original refined products, as you'll see in whole grain white breads.

If you're a fan of white bread and other refined grains, it's time to give whole grains a try. Start with products that aren't too far from what you're used to, such as a whole grain white bread or multigrain pasta. Then as you get used to the taste and texture of whole grains, add more of them to your diet.

DON'T FORGET FIBER!

Most people are far from meeting their fiber needs. You need 25–35 grams a day, but if your diet lacks whole grains and is low in fruits and vegetables, you probably don't come near that recommended range. Check labels and you'll quickly learn which foods are highest in fiber. Also eat plenty of fruits and vegetables, which are naturally high in fiber.

CHECK THE LABEL!

To search out whole grain products, don't just look at the front of the package. Go to the ingredient panel and make sure that the first or second ingredient says whole grain flour, whole oats, whole corn, etc. Also check the Nutrition Facts panel. If the product has 0–1 gram fiber per serving, it contains no or very little whole grains.

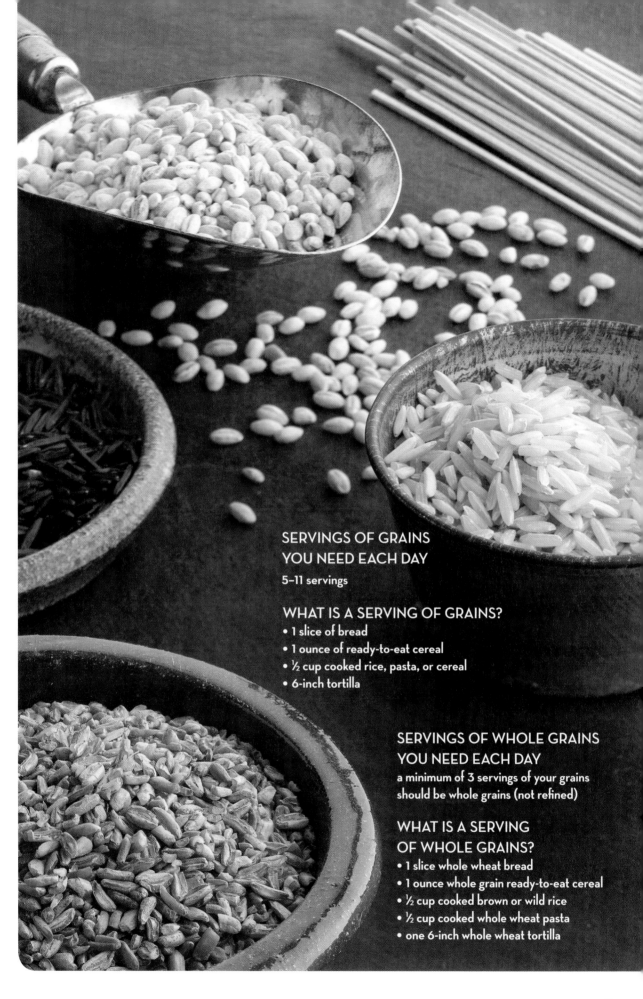

SERVINGS OF GRAINS YOU NEED EACH DAY

5–11 servings

WHAT IS A SERVING OF GRAINS?

- 1 slice of bread
- 1 ounce of ready-to-eat cereal
- ½ cup cooked rice, pasta, or cereal
- 6-inch tortilla

SERVINGS OF WHOLE GRAINS YOU NEED EACH DAY

a minimum of 3 servings of your grains should be whole grains (not refined)

WHAT IS A SERVING OF WHOLE GRAINS?

- 1 slice whole wheat bread
- 1 ounce whole grain ready-to-eat cereal
- ½ cup cooked brown or wild rice
- ½ cup cooked whole wheat pasta
- one 6-inch whole wheat tortilla

Are You Getting Enough?

Although the protein and dairy groups are separated on the food pyramid, many dairy foods are also high in protein. Both groups are discussed together here.

Protein Confusion

Many people worry that they aren't getting enough protein, but the truth is they probably get more protein than they need even when they're dieting. Protein is found in bread, milk, and many other foods, not just meat or fish, so it's easy to meet your needs.

As a dieter, you just need to know which proteins to eat and when to eat them. For maximum weight loss results, choose the leanest cuts of meat or choose naturally lean white meat chicken or fish. Add a little protein to each meal and you will feel full for longer since the body needs time to digest the protein. Between meals eat snacks that are mainly protein, such as some deli turkey or a small piece of low-fat cheese. Foods with protein are more satisfying than just a piece of fruit or some crackers.

Dairy: Last on Most Diets

Foods in the dairy group are often left out of diets. It's probably due to the calories and fat found in these foods, but with low-fat versions available, there's really no reason to leave this group out. Despite low-fat options, most diets either cut out dairy completely or suggest only 1 or 2 servings a day. But your body requires at least 3 servings to meet vital calcium needs. Of course, a calcium supplement is always an option, but since dairy foods also have protein, B vitamins, and other nutrients, you should think twice before eliminating them.

THE IMPORTANCE OF THE SUNSHINE VITAMIN

Recent studies have shown that people aren't getting enough vitamin D, the vitamin that's crucial for strong bones. Why? Because this vitamin isn't that easy to get. Milk is fortified with vitamin D, and it's the main source of vitamin D in our diets. But what if you don't drink milk? You also can get your body to make vitamin D if you expose your skin to about 20 minutes of sun each day. People in northern climates don't get much sun in the winter, so they could be vitamin D deficient. If you don't drink milk or get much sun, you may need a supplement.

DO YOU MEET YOUR CALCIUM NEEDS?

With all the talk about calcium, you would think we all get enough. But the majority of us still don't meet our needs, especially women. Calcium is found in most dairy products, and small amounts are in broccoli and dark, leafy greens. But lots of people don't like dairy products or can't eat them due to an allergy. And dieters often don't want to spend their limited calories on milk or other dairy products.

If dairy isn't in your diet, make sure you take a calcium supplement. But don't take all of your calcium at once. The body can absorb only a small amount at a time—no more than 500 mg—so be sure to divide up your calcium intake, from food or supplements, throughout the day.

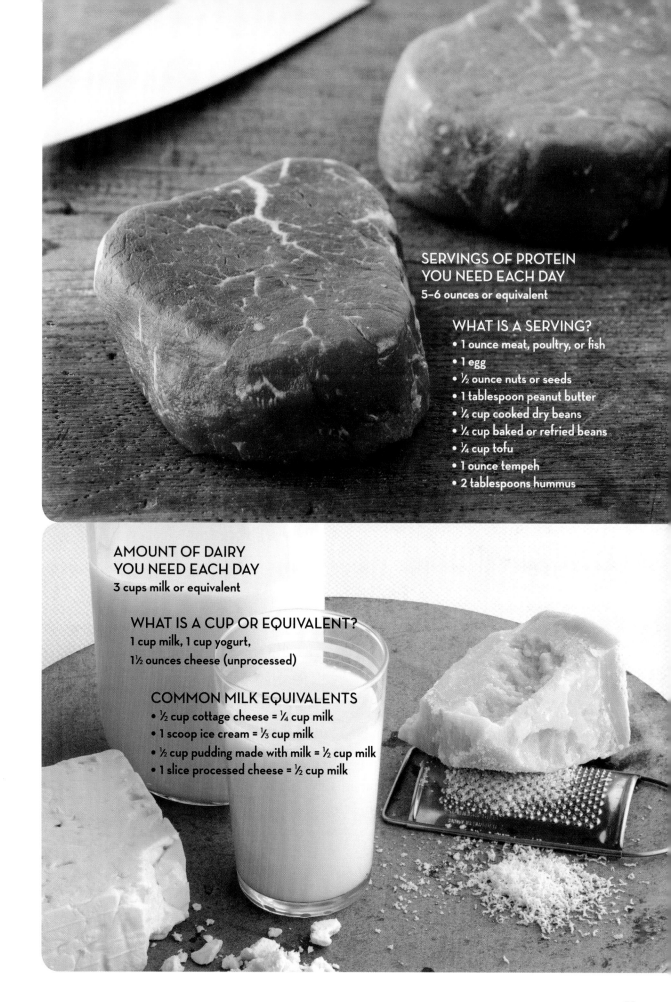

SERVINGS OF PROTEIN YOU NEED EACH DAY
5–6 ounces or equivalent

WHAT IS A SERVING?
- 1 ounce meat, poultry, or fish
- 1 egg
- ½ ounce nuts or seeds
- 1 tablespoon peanut butter
- ¼ cup cooked dry beans
- ¼ cup baked or refried beans
- ¼ cup tofu
- 1 ounce tempeh
- 2 tablespoons hummus

AMOUNT OF DAIRY YOU NEED EACH DAY
3 cups milk or equivalent

WHAT IS A CUP OR EQUIVALENT?
1 cup milk, 1 cup yogurt,
1½ ounces cheese (unprocessed)

COMMON MILK EQUIVALENTS
- ½ cup cottage cheese = ¼ cup milk
- 1 scoop ice cream = ⅓ cup milk
- ½ cup pudding made with milk = ½ cup milk
- 1 slice processed cheese = ½ cup milk

Add Color to Your Plate

Your mom always said to eat your fruits and veggies, right? But did she say which ones were best to eat? Sure, they are all good and eating a variety is best, but some fruits and vegetables are better than others. Iceberg lettuce, for example, is basically just water and a little fiber. You would be much better off eating dark green romaine and purple radicchio, which have more fiber and a lot more vitamins than plain old iceberg.

It's All About Color

When searching for the best fruits and vegetables, go for color. The latest research shows that those color pigments in fruits and vegetables are actually types of phytochemicals, a fancy word for nutrients that are believed to do everything from slowing the aging process to preventing cancer. There are many different types of phytochemicals, so eating a variety of foods from each color is your best bet for better health.

As a dieter, you need to sneak veggies in whenever you can. They are very low in calories, so you can fill up your plate with them. Starchier veggies, such as sweet potatoes, are also very filling, but they are higher in calories than other vegetables. Go ahead and enjoy them, but watch your serving sizes on the starchy vegetables.

Fruits are a great diet food too, but you need to watch the amounts. Fruit is high in natural sugar, making it higher in calories. Tropical fruits, such as mango or pineapple, are very high in sugar. You still can eat them, but the calories will add up quickly. Since most fruits are very sweet, they make the perfect diet dessert or snack.

Quick Color Guide

Which colors should you look for? Follow this quick guide. Try to eat from as many color groups as you can each day.

Green: kiwifruit, broccoli, Brussels sprouts, cabbage, avocado, green peppers, zucchini, leafy greens (spinach, kale)

Orange/Yellow: oranges, mangoes, cantaloupe, peaches, carrots, sweet potatoes, acorn squash, lemons, pineapple

Red: strawberries, pink grapefruit, watermelon, cranberries, tomatoes, red sweet peppers

Purple/Blue: grapes, plums, cherries, blueberries, raisins, eggplant, purple cabbage, beets

White: bananas, white peaches, garlic, onions, leeks, mushrooms, jicama, white potatoes, cauliflower

PRODUCE IN A PILL

Health food stores and supplement companies now sell pills that claim to have the same nutrients as a serving of fruit or vegetable. Some even claim to have multiple servings in one pill! Can that be? The answer is no. Fruits and vegetables are naturally very complex plants that can't be replicated in a single pill made in a laboratory. A pill may contain the same vitamins and minerals, but there are other nutrients—some we probably don't even know about yet—that make the real fruit or vegetable better than a pill.

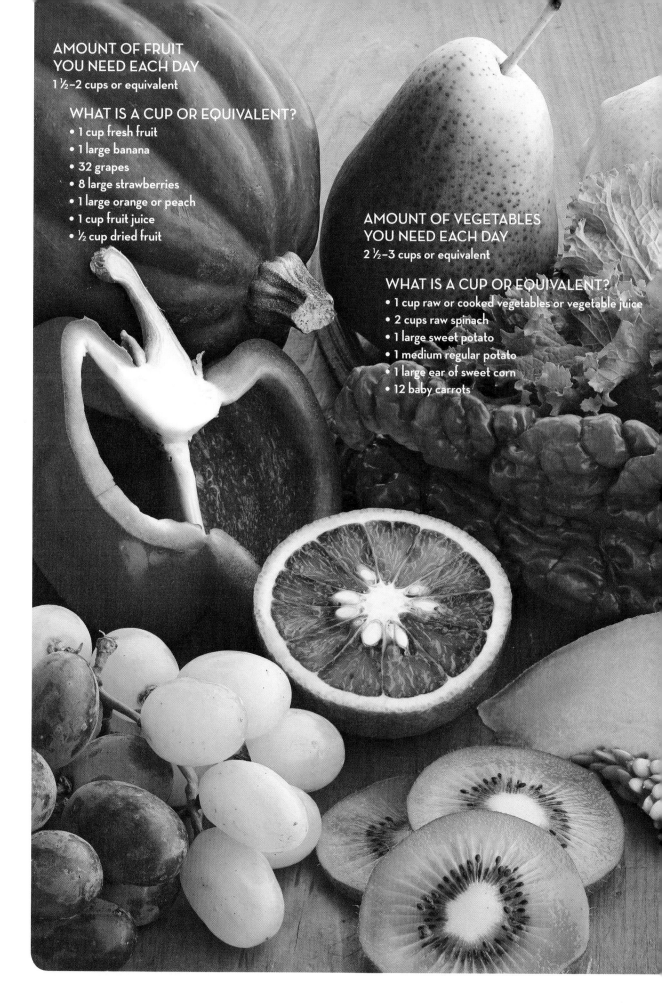

AMOUNT OF FRUIT YOU NEED EACH DAY
1½–2 cups or equivalent

WHAT IS A CUP OR EQUIVALENT?
- 1 cup fresh fruit
- 1 large banana
- 32 grapes
- 8 large strawberries
- 1 large orange or peach
- 1 cup fruit juice
- ½ cup dried fruit

AMOUNT OF VEGETABLES YOU NEED EACH DAY
2½–3 cups or equivalent

WHAT IS A CUP OR EQUIVALENT?
- 1 cup raw or cooked vegetables or vegetable juice
- 2 cups raw spinach
- 1 large sweet potato
- 1 medium regular potato
- 1 large ear of sweet corn
- 12 baby carrots

When is the last time you measured your plates?

If your plates are 10 years old, they are probably about 10 inches in diameter. If they are older than that, they might be 9 inches. If they are new, chances are your plates have a diameter of 12 or more inches. It's no coincidence that plate size has increased along with our waistlines. Nobody wants to eat from a half-empty plate of food. You want a nicely filled plate, especially if you paid good money for that food at a restaurant. If you think your home plates are big, restaurant plates are even bigger—more like platters than plates.

It's human nature to eat everything on your plate, even if you are full after eating just half.

That's why many diet books tell you to fill just the inner rim of your plate or to downsize to a plate that's a few inches smaller than the typical dinner plate.

Those are good ideas if you're eating at home, but if you eat out, you have to make a point of not eating the whole platterlike plateful, which is tough. Splitting a meal with a fellow diner is always an option. Or you could divide your plate in half as soon as you get it and eat only from one side. The trick is to make sure to stop as soon as you feel even a little bit full. Otherwise your natural habit to eat everything on your plate will take over.

PLATE CHECK

Still not convinced that the plate size is a big deal? Check out this visual. Each plate has a normal serving of spaghetti— 1 cup cooked pasta with ½ cup pasta sauce. Which serving looks most appealing?

8 ½-INCH PLATE

9¾-INCH PLATE

11 ¼-INCH PLATE

CHECK YOUR CUPS TOO!

Plates aren't the only serving pieces that have grown in size. Cups and glasses have too! Just look at the coffee cups below. The one on the left is a coffee cup today, which holds about 16 ounces. The one on the right is what was typical about 20 years ago. It holds 6 ounces. It's easy to see how calories add up fast with today's big cups and glasses. We may be drinking the same beverages as we did years ago, but now we're drinking twice the amount or more (and that means more calories!).

FOR MORE INFORMATION

Learn more about nutrition, portion sizes, and calorie control at these websites:

mypyramid.gov
Find the current USDA food pyramid, plus all kinds of interactive tools to help you plan your diet.

eatright.org
Find current nutrition news, advice on weight control, and other helpful tips at this website of the American Dietetic Association.

calorieking.com
Quickly look up calorie levels for thousands of foods at this site.

Think you're eating the right amount?

You could be eating three or four times what you really need. Check the difference in sizes of the following common foods. The first food in each photo shows a typical portion today. The second food shows what an actual serving should be. It's easy to see how your version of one serving actually could contain multiple portions. And with multiple portions, the calories add up quickly.

ORANGE JUICE

- 12 OUNCES (2 FRUIT SERVINGS)
  165 CALORIES
- 6 OUNCES (1 FRUIT SERVING)
  83 CALORIES

BAGEL

- 3.5 OUNCES (3 ½ GRAIN SERVINGS)
  250 CALORIES
- 2 OUNCES (2 GRAIN SERVINGS)
  140 CALORIES

CEREAL

- 2 ¼ CUPS (3 GRAIN SERVINGS)
  330 CALORIES
- 1 OUNCE OR ¾ CUP (1 GRAIN SERVING)
  110 CALORIES

APPLE

- 7 OUNCES (2 FRUIT SERVINGS)
  186 CALORIES
- 3 OUNCES (1 FRUIT SERVING)
  80 CALORIES

STEAK

- 12 OUNCES (3 MEAT SERVINGS)
  1,080 CALORIES
- 5 OUNCES (1½ MEAT SERVINGS)
  450 CALORIES

POTATO

- 9 OUNCES (2 VEGETABLE SERVINGS)
  350 CALORIES
- 4½ OUNCES (1 VEGETABLE SERVING)
  175 CALORIES

ICE CREAM

- 3 SCOOPS (1 MILK SERVING)
  450 CALORIES
- ONE ½-CUP SCOOP (⅓ MILK SERVING)
  150 CALORIES

CALORIE COUNT

Many dieters can roughly estimate the calories in food but don't know how many calories they should be eating in a day. Everyone is different, so it's easy to see why people get confused.

How can your friend, who seems to be the same size as you, eat more and not gain weight? It has to do with your activity level, your muscle mass, how much you fidget throughout the day, and your age, along with several other factors.

You can see how figuring this out can be complicated. Following is a basic calculation to help you ballpark your appropriate calorie level. Once you have that number, you can record what you eat for a few days and see how close your calorie intake is compared to what your body needs.

Eat less than what you need, you'll lose weight. Eat more and you'll gain weight. Or you can use up those extra calories by burning them off with exercise. It's a constant balancing act, but one that can be managed if you know your calorie needs and don't go over those limits.

Calculation

1. Take your weight in pounds and multiply by 10. This covers your basal metabolic needs—what you need to breathe and perform other basic bodily functions.
2. Add 10% for digestion. Eating and digesting food takes energy. The more often you eat, the harder your body has to work, which is why many diets suggest eating 5 mini meals a day rather than just 3 big meals.
3. Add 10% for light activity level. Add 20% for moderate activity level. Add 30% for high-intensity activity level. Activity level varies by person; larger people burn more calories than smaller people doing the same activity. So the add-on for activity calories is not precise,

but it works for the purpose of an estimate. If you move a little during the day doing basic household tasks, use the light activity number. If you stay fairly active all day and include a little exercise as well, go for moderate. If you do an intense workout each day or have a very active job, go for the 30% add-on.

Your Estimate of Total Calorie Needs

The calories you need are complex to calculate because there are other factors—besides activity level—that impact the number. These include your age and how much muscle you have. Your metabolism slows with age, meaning you need fewer calories, especially after age 30. Muscular people burn more calories than people who have a lot of fat. Since men are naturally more muscular, they tend to burn more calories than women.

The Weight-Loss Number

The number you calculated is the calorie amount you need to maintain your weight. To lose a pound of body weight, you need a deficit of 3,500 calories. So to lose a pound a week, you could either eat 500 fewer calories a day or burn off those 500 calories each day with exercise. To lose weight faster than that, you would need to shave off even more calories from your diet (or exercise more). But don't take your calories too low. Your body will think it's starving and will slow down your metabolism—something you don't want when trying to lose weight.

Breakfast

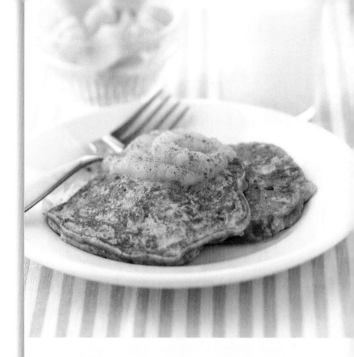

1	cooking apple (such as Jonathan or Granny Smith), cored and finely chopped (about ¾ cup)
1	teaspoon lemon juice
¾	cup whole wheat flour
1	tablespoon sugar
1	teaspoon baking powder
¼	teaspoon apple pie spice or ground cinnamon
⅛	teaspoon salt
¾	cup fat-free milk
1	egg white
2	tablespoons canola oil
	Nonstick cooking spray
1	cup unsweetened applesauce
⅛	teaspoon apple pie spice or ground cinnamon
	Apple pie spice or ground cinnamon (optional)
	Fresh fruit (optional)

Apple Griddle Cakes

PREP: 25 minutes

COOK: 2 minutes per batch

NUTRITION FACTS per serving:

- -

CALORIES 214
TOTAL FAT 7 g (1 g sat. fat)
CHOLESTEROL 1 mg
PROTEIN 6 g
CARBOHYDRATE 34 g
FIBER 4 g
SODIUM 169 mg

EXCHANGES 1.5 Starch, 0.5 Fruit, 1 Fat

1 In a small bowl combine apple and lemon juice; set aside. In a medium bowl combine whole wheat flour, sugar, baking powder, ¼ teaspoon apple pie spice, and salt. In another small bowl combine milk, egg white, and oil; beat with a rotary beater or wire whisk.

2 Add milk mixture all at once to flour mixture; stir just until moistened (batter should be lumpy). Gently fold in apple mixture.

3 Coat an unheated griddle or heavy nonstick skillet with nonstick cooking spray. Preheat over medium heat until a few drops of water dance across the surface. For each pancake, pour a scant ¼ cup batter onto the hot griddle; spread batter into a 3- to 4-inch circle.

4 Cook for 1 to 2 minutes on each side or until pancakes are golden brown, turning when pancake surfaces are bubbly and edges are slightly dry. In a small bowl stir together applesauce and ⅛ teaspoon apple pie spice; serve with pancakes.

5 If desired, sprinkle with additional apple pie spice. If desired, serve with fresh fruit. Makes 4 (2-pancake) servings.

1 cup all-purpose flour

⅓ cup yellow cornmeal

⅓ cup quick-cooking rolled oats

2 tablespoons packed brown sugar

1½ teaspoons baking powder

¼ teaspoon salt

1 egg

1 cup fat-free milk

2 tablespoons canola oil

Nonstick cooking spray

4 cups fresh strawberries, hulled

1 tablespoon granulated sugar

1 teaspoon vanilla

Grain Pancakes with Strawberry Sauce

START TO FINISH: 25 minutes

NUTRITION FACTS per serving:

CALORIES 242

TOTAL FAT 6 g (1 g sat. fat)

CHOLESTEROL 36 mg

PROTEIN 6 g

CARBOHYDRATE 40 g

FIBER 3 g

SODIUM 192 mg

EXCHANGES 2 Starch, 0.5 Fruit, 1 Fat

1 In a medium bowl combine flour, cornmeal, rolled oats, brown sugar, baking powder, and salt. Make a well in the center of the flour mixture; set aside.

2 In a small bowl combine egg, milk, and oil; beat with a fork or whisk until combined. Add the egg mixture all at once to the flour mixture. Stir just until moistened (batter should be lumpy).

3 Lightly coat an unheated griddle or large skillet with nonstick cooking spray. Preheat griddle over medium heat. For each pancake, pour a scant ¼ cup of the batter onto the hot griddle. Spread each to a 3- to 3½-inch circle. Cook over medium heat for 1 to 2 minutes on each side or until pancakes are golden brown, turning to second sides when pancakes have bubbly surfaces and slightly dry edges.

4 Meanwhile, for sauce, in a blender or food processor combine 2 cups strawberries, granulated sugar, and vanilla. Cover and blend or process until smooth. Transfer to a small saucepan; heat sauce until warm. Quarter remaining 2 cups strawberries. Serve pancakes with sauce and berries. Makes 6 servings (2 pancakes per serving).

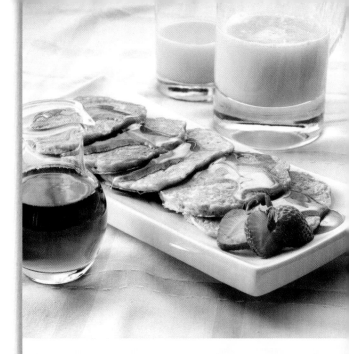

1¼   cups regular rolled oats
¾   cup all-purpose flour
½   cup whole wheat flour
1   tablespoon baking powder
¼   teaspoon salt
3   egg whites
2¼   cups buttermilk
2   tablespoons canola oil
2   tablespoons honey (optional)
1   teaspoon vanilla
     Nonstick cooking spray
     Bottled light pancake syrup
        (optional)

1 In a large bowl combine oats, all-purpose flour, whole wheat flour, baking powder, and salt. Make a well in the center of flour mixture; set aside.

2 In a medium bowl beat egg whites with a fork; stir in buttermilk, oil, honey (if desired), and vanilla. Add egg white mixture all at once to flour mixture. Stir just until moistened (batter should be lumpy). If you prefer softened oats, cover batter and allow to stand at room temperature for 15 to 30 minutes.

3 Coat an unheated griddle or heavy skillet with nonstick cooking spray. Preheat over medium-high heat. For each pancake, pour about ¼ cup of the batter onto the hot griddle or skillet. Spread batter into a circle about 4 inches in diameter. Cook over medium heat for 4 to 6 minutes or until the pancakes are golden, turning to cook second sides when pancakes have bubbly surfaces and edges are slightly dry. If desired, serve with syrup. Makes 8 servings (2 pancakes per serving).

Oat Pancakes

PREP: 25 minutes

COOK: 4 minutes per batch

NUTRITION FACTS per serving:

CALORIES 229
TOTAL FAT 6 g (1 g sat. fat)
CHOLESTEROL 3 mg
PROTEIN 10 g
CARBOHYDRATE 34 g
FIBER 4 g
SODIUM 257 mg

EXCHANGES 2 Starch, 0.5 Very Lean Meat, 1 Fat

NUTRITION NOTE

Whole wheat flour is made from the entire wheat grain—bran, germ, and endosperm—and has many more nutrients than refined flours, plus more fiber.

Breakfast Bread Pudding

PREP: 30 minutes   **BAKE:** 30 minutes
STAND: 15 minutes   **OVEN:** 325°F

NUTRITION FACTS per serving:

CALORIES 178
TOTAL FAT 4 g (1 g sat. fat)
CHOLESTEROL 107 mg
PROTEIN 9 g
CARBOHYDRATE 27 g
FIBER 3 g
SODIUM 179 mg

EXCHANGES 2 Starch, 0.5 Medium-Fat Meat

5   to 6 slices whole wheat cinnamon-swirl bread or cinnamon-raisin bread

   Nonstick cooking spray

1½ cups fat-free milk

3   eggs

2   tablespoons sugar

1   teaspoon vanilla

¼   teaspoon ground nutmeg

1   5½-ounce can apricot nectar or peach nectar (⅔ cup)

2   teaspoons cornstarch

1 Preheat oven to 325°F. Cut enough of the bread into cubes to make 4 cups. Place bread cubes in a shallow baking pan. Bake about 10 minutes or until bread is dry, stirring once. Cool on a wire rack.

2 Lightly coat six 6-ounce soufflé dishes or custard cups with nonstick cooking spray. Divide bread cubes among the prepared dishes. In a medium bowl combine milk, eggs, sugar, vanilla, and nutmeg; beat with a rotary beater or wire whisk. Pour milk mixture evenly over bread cubes. Press lightly with the back of a spoon to thoroughly moisten bread.

3 Place soufflé dishes in a 13×9×2-inch baking pan. Place baking pan on oven rack. Carefully pour hot tap water into the baking pan around dishes to a depth of 1 inch.

4 Bake for 30 to 35 minutes or until a knife inserted near centers comes out clean. Transfer dishes to a wire rack. Let stand for 15 minutes.

5 Meanwhile, for sauce, in a small saucepan gradually stir apricot nectar into cornstarch until combined. Cook and stir over medium heat until thickened and bubbly. Reduce heat. Cook and stir for 2 minutes more.

6 If desired, remove puddings from soufflé dishes. Spoon sauce over warm puddings. Makes 6 servings.

Make-Ahead Directions: Prepare as above through step 2. Place soufflé dishes in a 13×9×2-inch baking pan. Cover with plastic wrap. Chill overnight in the refrigerator. Uncover; add hot tap water to pan. Continue with steps 4 through 6.

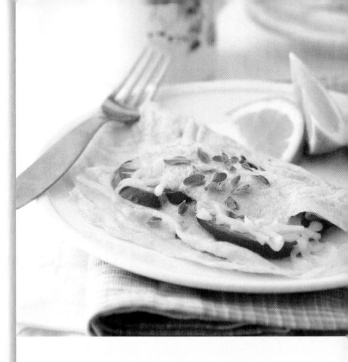

4	eggs
1/8	teaspoon salt
1/8	teaspoon black pepper
	Nonstick cooking spray
4	medium tomato slices
1/4	cup shredded reduced-fat mozzarella cheese (1 ounce)
1	teaspoon snipped fresh oregano or 1/4 teaspoon dried oregano, crushed

1 In a small bowl combine eggs, salt, and pepper; beat with a rotary beater or wire whisk. Coat an unheated 8-inch nonstick skillet with nonstick cooking spray. Preheat over medium heat. Pour half of the egg mixture into the hot skillet.

2 Using a wooden spoon or plastic spatula, immediately begin stirring egg mixture gently but continuously until mixture resembles small pieces of cooked egg surrounded by liquid egg. Stop stirring. Cook for 30 to 60 seconds more or until egg mixture is set but shiny.

3 Place two tomato slices on half of the egg mixture in skillet. Top with half of the mozzarella. Using a spatula, lift and fold opposite edge of the omelet over tomato slices. Sprinkle half of the oregano onto omelet. Transfer to a warm plate.

4 Repeat with remaining egg mixture, tomato, cheese, and oregano. Makes 2 servings.

COOK'S TIP

If you use fresh oregano in this recipe, select oregano that is bright green with no signs of wilting or yellowing. Oregano can be refrigerated in a plastic bag for up to three days.

Fresh Tomato Omelet with Mozzarella Cheese

START TO FINISH: 20 minutes

NUTRITION FACTS per serving:

CALORIES 228
TOTAL FAT 13 g (4 g sat. fat)
CHOLESTEROL 432 mg
PROTEIN 18 g
CARBOHYDRATE 11 g
FIBER 3 g
SODIUM 398 mg

EXCHANGES 2 Medium-Fat Meat, 2 Vegetable, 0.5 Fat

Omelet de Provence

START TO FINISH: 30 minutes

NUTRITION FACTS per serving:

- -

CALORIES 255
TOTAL FAT 16 g (6 g sat. fat)
CHOLESTEROL 436 mg
PROTEIN 21 g
CARBOHYDRATE 8 g
FIBER 2 g
SODIUM 422 mg

EXCHANGES 2.5 Lean Meat, 1.5 Vegetable, 1.5 Fat

Nonstick cooking spray
2 cups sliced fresh mushrooms
3 tablespoons sliced green onion
1 clove garlic, minced
4 eggs
¼ teaspoon herbes de Provence or dried thyme or basil, crushed
⅛ teaspoon salt
Dash black pepper
1 teaspoon olive oil
¼ cup shredded part-skim mozzarella cheese (1 ounce)
1 medium plum tomato, chopped
1 tablespoon finely shredded Asiago or Parmesan cheese
Snipped fresh parsley (optional)

1 Lightly coat an unheated 6- to 7-inch nonstick skillet with flared sides with nonstick cooking spray. Preheat skillet over medium heat. Add mushrooms, green onion, and garlic; cook and stir until mushrooms are tender. Using a slotted spoon, remove mushroom mixture from skillet; set aside. If necessary, drain skillet; carefully wipe out skillet with paper towels.

2 In a medium bowl combine eggs, herbes de Provence, salt, and pepper; beat with a rotary beater or wire whisk.

3 Add half of the oil to the skillet; heat skillet over medium heat. Pour half of the egg mixture into skillet. Using a wooden spoon or plastic spatula, immediately begin stirring the eggs gently but continuously until mixture resembles small pieces of cooked egg surrounded by liquid egg. Stop stirring. Cook for 30 to 60 seconds more or until egg mixture is set and shiny.

4 Sprinkle with half of the mozzarella cheese. Top with half of the mushroom mixture. Continue cooking until cheese just begins to melt. Using the spatula, lift and fold an edge of the omelet partially over filling. Remove from skillet; cover and keep warm.

5 Repeat with remaining oil, egg mixture, mozzarella cheese, and mushroom mixture. Top omelets with tomato, Asiago cheese, and, if desired, parsley. Makes 2 servings.

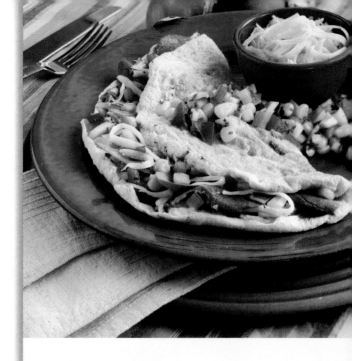

4	eggs
1	tablespoon snipped fresh cilantro
	Dash salt
	Dash ground cumin
	Nonstick cooking spray
¼	cup shredded Monterey Jack cheese with jalapeño chile peppers, reduced-fat cheddar cheese, or reduced-fat Swiss cheese (1 ounce)
¾	cup fresh baby spinach leaves
1	recipe Corn-Pepper Relish

1 In a medium bowl combine eggs, cilantro, salt, and cumin; beat with a rotary beater or wire whisk until frothy.

2 Coat an unheated 10-inch nonstick skillet with flared sides with nonstick cooking spray. Preheat skillet over medium-high heat.

3 Pour egg mixture into hot skillet; lower heat to medium. Using a wooden spoon or plastic spatula, immediately begin stirring the eggs gently but continuously until mixture resembles small pieces of cooked egg surrounded by liquid egg. Stop stirring. Cook for 30 to 60 seconds more or until egg mixture is set and shiny.

4 Sprinkle with cheese. Top with three-fourths of the spinach and half of the Corn-Pepper Relish. Using the spatula, lift and fold an edge of the omelet partially over filling. Top with remaining spinach and remaining Corn-Pepper Relish. Cut omelet in half; transfer omelet to warm plates. Makes 2 servings.

Corn-Pepper Relish: In a small bowl combine ¼ cup chopped red sweet pepper; ¼ cup loose-pack frozen whole kernel corn, thawed; 2 tablespoons chopped red onion; and 1 tablespoon snipped fresh cilantro.

Tex-Mex Spinach Omelet

START TO FINISH: 25 minutes

NUTRITION FACTS per serving:
- -

CALORIES 232
TOTAL FAT 15 g (6 g sat. fat)
CHOLESTEROL 438 mg
PROTEIN 17 g
CARBOHYDRATE 8 g
FIBER 1 g
SODIUM 322 mg

EXCHANGES 0.5 Starch, 2.5 Lean Meat, 0.5 Vegetable, 1.5 Fat

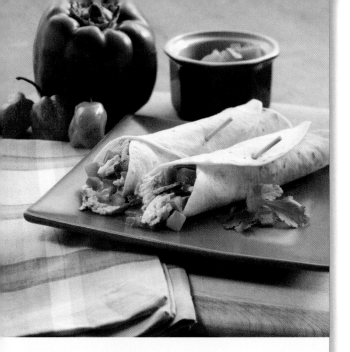

Breakfast Tortilla Wrap

START TO FINISH: 15 minutes

NUTRITION FACTS per serving:

CALORIES 248
TOTAL FAT 11 g (4 g sat. fat)
CHOLESTEROL 227 mg
PROTEIN 17 g
CARBOHYDRATE 17 g
FIBER 11 g
SODIUM 573 mg

EXCHANGES 1 Starch, 2 Medium-Fat Meat

Nonstick cooking spray
2 slices turkey bacon, chopped
¼ cup chopped green sweet pepper
¼ teaspoon ground cumin
⅛ teaspoon crushed red pepper
2 eggs
¼ cup chopped tomato
2 8-inch whole wheat flour tortillas, warmed*
Bottled salsa (optional)

1 Coat an unheated large nonstick skillet with nonstick cooking spray. Preheat over medium heat. Add bacon; cook until browned. Add sweet pepper, cumin, and crushed red pepper. Cook for 3 minutes, stirring occasionally.

2 In a small bowl lightly beat eggs with a fork. Add eggs to skillet; cook without stirring until eggs begin to set on the bottom and around edges. Using a spatula or wooden spoon, lift and fold the partially cooked egg mixture so the uncooked portion flows underneath. Continue cooking for 1 to 2 minutes or until egg mixture is cooked through but is still glossy and moist. Remove from heat. Stir in tomato. Spoon onto tortillas and roll up. If desired, secure with wooden picks. If desired, serve with salsa. Makes 2 servings.

*To warm tortillas, preheat oven to 350°F. Wrap tortillas tightly in foil; bake for 5 to 8 minutes or until warm. (Or wrap tortillas in white microwave-safe paper towels; microwave on 100% power [high] for 20 to 30 seconds or until tortillas are softened.)

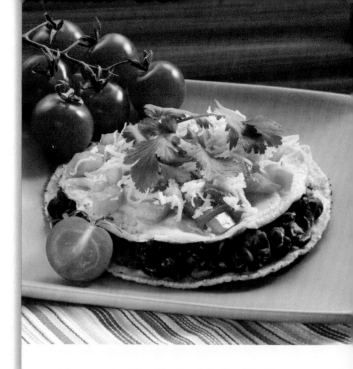

- 2   6-inch corn tortillas
- ½   cup canned black beans, rinsed and drained
- 2   eggs
- 1   tablespoon fat-free milk
- ⅛   teaspoon black pepper
-     Dash salt
-     Nonstick cooking spray
- ½   cup chopped tomato
- 2   tablespoons crumbled queso fresco or shredded Monterey Jack cheese
- 2   teaspoons snipped fresh cilantro
-     Fresh cilantro sprigs (optional)
-     Purchased chunky salsa (optional)

Southwestern Breakfast Tostadas

START TO FINISH: 20 minutes

1 Warm tortillas according to package directions. Meanwhile, in a small bowl use a potato masher or fork to slightly mash beans; set aside. In another small bowl or 1-cup glass measure combine eggs, milk, pepper, and salt; beat with a rotary beater or wire whisk.

2 Lightly coat an unheated medium nonstick skillet with nonstick cooking spray. Preheat over medium heat. Pour egg mixture into hot skillet. Cook, without stirring, until egg mixture begins to set on the bottom and around edge. With a spatula or large spoon, lift and fold the partially cooked egg mixture so the uncooked portion flows underneath. Cook for 2 to 3 minutes more or until egg mixture is cooked through but is still glossy and moist. Immediately remove from heat.

3 Spread one tortilla with mashed beans. Top with remaining tortilla, cooked egg mixture, tomato, cheese, and snipped cilantro. If desired, garnish with cilantro sprigs. If desired, serve with salsa. Serve immediately. Makes 2 servings.

NUTRITION FACTS per serving:

- -

CALORIES 213
TOTAL FAT 7 g (2 g sat. fat)
CHOLESTEROL 217 mg
PROTEIN 12 g
CARBOHYDRATE 26 g
FIBER 5 g
SODIUM 446 mg

EXCHANGES 2 Starch, 1 Lean Meat, 0.5 Fat

COOK'S TIP

Queso fresco, also known as queso blanco, is a fresh white Mexican cheese with a slightly salty, mild flavor. If you can't find it at the supermarket, try a local Mexican market.

Asparagus and Zucchini Frittata

PREP: 30 minutes **BAKE:** 40 minutes
STAND: 10 minutes **OVEN:** 350°F

NUTRITION FACTS per serving:

CALORIES 176
TOTAL FAT 9 g (3 g sat. fat)
CHOLESTEROL 353 mg
PROTEIN 15 g
CARBOHYDRATE 11 g
FIBER 3 g
SODIUM 527 mg

EXCHANGES 1.5 Medium-Fat Meat,
2 Vegetable

NUTRITION NOTE

Asparagus, which is at its best from
February to June, is one vegetable choice
for health-conscious consumers. Low in
calories, without fat and cholesterol, it
boasts potassium, fiber, and folic acid.

Nonstick cooking spray
1½ pounds fresh asparagus, trimmed
and cut into 1-inch-long pieces
1 medium yellow sweet pepper,
cut into strips
⅓ cup chopped onion
¼ cup bottled roasted red sweet
peppers, drained and chopped
1 small zucchini, halved lengthwise
and cut into ¼-inch-thick slices
(about 1 cup)
10 eggs
1 cup fat-free milk
2 tablespoons snipped fresh dill or
½ teaspoon dried dill
1 teaspoon salt
½ teaspoon black pepper
Fresh dill sprigs (optional)

1 Preheat oven to 350°F. Coat a 3-quart oval
or rectangular baking dish with nonstick
cooking spray; set aside.

2 In a large saucepan bring about 1 inch water
to boiling. Add asparagus, sweet pepper
strips, and onion. Return to boiling; reduce heat.
Cover and simmer about 1 minute or until crisp-
tender. Drain well. Stir in roasted red peppers.
Evenly spread asparagus mixture in prepared
baking dish. Layer zucchini slices on top.

3 In a large bowl beat eggs with a rotary
beater or wire whisk until combined. Beat
in milk, snipped or dried dill, salt, and black
pepper. Pour over vegetables in baking dish.
Bake, uncovered, for 40 to 45 minutes or until a
knife inserted near center comes out clean. Let
stand for 10 minutes before serving. If desired,
garnish with dill sprigs. Makes 6 servings.

Nonstick cooking spray

1 cup chopped cooked ham
(5 ounces)

½ cup sliced green onion or chopped
onion

½ cup chopped green or red
sweet pepper

6 eggs

¾ cup low-fat cottage cheese

⅛ teaspoon black pepper

2 plum tomatoes, thinly sliced

¼ cup shredded reduced-fat
cheddar cheese (1 ounce)

Sliced green onions (optional)

1 Preheat broiler. Lightly coat an unheated 10-inch ovenproof skillet with nonstick cooking spray. Preheat skillet over medium heat. Add ham, ½ cup green onion, and sweet pepper. Cook and stir about 4 minutes or until vegetables are tender and ham is lightly browned.

2 Meanwhile, in a medium bowl beat eggs with a rotary beater or wire whisk. Beat in cottage cheese and black pepper. Pour over ham mixture in skillet. Cook over medium-low heat. As egg mixture sets, run a spatula around the edge of the skillet, lifting egg mixture so the uncooked portion flows underneath. Continue cooking and lifting edge until egg mixture is almost set but still glossy and moist.

3 Broil 5 inches from heat for 1 to 2 minutes or until eggs are set. Arrange tomato slices on frittata. Sprinkle cheese over tomato. Broil for 1 minute more. If desired, garnish with additional green onions. Makes 6 servings.

Ham and Cheese Skillet

START TO FINISH: 25 minutes

NUTRITION FACTS per serving:

CALORIES 148
TOTAL FAT 7 g (3 g sat. fat)
CHOLESTEROL 228 mg
PROTEIN 16 g
CARBOHYDRATE 5 g
FIBER 1 g
SODIUM 581 mg

EXCHANGES 2.5 Lean Meat, 0.5 Vegetable

2 cups water

¼ teaspoon salt

1 cup rolled oats

1 cup chopped apple or chopped peeled peach

¼ cup raisins or snipped whole pitted dates

1 teaspoon vanilla

¼ teaspoon ground cinnamon

Fat-free milk (optional)

1 In a medium saucepan bring water and salt to boiling. Stir in oats, apple, raisins, vanilla, and cinnamon. Reduce heat. Simmer, uncovered, for 3 minutes (for quick oats) or 5 minutes (for regular oats), stirring occasionally. Remove from heat. Cover and let stand for 2 minutes before serving. If desired, serve with fat-free milk. Makes 4 servings.

Fruity Oatmeal

START TO FINISH: 15 minutes

NUTRITION FACTS per serving:

- -

CALORIES 140
TOTAL FAT 2 g (0 g sat. fat)
CHOLESTEROL 0 mg
PROTEIN 4 g
CARBOHYDRATE 28 g
FIBER 4 g
SODIUM 151 mg

EXCHANGES 1.5 Starch, 0.5 Fat

NUTRITION NOTE

Rolled oats are highly nutritious. They contain plenty of thiamine, iron, and cholesterol-fighting soluble fiber.

- 2 cups fat-free milk
- 2 tablespoons sugar
- ⅓ cup quick-cooking wheat cereal (farina)
- ¼ cup raisins
- 1 teaspoon ground cinnamon
  Ground cinnamon (optional)

1 In a medium saucepan combine milk and sugar. Bring just to boiling; reduce heat. Add cereal, stirring constantly. Stir in raisins and cinnamon.

2 Cook, uncovered, for 2 to 3 minutes or until thickened, stirring frequently. Serve warm. If desired, sprinkle with additional cinnamon. Makes 4 (½-cup) servings.

Spiced Oatmeal: Prepare as above, except substitute 1 cup quick-cooking rolled oats for quick-cooking wheat cereal.

Spiced Hot Cereal

START TO FINISH: 10 minutes

NUTRITION FACTS per serving:
- -

CALORIES 120
TOTAL FAT 0 g (0 g sat. fat)
CHOLESTEROL 2 mg
PROTEIN 5 g
CARBOHYDRATE 25 g
FIBER 1 g
SODIUM 53 mg

EXCHANGES 0.5 Starch, 0.5 Fruit, 0.5 Milk

1 cup orange juice

1 cup loose-pack frozen strawberries, raspberries, and/or blackberries

1 medium banana, peeled and cut up

¼ cup plain low-fat yogurt

Fresh strawberries, sliced (optional)

1 In a blender combine orange juice, frozen berries, banana, and yogurt. Cover and blend until smooth.

2 To serve, pour into two glasses. If desired, garnish with fresh strawberries.
Makes 2 (about 9-ounce) servings.

Berry-Banana Smoothie

START TO FINISH: 10 minutes

NUTRITION FACTS per serving:
- -

CALORIES 151
TOTAL FAT 1 g (0 g sat. fat)
CHOLESTEROL 2 mg
PROTEIN 4 g
CARBOHYDRATE 34 g
FIBER 3 g
SODIUM 24 mg

EXCHANGES 2 Fruit, 0.5 Milk

Chapter 3

Breads

On the opener: Pear-Almond Muffins (see recipe, page 38)

Nonstick cooking spray

- 1 cup all-purpose flour
- 1 cup whole wheat flour or white whole wheat flour
- ⅓ cup packed brown sugar
- 2½ teaspoons baking powder
- 1 teaspoon apple pie spice
- ¼ teaspoon salt
- 2 eggs
- 1 cup buttermilk
- 2 tablespoons canola oil
- ¾ cup shredded, peeled apple (1 medium)
- 2 tablespoons finely chopped pecans
- 1 tablespoon flaxseed meal or toasted wheat germ
- 1 tablespoon packed brown sugar
- 1 tablespoon butter

1 Preheat oven to 375°F. Lightly coat twelve 2½-inch muffin cups with nonstick cooking spray or line with paper bake cups and coat insides of paper cups with nonstick cooking spray; set aside. In a large bowl stir together all-purpose flour, whole wheat flour, ⅓ cup brown sugar, baking powder, apple pie spice, and salt. Make a well in the center of the flour mixture; set aside.

2 In a medium bowl lightly beat eggs with a fork; stir in buttermilk and oil. Add egg mixture all at once to flour mixture; stir just until moistened (batter should be lumpy). Fold in shredded apple. Spoon batter into prepared muffin cups, filling each about three-fourths full.

3 In a small bowl combine pecans, flaxseed meal, and 1 tablespoon brown sugar. Using a pastry blender, cut in butter until mixture resembles coarse crumbs. Spoon pecan mixture on top of muffin batter.

4 Bake for 18 to 20 minutes or until a toothpick inserted in centers comes out clean. Cool in muffin cups on a wire rack for 5 minutes. Remove muffins from muffin cups. Serve warm. Makes 12 muffins.

Apple-Streusel Muffins

PREP: 25 minutes   **BAKE:** 18 minutes
COOL: 5 minutes   **OVEN:** 375°F

NUTRITION FACTS per muffin:

CALORIES 163
TOTAL FAT 6 g (1 g sat. fat)
CHOLESTEROL 39 mg
PROTEIN 4 g
CARBOHYDRATE 25 g
FIBER 2 g
SODIUM 167 mg

EXCHANGES 1.5 Starch, 1 Fat

Pear-Almond Muffins

PREP: 20 minutes   **BAKE:** 15 minutes
COOL: 5 minutes   **OVEN:** 400°F

NUTRITION FACTS per muffin:

CALORIES 154
TOTAL FAT 5 g (1 g sat. fat)
CHOLESTEROL 5 mg
PROTEIN 4 g
CARBOHYDRATE 24 g
FIBER 2 g
SODIUM 163 mg

EXCHANGES 1.5 Other Carbohydrates, 1 Fat

Nonstick cooking spray
1   cup all-purpose flour
½   cup packed brown sugar
2   teaspoons baking powder
½   teaspoon ground ginger
¼   teaspoon salt
¾   cup whole bran cereal
¾   cup fat-free milk
¾   cup chopped, peeled pear
2   egg whites, lightly beaten
3   tablespoons canola oil
2   tablespoons finely
        chopped almonds
1   recipe Ginger-Cream Spread

1 Preheat oven to 400°F. Lightly coat twelve 2½-inch muffin cups with nonstick cooking spray or line with paper bake cups and coat insides of paper cups with nonstick cooking spray; set aside. In a large bowl stir together flour, brown sugar, baking powder, ginger, and salt. Make a well in the center of the flour mixture; set aside.

2 In a medium bowl stir together cereal and milk; let mixture stand for 5 minutes. Stir in pear, egg whites, and oil. Add cereal mixture all at once to flour mixture; stir just until moistened (batter should be lumpy).

3 Spoon batter into prepared muffin cups, filling each three-fourths full. Sprinkle with almonds. Bake for 15 to 18 minutes or until a toothpick inserted near centers comes out clean.

4 Cool in muffin cups on a wire rack for 5 minutes. Remove muffins from muffin cups. Serve warm with Ginger-Cream Spread. Makes 12 muffins.

Ginger-Cream Spread: In a small bowl stir together half of an 8-ounce tub light cream cheese, 2 teaspoons finely chopped crystallized ginger or ¼ teaspoon ground ginger, and 2 teaspoons honey.

Make-Ahead Directions: Store the batter in the refrigerator for up to 3 days and bake a few at a time, if you like.

Nonstick cooking spray

1¼	cups all-purpose flour
⅔	cup oat bran
½	cup packed brown sugar
2	teaspoons baking powder
⅛	teaspoon salt
1	egg or 2 egg whites
½	cup light dairy sour cream
¼	cup fat-free milk
2	tablespoons canola oil
1	cup chopped fresh mango or chopped thawed frozen unsweetened mango chunks, drained
⅓	cup pistachio nuts, chopped

1 Preheat oven to 400°F. Coat twelve 2½-inch muffin cups with nonstick cooking spray or line with paper bake cups and coat insides of paper cups with nonstick cooking spray; set aside. In a large bowl combine flour, oat bran, brown sugar, baking powder, and salt. Make a well in the center of the flour mixture; set aside.

2 In a medium bowl whisk together egg, sour cream, milk, and oil. Add egg mixture all at once to flour mixture; stir just until moistened (batter should be lumpy). Fold in mango and pistachio nuts.

3 Spoon batter into prepared muffin cups, filling each about three-fourths full. Bake about 18 minutes or until golden brown and a toothpick inserted in centers comes out clean.

4 Cool in muffin cups on a wire rack for 5 minutes. Remove muffins from muffin cups. Serve warm. Makes 12 muffins.

Pistachio-Mango Muffins

PREP: 25 minutes **BAKE:** 18 minutes
COOL: 5 minutes **OVEN:** 400°F

NUTRITION FACTS per muffin:

CALORIES 162
TOTAL FAT 6 g (1 g sat. fat)
CHOLESTEROL 21 mg
PROTEIN 4 g
CARBOHYDRATE 27 g
FIBER 2 g
SODIUM 103 mg

EXCHANGES 2 Other Carbohydrates, 1 Fat

NUTRITION NOTE

Nuts, which are high in calories and fat, should be eaten in moderate amounts. Fortunately, the fat in nuts such as pistachios is mostly monounsaturated fat, which can help lower bad cholesterol and raise good cholesterol.

1½ cups all-purpose flour

½ cup rolled oats

½ cup sugar

3 tablespoons unsweetened cocoa powder

1 tablespoon instant espresso coffee powder or instant coffee crystals

2 teaspoons baking powder

¼ teaspoon salt

¼ cup butter, cut into pieces

1 6-ounce carton plain fat-free or low-fat yogurt

1 egg white, lightly beaten

⅓ cup semisweet chocolate pieces

Rolled oats (optional)

Mocha Scones

PREP: 15 minutes   **BAKE:** 13 minutes

COOL: 5 minutes   **OVEN:** 400°F

NUTRITION FACTS per scone:

CALORIES 185
TOTAL FAT 6 g (4 g sat. fat)
CHOLESTEROL 10 mg
PROTEIN 4 g
CARBOHYDRATE 30 g
FIBER 2 g
SODIUM 153 mg

EXCHANGES 2 Other Carbohydrates, 1 Fat

1 Preheat oven to 400°F. Lightly grease a large baking sheet or line with parchment paper; set aside.

2 In a medium bowl combine flour, ½ cup oats, sugar, cocoa powder, espresso powder, baking powder, and salt. Using a pastry blender, cut in butter until mixture resembles coarse crumbs. Make a well in the center of the flour mixture; set aside.

3 In a medium bowl combine yogurt and egg white. Stir in chocolate pieces. Add yogurt mixture all at once to flour mixture; stir just until moistened.

4 Turn out dough on a lightly floured surface. Knead by folding and gently pressing dough for 10 to 12 strokes or until nearly smooth. Pat or lightly roll dough into an 8×6-inch rectangle. Cut rectangle crosswise into 4 strips. Cut each strip into 3 rectangles to make 12 pieces.

5 Place dough pieces 1 inch apart on prepared baking sheet. If desired, sprinkle with additional rolled oats. Bake for 13 to 15 minutes or until tops are set. Remove scones from baking sheet. Cool on a wire rack for 5 minutes. Serve warm. Makes 12 scones.

Nonstick cooking spray

1½ cups all-purpose flour

½ cup white whole wheat flour or whole wheat flour

¼ cup sugar

1 tablespoon baking powder

1 tablespoon finely shredded orange peel

¼ teaspoon baking soda

¼ teaspoon salt

¼ cup butter

1 egg

½ cup buttermilk or sour fat-free milk*

1 teaspoon vanilla

1 cup fresh or frozen blueberries

1 recipe Orange Glaze (optional)

Blueberry Breakfast Scones

PREP: 30 minutes   **BAKE:** 15 minutes
OVEN: 400°F

NUTRITION FACTS per scone:

CALORIES 171
TOTAL FAT 5 g (3 g sat. fat)
CHOLESTEROL 34 mg
PROTEIN 4 g
CARBOHYDRATE 27 g
FIBER 1 g
SODIUM 215 mg

EXCHANGES 2 Other Carbohydrates, 1 Fat

1 Preheat oven to 400°F. Lightly coat a baking sheet with nonstick cooking spray; set aside. In a large bowl stir together all-purpose flour, whole wheat flour, sugar, baking powder, orange peel, baking soda, and salt. Using a pastry blender, cut in butter until mixture resembles coarse crumbs. Make a well in the center of the flour mixture.

2 In a small bowl whisk together egg, buttermilk, and vanilla. Add egg mixture all at once to flour mixture; stir just until moistened. Gently stir in blueberries. (Do not thaw frozen blueberries; thawed berries will discolor the dough.) (Mixture will not completely come together in a ball.)

3 Turn out dough on a lightly floured surface. Knead dough by folding and gently pressing dough for 10 to 12 strokes or until nearly smooth. Transfer dough to the prepared baking sheet; pat or lightly roll dough to a 7-inch circle. Cut circle into 10 wedges. Separate wedges so they are about 1 inch apart.

4 Bake about 15 minutes or until golden brown. Remove from baking sheet. Cool slightly on a wire rack. If desired, drizzle scones with Orange Glaze. Serve warm. Makes 10 scones.

*To make ½ cup sour fat-free milk, place 1½ teaspoons lemon juice or vinegar in a glass measuring cup. Add enough fat-free milk to make ½ cup total liquid; stir. Let stand for 5 minutes before using.

Orange Glaze: In a small bowl stir together ¾ cup powdered sugar and ¼ teaspoon finely shredded orange peel. Stir in enough orange juice or fat-free milk (3 to 4 teaspoons) to make drizzling consistency.

Blueberry-Peach Coffee Cake

PREP: 25 minutes **BAKE:** 40 minutes
COOL: 30 minutes **OVEN:** 350°F

NUTRITION FACTS per serving:

- -

CALORIES 206
TOTAL FAT 7 g (1 g sat. fat)
CHOLESTEROL 1 mg
PROTEIN 4 g
CARBOHYDRATE 35 g
FIBER 1 g
SODIUM 201 mg

EXCHANGES 1.5 Starch, 1 Other
Carbohydrates, 1 Fat

Nonstick cooking spray
1   cup all-purpose flour
⅓   cup yellow cornmeal
1½   teaspoons finely shredded
     lemon peel
1   teaspoon baking powder
½   teaspoon baking soda
¼   teaspoon salt
1   6-ounce carton plain low-fat yogurt
2   egg whites
¼   cup sugar
¼   cup honey
¼   cup canola oil
1   cup fresh or frozen blueberries
½   cup chopped fresh peach or
     chopped thawed frozen
     unsweetened peach slices,
     drained
1   tablespoon all-purpose flour

1 Preheat oven to 350°F. Lightly coat an
8×8×2-inch baking pan with nonstick
cooking spray; set aside. In a large bowl stir
together 1 cup flour, cornmeal, lemon peel,
baking powder, baking soda, and salt. Make a
well in the center of the flour mixture; set aside.

2 In a medium bowl combine yogurt, egg
whites, sugar, honey, and oil. Add yogurt
mixture all at once to flour mixture; stir just
until combined. In a small bowl combine
blueberries, peach, and the 1 tablespoon flour;
toss gently to coat.

3 Spread about half of the batter in the
prepared baking pan. Sprinkle with fruit
mixture. Spoon mounds of remaining batter
over the fruit mixture. Spread evenly over fruit
(the batter may not completely cover the fruit).

4 Bake about 40 minutes or until coffee cake
is golden brown and a toothpick inserted
near the center comes out clean. Cool in pan on
a wire rack for 30 minutes. Serve warm. Makes
9 servings.

Nonstick cooking spray

- 1 cup all-purpose flour
- ½ cup white whole wheat flour or whole wheat flour
- 1 teaspoon baking powder
- ¼ teaspoon salt
- ¼ teaspoon ground cinnamon
- ⅛ teaspoon ground ginger
- 1 egg
- ½ cup snipped dried apricots
- ½ cup fat-free milk
- ¼ cup sugar
- ¼ cup unsweetened applesauce
- ¼ cup canola oil
- 2 tablespoons reduced-sugar apricot preserves, melted
- 2 tablespoons sliced almonds, toasted

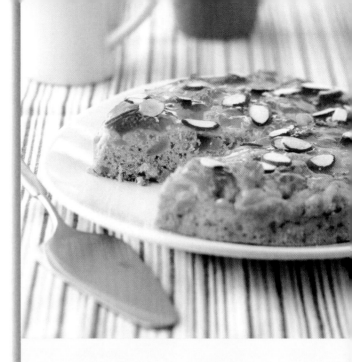

Apricot-Almond Coffee Cake

PREP: 20 minutes   **BAKE:** 25 minutes
COOL: 10 minutes   **OVEN:** 350°F

NUTRITION FACTS per serving:

CALORIES 182
TOTAL FAT 7 g (1 g sat. fat)
CHOLESTEROL 21 mg
PROTEIN 4 g
CARBOHYDRATE 28 g
FIBER 2 g
SODIUM 97 mg

EXCHANGES 2 Other Carbohydrates, 1 Fat

1 Preheat oven to 350°F. Lightly coat an 8×1½-inch round baking pan with nonstick cooking spray; set aside. In a medium bowl stir together all-purpose flour, whole wheat flour, baking powder, salt, cinnamon, and ginger.

2 In a medium bowl lightly beat egg with a fork; stir in dried apricots. Stir in milk, sugar, applesauce, and oil. Add apricot mixture all at once to flour mixture; stir until combined. Spread batter in the prepared baking pan.

3 Bake for 25 to 30 minutes or until a toothpick inserted near the center comes out clean. Cool in pan on a wire rack for 10 minutes. Cut up any large pieces of fruit in preserves; spoon over coffee cake. Sprinkle with toasted almonds. Serve warm. Makes 10 servings.

COOK'S TIP

Because whole wheat flour contains the whole grain, it has shorter shelf life than refined products. Refrigerate whole wheat flour in an air-tight container to keep it fresh.

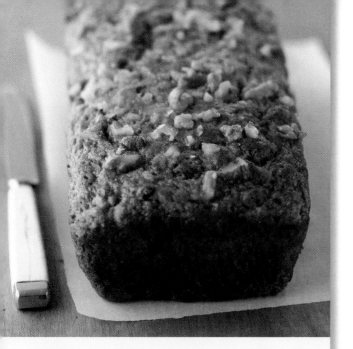

Nonstick cooking spray
- 1 cup all-purpose flour
- ½ cup white whole wheat flour or whole wheat flour
- 2 teaspoons baking powder
- ½ teaspoon pumpkin pie spice
- ¼ teaspoon baking soda
- ¼ teaspoon salt
- 1 cup mashed banana (2 to 3 medium)
- ¾ cup packed brown sugar
- ¼ cup fat-free milk
- 2 egg whites
- 2 tablespoons canola oil
- ¼ cup chopped walnuts, toasted (optional)

Banana Bread

PREP: 20 minutes **BAKE:** 45 minutes
COOL: 2 hours **STAND:** overnight
OVEN: 350°F

NUTRITION FACTS per serving:

CALORIES 143
TOTAL FAT 2 g (0 g sat. fat)
CHOLESTEROL 0 mg
PROTEIN 3 g
CARBOHYDRATE 28 g
FIBER 1 g
SODIUM 152 mg

EXCHANGES 2 Other Carbohydrates

1 Preheat oven to 350°F. Lightly coat the bottom and about ½ inch up the sides of an 8×4×2-inch loaf pan with nonstick cooking spray; set aside.

2 In a large bowl stir together all-purpose flour, whole wheat flour, baking powder, pumpkin pie spice, baking soda, and salt. Make a well in the center of the flour mixture; set aside.

3 In a medium bowl combine mashed banana, brown sugar, milk, egg whites, and oil. Add banana mixture all at once to flour mixture; stir just until moistened (batter should be lumpy). If desired, fold in 2 tablespoons walnuts. Spoon batter into prepared loaf pan. If desired, sprinkle with remaining 2 tablespoons walnuts.

4 Bake for 45 to 50 minutes or until a toothpick inserted near the center comes out clean. Cool in pan on a wire rack for 10 minutes. Remove bread from pan. Cool on wire rack. Wrap and store overnight before slicing. Makes 1 loaf (12 servings).

- ¾ cup packed brown sugar
- ⅓ cup creamy peanut butter
- 1½ teaspoons baking powder
- ¼ teaspoon baking soda
- ¼ teaspoon salt
- 2 egg whites
- 2 tablespoons canola oil
- 1 cup all-purpose flour
- ½ cup white whole wheat flour or whole wheat flour
- 1 cup fat-free milk
- 2 tablespoons unsweetened cocoa powder
- 1 tablespoon fat-free milk

1 Preheat oven to 350°F. Grease the bottom(s) and ½ inch up the sides of one 8×4×2-inch loaf pan or four 4½×2½×1½-inch individual loaf pans; set aside.

2 In a large bowl combine brown sugar, peanut butter, baking powder, baking soda, and salt. Beat with an electric mixer until combined. Beat in egg whites and oil until combined. In a small bowl combine all-purpose flour and whole wheat flour. Alternately add flour mixture and 1 cup milk to peanut butter mixture, beating on low speed after each addition just until combined. Transfer ½ cup of the batter to a small bowl; stir in cocoa powder and 1 tablespoon milk.

3 Spoon half of the light-color batter evenly into prepared loaf pan(s). Drop all of the chocolate batter by small spoonfuls on top of batter in pans. Spoon remaining light-color batter evenly over chocolate batter. Using a narrow metal spatula, swirl batters to create a marbled effect.

4 Bake for 50 to 55 minutes for the 8-inch pan, 30 to 35 minutes for the 4½-inch pans, or until a toothpick inserted near center(s) comes out clean. Cool in pan(s) on a wire rack for 10 minutes. Remove bread from pan(s). Cool on wire rack. Wrap and store overnight before slicing. Makes 12 servings.

Peanut Butter and Chocolate Swirl Bread

PREP: 25 minutes   **BAKE:** 50 minutes

COOL: 2 hours   **STAND:** overnight

OVEN: 350°F

NUTRITION FACTS per serving:

CALORIES 181
TOTAL FAT 6 g (1 g sat. fat)
CHOLESTEROL 0 mg
PROTEIN 5 g
CARBOHYDRATE 28 g
FIBER 1 g
SODIUM 177 mg

EXCHANGES 1 Starch, 1 Other Carbohydrates, 1 Fat

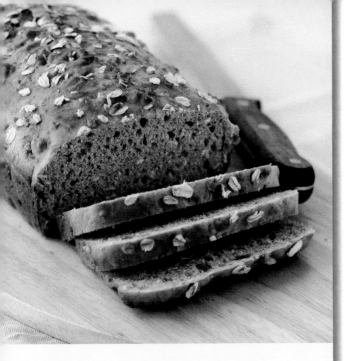

1 cup warm fat-free milk
(105°F to 115°F)

¼ cup honey or packed brown sugar

1 package active dry yeast

½ teaspoon salt

1¾ cups bread flour or
all-purpose flour

1 egg, lightly beaten

1 tablespoon canola oil

¾ cup whole wheat flour

½ cup rolled oats

Nonstick cooking spray

Water (optional)

Rolled oats (optional)

Easy Oatmeal Bread

PREP: 25 minutes   **RISE:** 1¼ hours

BAKE: 40 minutes   **COOL:** 2 hours

OVEN: 350°F

NUTRITION FACTS per serving:

- -

CALORIES 156

TOTAL FAT 2 g (0 g sat. fat)

CHOLESTEROL 18 mg

PROTEIN 5 g

CARBOHYDRATE 29 g

FIBER 2 g

SODIUM 113 mg

EXCHANGES 2 Starch

1 In a large bowl combine milk, honey or brown sugar, yeast, and salt, stirring to dissolve yeast. Let stand for 5 minutes.

2 Add bread flour, egg, and oil to yeast mixture. Beat with an electric mixer on low to medium speed until combined. Beat on high speed for 3 minutes, scraping side of bowl occasionally. Using a wooden spoon, stir in whole wheat flour and ½ cup oats until combined. Cover and let rise in a warm place until double in size (45 to 60 minutes).

3 Lightly coat a 9×5×3-inch loaf pan with nonstick cooking spray. Stir down dough and spoon into prepared loaf pan. Cover and let rise in a warm place until double in size (about 30 minutes). If desired, lightly brush top of loaf with water and sprinkle with additional rolled oats.

4 Preheat oven to 350°F. Bake about 40 minutes or until bread is golden brown and sounds hollow when lightly tapped. Immediately remove bread from pan. Cool on a wire rack. Makes 12 servings.

1 cup Sourdough Starter (see page 54)
3½ to 4 cups all-purpose flour
1 package active dry yeast
1½ cups water
¼ cup honey
3 tablespoons canola oil
1½ teaspoons salt
1½ cups white whole wheat flour or whole wheat flour
¼ cup flaxseed meal or toasted wheat germ
2 teaspoons flaxseeds
½ teaspoon baking soda
Water (optional)
Flaxseeds (optional)
Flaxseed meal (optional)

1 Measure Sourdough Starter; let stand at room temperature for 30 minutes. In a large bowl combine 2½ cups all-purpose flour and yeast; set aside. In a medium saucepan heat and stir 1½ cups water, honey, oil, and salt just until warm (120°F to 130°F). Add water mixture to yeast mixture; add Sourdough Starter. Beat with an electric mixer on low to medium speed for 30 seconds, scraping side of bowl constantly. Beat on high speed for 3 minutes. In a medium bowl combine ½ cup remaining all-purpose flour, whole wheat flour, ¼ cup flaxseed meal, 2 teaspoons flaxseeds, and baking soda; add to yeast mixture. Using a wooden spoon, stir until combined. Stir in as much of the remaining all-purpose flour as you can.

2 Turn out dough on a lightly floured surface. Knead in enough of the remaining all-purpose flour to make a moderately stiff dough that is smooth and elastic (6 to 8 minutes total). Shape dough into a ball. Place in a lightly greased bowl, turning once to grease surface. Cover and let rise in a warm place until double in size (45 to 60 minutes). Punch down dough. Turn out on a lightly floured surface. Divide dough in half. Cover; let rest for 10 minutes. Meanwhile, lightly grease two baking sheets.

3 Shape each dough portion by gently pulling it into a ball, tucking edges underneath. Place dough balls on prepared baking sheets. Flatten each dough ball slightly to about 6 inches in diameter. Using a sharp knife, make crisscross slashes across tops of loaves. Cover; let rise in a warm place until nearly double in size (about 30 minutes). If desired, lightly brush tops of loaves with water and sprinkle with additional flaxseeds and flaxseed meal.

4 Preheat oven to 375°F. Bake for 30 to 35 minutes or until bread sounds hollow when lightly tapped. (If necessary to prevent overbrowning, cover loosely with foil for the last 10 minutes of baking.) Remove bread from baking sheets. Cool on wire racks. Makes 2 loaves (24 servings).

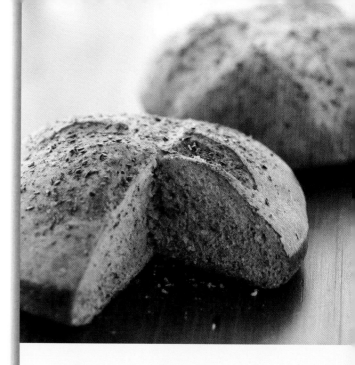

Honey-Flax Sourdough Bread

See page 54 for Sourdough Starter recipe.

PREP: 45 minutes   **STAND:** 30 minutes
RISE: 1¼ hours   **REST:** 10 minutes
BAKE: 30 minutes   **COOL:** 2 hours
OVEN: 375°F

NUTRITION FACTS per serving:

CALORIES 140
TOTAL FAT 2 g (0 g sat. fat)
CHOLESTEROL 0 mg
PROTEIN 4 g
CARBOHYDRATE 26 g
FIBER 2 g
SODIUM 173 mg
EXCHANGES 1.5 Starch

Dried Tomato-Feta Focaccia

PREP: 35 minutes   **STAND:** 8 hours

RISE: 1 hour   **REST:** 30 minutes

BAKE: 15 minutes   **COOL:** 15 minutes

OVEN: 475°F

NUTRITION FACTS per serving:

CALORIES 166
TOTAL FAT 2 g (1 g sat. fat)
CHOLESTEROL 2 mg
PROTEIN 6 g
CARBOHYDRATE 30 g
FIBER 2 g
SODIUM 311 mg

EXCHANGES 2 Starch

*If you don't have a bread stone, preheat a greased baking sheet in the oven for 5 minutes (do not preheat longer). Carefully transfer the shaped dough to the preheated baking sheet.

2¾ to 3¼ cups all-purpose flour
½ cup warm water (105°F to 115°F)
1 teaspoon active dry yeast
1 cup warm water (120°F to 130°F)
⅓ cup snipped dried tomatoes (not oil pack)
1 cup white whole wheat flour or whole wheat flour
½ cup crumbled reduced-fat feta cheese (2 ounces)
1 clove garlic, minced
1 teaspoon salt
1 tablespoon olive oil
1 tablespoon grated Parmesan cheese

1 In a large bowl combine ½ cup all-purpose flour, ½ cup warm water, and yeast. Beat with a wooden spoon until smooth. Cover loosely with plastic wrap. Let stand at room temperature for at least 8 hours or overnight to ferment.

2 In a small bowl combine 1 cup warm water and dried tomatoes. Let stand for 5 minutes. Gradually stir tomato mixture into the yeast mixture. Stir in whole wheat flour, feta cheese, garlic, and salt. Stir in as much of the remaining all-purpose flour as you can. Turn out dough onto a lightly floured surface. Knead in enough of the remaining all-purpose flour to make a stiff dough that is smooth and elastic (8 to 10 minutes total). Shape dough into a ball. Place in a lightly greased bowl, turning once to grease surface. Cover and let rise in a warm place until double in size (about 1 hour).

3 Punch down dough. Turn out on a well-floured baking sheet. Place a large bowl upside down over dough to cover it; let rest for 30 minutes.

4 Preheat oven and a bread stone* to 475°F. Shape dough on the baking sheet into an 11-inch circle by gently pulling and pressing with your fingertips, taking care to keep dough air bubbles intact. Using your fingers, make ½-inch-deep indentations every 2 inches in dough (dust your fingers with flour if necessary). Brush dough with oil; sprinkle with Parmesan cheese. Carefully slide dough from baking sheet to preheated bread stone.

5 Bake about 15 minutes or until golden brown, checking after 8 minutes and using a sharp knife to pop any large air bubbles. Using a large spatula, transfer focaccia to a wire rack. Cool about 15 minutes. Cut into 12 wedges. Serve warm. Makes 12 servings.

Nonstick cooking spray

1 medium tomato, seeded and chopped (⅔ cup)

⅓ cup reduced-fat shredded mozzarella cheese

1 clove garlic, minced

½ teaspoon dried basil or Italian seasoning, crushed

1 16-ounce loaf frozen whole wheat bread dough, thawed

Fat-free milk

2 tablespoons finely shredded Parmesan cheese

1 Lightly coat an 8×8×2-inch baking pan with nonstick cooking spray; set aside. In a small bowl combine tomato, mozzarella cheese, garlic, and basil; set aside.

2 Divide bread dough into 12 portions. On a lightly floured surface flatten each dough portion to a 3-inch round. Spoon about 1 tablespoon of the tomato mixture into center of each dough round; shape dough around tomato mixture into a ball, pinching the dough together to seal.

3 Place rolls, seam sides down, in the prepared baking pan. Cover and let rise in a warm place until nearly double in size (30 to 45 minutes). Lightly brush tops of rolls with milk and sprinkle with Parmesan cheese.

4 Preheat oven to 375°F. Bake about 20 minutes or until tops are golden brown. Cool in pan on a wire rack for 20 minutes. Serve warm. Makes 12 rolls.

See page 54 for recipe variations (Seeded Pull-Apart Rolls and Gremolata-Stuffed Parker House Rolls).

Italian-Style Dinner Rolls

PREP: 25 minutes   **RISE:** 30 minutes

BAKE: 20 minutes   **COOL:** 20 minutes

OVEN: 375°F

NUTRITION FACTS per roll:

CALORIES 110
TOTAL FAT 2 g (0 g sat. fat)
CHOLESTEROL 2 mg
PROTEIN 5 g
CARBOHYDRATE 19 g
FIBER 2 g
SODIUM 243 mg

EXCHANGES 1.5 Starch

1 16-ounce loaf frozen whole wheat bread dough, thawed

½ of an 8-ounce tub light cream cheese spread with strawberries, softened

½ cup fresh pitted tart red or dark sweet cherries

½ cup fresh blueberries

½ cup fresh raspberries

1 egg white

1 tablespoon water

1 recipe Orange Glaze (optional)

1 Line a large baking sheet with parchment paper or foil. If using foil, lightly grease foil. Set aside.

2 On a lightly floured surface roll bread dough into a 16×9-inch rectangle. If dough is difficult to roll out, let it rest for 5 to 10 minutes. Transfer dough rectangle to prepared baking sheet. Spread cream cheese lengthwise down the center third of the dough, leaving ½ inch unfilled along each end. Top cream cheese with cherries, blueberries, and raspberries.

3 On both long sides make 3-inch cuts from the edges toward the center, spacing the cuts 1 inch apart. Starting at an end, alternately fold opposite strips of dough, at an angle, across the filling. Slightly press ends together in center to seal. Cover and let rise in a warm place for 45 minutes.

4 Preheat oven to 350°F. In a small bowl whisk together egg white and water; brush mixture over braid. Bake for 25 to 30 minutes or until top and bottom are golden brown. Cool on baking sheet on a wire rack for 15 minutes. Cut crosswise into slices. If desired, drizzle with Orange Glaze. Serve warm. Makes 14 to 16 servings.

Orange Glaze: In a small bowl stir together ¾ cup powdered sugar and ¼ teaspoon finely shredded orange peel. Stir in enough orange juice or fat-free milk (3 to 4 teaspoons) to make drizzling consistency.

Berry-Cream Tea Braid

PREP: 30 minutes   **RISE:** 45 minutes

BAKE: 25 minutes   **COOL:** 15 minutes

OVEN: 350°F

NUTRITION FACTS per serving:

CALORIES 111
TOTAL FAT 2 g (1 g sat. fat)
CHOLESTEROL 4 mg
PROTEIN 5 g
CARBOHYDRATE 19 g
FIBER 2 g
SODIUM 214 mg

EXCHANGES 1.5 Starch

COOK'S TIP

When selecting berries look for bright color. Avoid those with mold, soft spots, or discoloration. When berries come in a box, tip the box to see whether the berries move freely; if they stick together, chances are they're moldy.

2½ to 2¾	cups all-purpose flour
1	package active dry yeast
1¼	cups water
5	tablespoons sugar
3	tablespoons pareve margarine
1	teaspoon salt
2	eggs
1½	cups white whole wheat flour
1	tablespoon shredded orange peel
3	tablespoons unsweetened cocoa powder
	Nonstick cooking spray
1	egg white, lightly beaten
1	recipe Orange Drizzle

1 In a large bowl stir together 2 cups all-purpose flour and yeast; set aside. In a small saucepan heat and stir water, 2 tablespoons sugar, margarine, and salt just until warm (120°F to 130°F) and margarine almost melts. Add water mixture to yeast mixture; add 2 eggs. Beat with an electric mixer on low to medium speed for 30 seconds, scraping side of bowl constantly. Beat on high speed for 3 minutes. Using a wooden spoon, stir in whole wheat flour.

2 Transfer half of the batter to a medium bowl; stir in orange peel. Turn out onto a lightly floured surface. Knead in enough of the remaining all-purpose flour (you will not use all of the flour) to make a moderately soft dough that is smooth and elastic (3 to 5 minutes total). Shape dough into a ball. Place in a lightly greased small bowl, turning once to grease surface. Cover and set aside.

3 To the remaining batter stir in 3 tablespoons sugar and cocoa powder. Turn out onto a lightly floured surface. Knead in enough all-purpose flour to make a moderately soft dough that is smooth and elastic (3 to 5 minutes total). Shape dough into a ball. Place in a lightly greased small bowl, turning once. Cover dough. Let both portions of dough rise in a warm place until double in size (1 to 1¼ hours).

4 Punch down dough. Turn out on a lightly floured surface. Cover; let rest for 10 minutes. Lightly coat a large baking sheet with nonstick cooking spray; set aside.

5 Roll each dough portion into a 22-inch-long rope. Place ropes side by side. Twist ropes together several times. Place twist on prepared baking sheet. Shape twist into a circle, leaving a 3-inch hole in center. Pinch ends together to seal. Crumple a piece of foil into a 2-inch ball; lightly coat with nonstick cooking spray. Place foil ball in the center of the dough ring. Cover and let rise in a warm place until nearly double in size (30 to 40 minutes).

6 Preheat oven to 375°F. Brush bread with egg white. Bake for 25 to 30 minutes or until bread sounds hollow when lightly tapped. (If necessary to prevent overbrowning, cover loosely with foil for the last 10 minutes of baking.) Immediately remove ball of foil. Remove bread from baking sheet. Cool on a wire rack. Before serving, top with Orange Drizzle. Makes 24 servings.

Chocolate-Orange Challah Wreath

PREP: 45 minutes **RISE:** 1½ hours
REST: 10 minutes **BAKE:** 25 minutes
COOL: 2 hours **OVEN:** 375°F

NUTRITION FACTS per serving:

CALORIES 120
TOTAL FAT 2 g (0 g sat. fat)
CHOLESTEROL 18 mg
PROTEIN 3 g
CARBOHYDRATE 22 g
FIBER 1 g
SODIUM 123 mg
EXCHANGES 1.5 Starch

Orange Drizzle: In a small bowl stir together ¾ cup powdered sugar and enough orange juice or fat-free milk (3 to 4 teaspoons) to reach drizzling consistency.

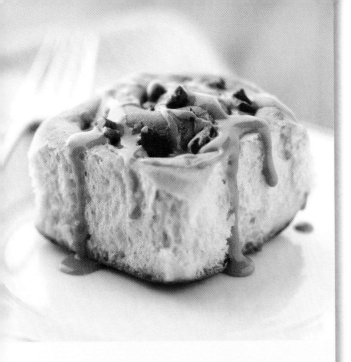

Cranberry-Maple Cinnamon Rolls

PREP: 30 minutes   **SATND:** 10 minutes

RISE: 1½ hours   **REST:** 10 minutes

BAKE: 25 minutes   **COOL:** 5 minutes

OVEN: 375°F

NUTRITION FACTS per roll:

CALORIES 180
TOTAL FAT 4 g (1 g sat. fat)
CHOLESTEROL 18 mg
PROTEIN 5 g
CARBOHYDRATE 33 g
FIBER 2 g
SODIUM 180 mg

EXCHANGES 2 Starch, 0.5 Fat

Maple-Brown Sugar Icing: In a small bowl combine 2 tablespoons packed brown sugar and 1 tablespoon very hot water; stir to dissolve brown sugar. Stir in ¾ cup powdered sugar and ¼ teaspoon maple flavoring. Stir in enough fat-free milk (1 to 2 teaspoons) to make drizzling consistency.

1   cup fat-free milk
2   tablespoons pure maple syrup
2   tablespoons butter
1   teaspoon salt
¼   cup warm water (110°F to 115°F)
1   package active dry yeast
1   egg, lightly beaten
1¼   cups white whole wheat flour or whole wheat flour
2½   to 3 cups all-purpose flour
⅓   cup packed brown sugar
2   teaspoons ground cinnamon
¼   cup snipped dried cranberries
¼   cup chopped pecans, toasted
1   recipe Maple-Brown Sugar Icing (optional)

1 In a small saucepan heat and stir milk, maple syrup, butter, and salt just until warm (110°F to 115°F); set aside. In a large bowl combine warm water and yeast; let stand for 10 minutes. Add milk mixture and egg to yeast mixture. Stir in whole wheat flour. Stir in as much of the all-purpose flour as you can.

2 Turn out dough on a lightly floured surface. Knead in enough all-purpose flour to make a moderately soft dough that is smooth and elastic (3 to 5 minutes total). Shape dough into a ball. Place in a lightly greased bowl, turning once to grease surface. Cover and let rise in a warm place until double in size (about 1 hour). Punch down dough. Turn out on a lightly floured surface. Cover; let rest for 10 minutes.

3 Meanwhile, lightly grease a 13×9×2-inch baking pan; set aside. In a small bowl combine brown sugar and cinnamon. Stir in dried cranberries and pecans.

4 Roll dough into a 15×8-inch rectangle. Sprinkle with pecan mixture, leaving 1 inch unfilled along one of the long sides. Starting from the long filled side, roll up rectangle. Pinch dough to seal seam; slice into 15 equal pieces. Arrange pieces, cut sides up, in prepared baking pan. Cover and let rise in a warm place until nearly double in size (about 30 minutes).

5 Preheat oven to 375°F. Bake for 25 minutes or until golden brown. Cool in pan on a wire rack for 5 minutes. Remove rolls from pan. If desired, drizzle with Maple-Brown Sugar Icing. Serve warm. Makes 15 rolls.

Nonstick cooking spray

¼ cup flaxseed meal or toasted wheat germ

3 tablespoons sugar

2 teaspoons ground cinnamon

1 16-ounce loaf frozen whole wheat bread dough, thawed

½ cup Cream Cheese Frosting

1 Line a large baking sheet with foil. Lightly coat foil with nonstick cooking spray; set aside. In a small bowl combine flaxseed meal, sugar, and cinnamon. Spread sugar mixture on a piece of waxed paper; set aside.

2 Divide bread dough into 24 portions. On a lightly floured surface, roll each dough portion into an 8-inch-long rope.* Lightly brush dough ropes with a little water. Roll dough ropes in sugar mixture to coat.

3 Place two ropes side by side on prepared baking sheet. Twist ropes together several times and pinch ends together to seal. Repeat with remaining ropes to make 12 twists, placing twists 2 inches apart on baking sheet. Cover and let rise in a warm place until nearly double in size and dough feels light when touched (30 to 45 minutes).

4 Preheat oven to 375°F. Bake for 12 to 15 minutes or until golden brown. Remove twists from baking sheet. Cool on a wire rack for 5 minutes. Frost or drizzle** with Cream Cheese Frosting. Serve warm. Makes 12 sticks.

*Dough ropes will shrink after shaping. Roll all of the ropes, letting each one rest while rolling the others. Then reroll each rope to desired length.

**To drizzle frosting, place it in a resealable heavy plastic bag; seal. Cut a small piece off of one corner of the bag; pipe frosting.

Cinnamon Buns: Prepare as directed, except do not twist dough ropes together. For each bun, place two ropes side by side on prepared baking sheet. Coil ropes together into a flat spiral. Pinch ends of ropes to seal. Continue as directed.

Frosted Cinnamon Sticks

PREP: 40 minutes   **RISE:** 30 minutes

BAKE: 12 minutes   **COOL:** 5 minutes

OVEN: 375°F

NUTRITION FACTS per stick:

CALORIES 171
TOTAL FAT 3 g (1 g sat. fat)
CHOLESTEROL 2 mg
PROTEIN 5 g
CARBOHYDRATE 32 g
FIBER 2 g
SODIUM 224 mg

EXCHANGES 1.5 Starch, 0.5 Other Carbohydrates

Cream Cheese Frosting: In a medium bowl combine one-fourth of an 8-ounce package reduced-fat cream cheese (Neufchâtel), softened; ½ teaspoon vanilla; and, if desired, ¼ teaspoon butter flavoring. Beat with an electric mixer on medium speed until smooth. Gradually beat in 1½ cups powdered sugar. Beat in 1 to 2 teaspoons fat-free milk to make frosting of drizzling consistency. Makes about ¾ cup.

Continued from page 49

Italian-Style Dinner Roll Variations

Seeded Pull-Apart Rolls: Lightly grease a 10-inch fluted tube pan; set aside. In a shallow dish combine 1 egg white and 1 tablespoon water. In a small bowl combine ¼ cup flaxseeds; 3 tablespoons sesame seeds, toasted; 2 tablespoons poppy seeds; and 1 tablespoon cumin seeds, toasted.

Divide one 16-ounce loaf frozen whole wheat bread dough, thawed, into 36 portions. Roll each portion of dough into a ball. Roll each ball in egg white mixture, allowing excess to drip off. Roll in seed mixture to coat. Place coated rolls in prepared tube pan. Cover and let rise in a warm place until nearly double in size (30 to 60 minutes).

Preheat oven to 375°F. Bake for 20 to 25 minutes or until rolls sound hollow when lightly tapped. Invert onto a wire rack. Serve slightly warm or cool. Makes 12 servings.

Per serving: 140 cal., 5 g total fat (0 g sat. fat), 0 mg chol., 216 mg sodium, 20 g carbo., 3 g fiber, 6 g pro.

Exchanges: 1.5 Starch, 0.5 Fat

Gremolata-Stuffed Parker House Rolls: Lightly grease a baking sheet; set aside. In a small bowl combine ½ cup snipped fresh flat-leaf parsley, 2 tablespoons finely chopped walnuts or pecans, 1 tablespoon finely shredded lemon peel, and 4 to 6 cloves garlic, minced; set aside.

Divide one 16-ounce loaf frozen whole wheat bread dough, thawed, into 16 portions. On a lightly floured surface flatten each dough portion to a 3-inch round. Using the dull edge of a table knife, make an off-center crease in each dough round. Spoon about 2 teaspoons of the parsley mixture onto the small side of each round. Fold larger side over parsley mixture along the crease; press folded edge firmly. Place rolls, large halves up, 2 to 3 inches apart on prepared baking sheet. Cover and let rise in a warm place until nearly double in size (30 to 45 minutes).

Preheat oven to 375°F. Bake for 12 to 15 minutes or until golden brown. Serve warm. Makes 16 rolls.

Per roll: 83 cal., 2 g total fat (0 g sat. fat), 0 mg chol., 159 mg sodium, 14 g carbo., 1 g fiber, 4 g pro.

Exchanges: 1 Starch

Continued from page 47

Honey-Flax Sourdough Bread

Sourdough Starter: Dissolve 1 package active dry yeast in ½ cup warm water (105°F to 115°F). Add 2 cups all-purpose flour, 2 cups warm water (105°F to 115°F), and 1 tablespoon honey. Using a wooden spoon, beat until smooth. Cover with 100%-cotton cheesecloth. Let stand at room temperature (75°F to 85°F) for 5 to 10 days or until mixture has a fermented aroma and vigorous bubbling stops, stirring two or three times a day. (Fermentation time depends on room temperature; a warmer room will hasten the fermentation process.) To store, transfer Sourdough Starter to a 1-quart plastic container. Cover and chill.

To use, stir starter. Measure amount of cold starter called for in recipe; bring to room temperature. Replenish starter after each use. For each 1 cup starter removed, stir ¾ cup all-purpose flour, ¾ cup water, and 1 teaspoon honey into remaining starter. Cover with cheesecloth; let stand at room temperature about 1 day or until bubbly. Cover with lid; chill for later use. If starter is not used within 10 days, stir in 1 teaspoon honey. Continue to add 1 teaspoon honey every 10 days unless starter is replenished.

On the opener: Fajita-Ranch Chicken Wraps (*see recipe, page 63*)

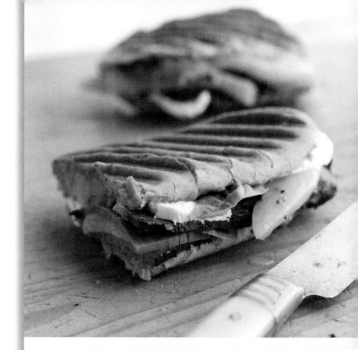

4 6-inch whole wheat
   hoagie rolls, split

   Olive oil nonstick cooking spray

10 ounces thinly sliced cooked
    roast beef

½ cup fresh basil leaves or fresh
   baby spinach

12 refrigerated mango slices,
    well drained

1 teaspoon black pepper

¼ cup semisoft goat cheese (chèvre)
   or 4 ounces provolone cheese,
   sliced

1 To assemble sandwiches, lightly coat outsides of hoagie rolls with nonstick cooking spray. Turn roll bottoms coated sides down; divide roast beef among roll bottoms. Top each with some basil and 3 mango slices. Sprinkle with pepper. Turn roll tops coated sides down; spread each with goat cheese. Place on sandwiches, cheese sides down.

2 Preheat an electric sandwich press, panini griddle, or covered indoor grill according to manufacturer's directions. (Or coat an unheated grill pan or large skillet with nonstick cooking spray. Preheat over low to medium-low heat for 1 to 2 minutes.) Add sandwiches in batches, if necessary. If using sandwich press, panini griddle, or covered indoor grill, close lid and grill for 4 or 5 minutes or until rolls are toasted and cheese melts. (If using grill pan or skillet, place a heavy skillet on sandwiches. Cook over medium-low heat for 7 to 10 minutes or until bottoms are toasted. Carefully remove top skillet, which may be hot. Turn sandwiches and top again with the skillet. Cook for 7 to 10 minutes more or until rolls are toasted and cheese melts.) Makes 4 servings.

Turkey-Sweet Pepper Panini: Prepare as above, except substitute thinly sliced turkey breast for the roast beef and ½ cup bottled roasted red sweet peppers, drained and cut into strips, for the mango. Makes 4 servings.

Per serving: 306 cal., 6 g total fat (2 g sat. fat), 42 mg chol., 1,277 mg sodium, 47 g carbo., 3 g fiber, 17 g pro.
Exchanges: 3 Starch, 2 Very Lean Meat

Roast Beef-Mango Panini

PREP: 20 minutes

COOK: 4 minutes per batch

NUTRITION FACTS per serving:

CALORIES 381
TOTAL FAT 5 g (3 g sat. fat)
CHOLESTEROL 35 mg
PROTEIN 20 g
CARBOHYDRATE 61 g
FIBER 2 g
SODIUM 1,042 mg

EXCHANGES 3 Starch, 1 Fruit, 2 Very Lean Meat

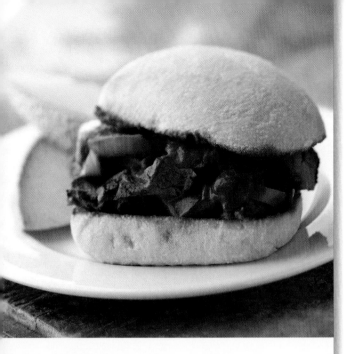

1   8-ounce can tomato sauce with roasted garlic or one 8-ounce can tomato sauce plus 1 clove garlic, minced

3   tablespoons tomato paste

2   tablespoons water

1   tablespoon Dijon-style mustard

1   tablespoon Worcestershire sauce

2   teaspoons honey

1   teaspoon finely chopped chipotle chile peppers in adobo sauce*

1   12-ounce beef flank steak

1   medium green sweet pepper, seeded and quartered

4   ½-inch-thick slices sweet onion (such as Vidalia, Walla Walla, or Maui)

     Nonstick cooking spray

4   ciabatta rolls, split and toasted

Chipotle-BBQ Steak Sandwiches

PREP: 25 minutes   **MARINATE:** 4 to 6 hours

GRILL: 17 minutes

NUTRITION FACTS per serving:

CALORIES 378

TOTAL FAT 9 g (3 g sat. fat)

CHOLESTEROL 35 mg

PROTEIN 25 g

CARBOHYDRATE 47 g

FIBER 4 g

SODIUM 1,030 mg

EXCHANGES 2 Starch, 2.5 Lean Meat

COOK'S TIP

Avoid marinating meat for longer than the recipe suggests. Overmarinating cuts such as flank steak breaks down the tissue and causes meat to become tough rather than tender.

1 For marinade, in a small bowl combine tomato sauce, tomato paste, water, mustard, Worcestershire sauce, honey, and chile peppers. Set aside. Trim fat from steak. Score both sides of steak in a diamond pattern by making shallow diagonal cuts at 1-inch intervals. Place steak in a large resealable plastic bag. Pour marinade over steak in bag. Seal bag; turn to coat steak. Marinate steak in the refrigerator for 4 to 6 hours, turning bag occasionally.

2 Drain steak, reserving marinade. Lightly coat sweet pepper quarters and onion slices with nonstick cooking spray.

3 For a charcoal grill, place steak, sweet pepper quarters, and onion slices on the rack of an uncovered grill directly over medium coals. Grill until steak is medium doneness (160°F) and vegetables are tender, turning all once halfway through grilling. Allow 17 to 21 minutes for the steak and 8 to 12 minutes for the vegetables. (For a gas grill, preheat grill. Reduce heat to medium. Place steak, sweet pepper quarters, and onion slices on grill rack over heat. Cover and grill as above.)

4 Meanwhile, for BBQ sauce, pour reserved marinade into a small saucepan. Bring to boiling; reduce heat. Simmer, uncovered, about 5 minutes or until desired consistency.

5 Thinly slice steak across the grain. Thinly slice sweet pepper quarters lengthwise. Place steak slices and sweet pepper strips on the bottom halves of ciabatta rolls. Top with onion slices. Spoon BBQ sauce on onions. Add ciabatta roll tops. Makes 4 servings.

*See handling note, page 67.

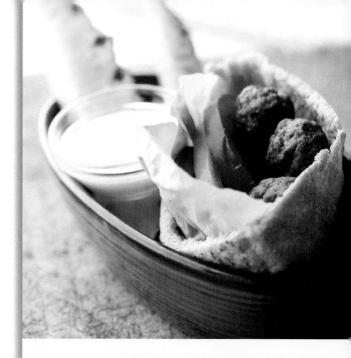

- ½ cup low-fat plain yogurt
- 1 teaspoon lemon juice
- 2 cloves garlic, minced
- ¼ teaspoon salt
- 12 ounces lean ground beef
- 1 tablespoon snipped fresh oregano or 1 teaspoon dried oregano, crushed
- ¾ teaspoon salt
- ⅛ to ¼ teaspoon cayenne pepper
- 4 large whole wheat pita bread rounds
- 8 lettuce leaves
- 2 medium red and/or yellow tomatoes, sliced

1 Preheat oven to 350°F. For sauce, in a small bowl combine yogurt, lemon juice, half of the garlic, and ¼ teaspoon salt. Set aside.

2 For meatballs, in a medium bowl combine ground beef, oregano, ¾ teaspoon salt, cayenne pepper, and remaining garlic; mix well. Form beef mixture into 24 meatballs, each about 1 inch in diameter. Place meatballs in a 15×10×1-inch baking pan.

3 Bake meatballs, uncovered, about 20 minutes or until cooked through.

4 Cut pita rounds in half crosswise; open pita halves to make pockets. Line pita pockets with lettuce leaves. Fill pitas with tomato slices and meatballs. Serve with sauce. Makes 8 servings.

Meatball Pitas

PREP: 25 minutes   **BAKE:** 20 minutes
OVEN: 350°F

NUTRITION FACTS per serving:

CALORIES 180
TOTAL FAT 5 g (2 g sat. fat)
CHOLESTEROL 29 mg
PROTEIN 13 g
CARBOHYDRATE 21 g
FIBER 3 g
SODIUM 508 mg

EXCHANGES 1 Starch, 1.5 Lean Meat, 0.5 Vegetable

NUTRITION NOTE

When shopping for ground beef, look for 95% to 98% lean. Although a little fat is necessary for flavor and moistness, cut it down to the smallest amount possible.

1 tablespoon olive oil

2 cups sliced fresh mushrooms

1 large red or green sweet pepper, seeded and chopped

2 teaspoons snipped fresh oregano or ½ teaspoon dried oregano, crushed

1 8-ounce can pizza sauce

4 oval multigrain wraps

6 ounces thinly sliced low-sodium cooked ham, coarsely chopped

½ cup shredded reduced-fat cheddar cheese or reduced-fat mozzarella cheese (2 ounces)

1 Preheat oven to 375°F. In a large skillet heat oil over medium heat. Add mushrooms and sweet pepper; cook for 5 to 10 minutes or until vegetables are tender, stirring occasionally. Stir in oregano.

2 Meanwhile, spread some pizza sauce on one side of each wrap, leaving a ½-inch border around the edge. Divide ham among wraps, arranging it on top of sauce on half of each wrap. Top ham with mushroom mixture. Sprinkle with cheese. Fold wraps in half. Place on a large baking sheet. Bake for 8 to 10 minutes or until heated through. Makes 4 servings.

Mushroom and Ham Fold-Overs

PREP: 25 minutes   **BAKE:** 8 minutes
OVEN: 375°F

NUTRITION FACTS per serving:

CALORIES 284
TOTAL FAT 13 g (4 g sat. fat)
CHOLESTEROL 34 mg
PROTEIN 25 g
CARBOHYDRATE 26 g
FIBER 11 g
SODIUM 1,232 mg

EXCHANGES 1.5 Starch, 2.5 Medium-Fat Meat, 1 Vegetable

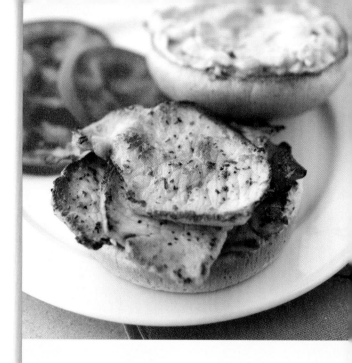

1　12-ounce boneless pork top loin roast (single loin)

1　small avocado, halved, pitted, and peeled

2　tablespoons snipped fresh flat-leaf parsley

2　teaspoons lemon juice

1　clove garlic, minced

¼　teaspoon salt

½　teaspoon Greek seasoning

　　Nonstick cooking spray

4　whole grain hamburger buns, split and toasted

1　medium tomato, sliced

1 For easier slicing, wrap and freeze pork for 1 hour. Meanwhile, in a small bowl mash avocado with a fork. Stir in parsley, lemon juice, garlic, and ⅛ teaspoon salt. Cover surface of the mixture with plastic wrap and set aside.

2 Working from one end of the roast, cut pork crosswise into twelve to sixteen ⅛- to ¼-inch-thick slices. Sprinkle pork slices with Greek seasoning and remaining ⅛ teaspoon salt.

3 Coat an unheated large nonstick skillet with nonstick cooking spray. Preheat over medium-high heat. Cook pork slices, half at a time, in hot skillet for 2 to 3 minutes or until pork slices are no longer pink on outside, turning once to brown evenly. Keep cooked pork slices warm while cooking the remaining pork.

4 To serve, layer cooked pork slices on bun bottoms. Top with sliced tomato. Spread avocado mixture on cut sides of bun tops. Place bun tops on tomato, avocado spread sides down. Makes 4 servings.

Mediterranean Pork Sandwiches with Avocado Spread

PREP: 25 minutes

FREEZE: 1 hour

NUTRITION FACTS per serving:

CALORIES 328
TOTAL FAT 15 g (4 g sat. fat)
CHOLESTEROL 50 mg
PROTEIN 22 g
CARBOHYDRATE 25 g
FIBER 4 g
SODIUM 407 mg

EXCHANGES 1.5 Starch, 2.5 Lean Meat, 1.5 Fat

12 ounces skinless, boneless chicken breast strips for stir-frying

¼ teaspoon garlic salt

⅛ teaspoon black pepper

Nonstick cooking spray

2 cups packaged shredded broccoli (broccoli slaw mix)

¼ teaspoon ground ginger

3 10-inch whole wheat flour tortillas, warmed*

1 recipe Peanut Sauce

Thai Chicken-Broccoli Wraps

START TO FINISH: 25 minutes

NUTRITION FACTS per serving:

CALORIES 191
TOTAL FAT 6 g (1 g sat. fat)
CHOLESTEROL 33 mg
PROTEIN 18 g
CARBOHYDRATE 16 g
FIBER 2 g
SODIUM 460 mg

EXCHANGES 1 Starch, 2 Very Lean Meat, 0.5 Vegetable, 0.5 Fat

1 Sprinkle chicken strips with garlic salt and pepper. Coat an unheated large nonstick skillet with nonstick cooking spray. Preheat skillet over medium-high heat. Add seasoned chicken; cook and stir for 2 to 3 minutes or until chicken is no longer pink. Remove chicken from skillet; keep warm. Add broccoli and ginger to skillet. Cook and stir for 2 to 3 minutes or until vegetables are crisp-tender.

2 Spread tortillas with Peanut Sauce. Top with chicken strips and vegetable mixture. Roll up tortillas. Cut each wrap in half. Serve immediately. Makes 6 servings.

*See tortilla warming note, page 63.

Peanut Sauce: In a small saucepan combine 3 tablespoons creamy peanut butter; 2 tablespoons water; 1 tablespoon reduced-sodium soy sauce; 1 clove garlic, minced; and ¼ teaspoon ground ginger. Heat over very low heat until melted and smooth, whisking constantly.

COOK'S TIP

If you're pressed for time and can't make your own peanut sauce, look for organic and/or health-conscious brands of bottled peanut sauces.

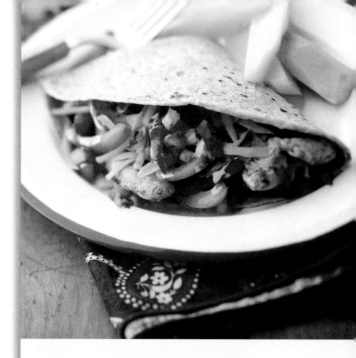

- 12 ounces skinless, boneless chicken breast strips for stir-frying
- ½ teaspoon chili powder
- ¼ teaspoon garlic powder

    Nonstick cooking spray
- 2 small red, yellow, and/or green sweet peppers, seeded and cut into thin strips
- 2 tablespoons bottled reduced-calorie ranch salad dressing
- 2 10-inch whole wheat, tomato, or jalapeño flour tortillas, warmed*
- ½ cup purchased deli-style fresh salsa
- ⅓ cup shredded reduced-fat cheddar cheese

1 Sprinkle chicken strips with chili powder and garlic powder. Coat an unheated large nonstick skillet with nonstick cooking spray. Preheat over medium-high heat. Cook chicken in hot skillet over medium heat for 4 to 6 minutes or until chicken is no longer pink. Remove chicken from skillet. Add sweet peppers to skillet; cook about 5 minutes or until peppers are tender. Return chicken to skillet; add salad dressing. Lightly toss to coat.

2 Divide chicken and pepper mixture between warmed tortillas, placing it on one side of each tortilla. Top with salsa and cheese. Fold each tortilla over; cut in half. Makes 4 servings.

*To warm tortillas, preheat oven to 350°F. Wrap tortillas tightly in foil; bake for 5 to 8 minutes or until warm. (Or wrap tortillas in white microwave-safe paper towels; microwave on 100% power [high] for 20 to 30 seconds or until tortillas are softened.)

Fajita-Ranch Chicken Wraps

START TO FINISH: 30 minutes

OVEN: 350°F

NUTRITION FACTS per serving:

CALORIES 267
TOTAL FAT 7 g (2 g sat. fat)
CHOLESTEROL 57 mg
PROTEIN 26 g
CARBOHYDRATE 24 g
FIBER 5 g
SODIUM 706 mg

EXCHANGES 1.5 Starch, 3 Very Lean Meat, 0.5 Vegetable, 0.5 Fat

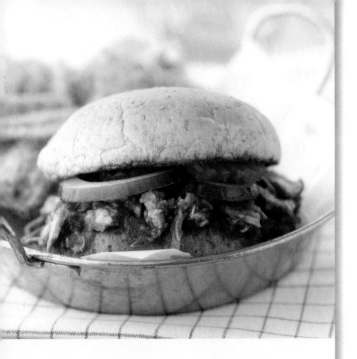

1 recipe Barbecue Sauce
2 cups shredded cooked chicken*
6 whole wheat hamburger buns, split and, if desired, toasted
Red onion slices (optional)
Dill pickle slices (optional)

1 Prepare Barbecue Sauce. Add shredded chicken to sauce. Heat through, stirring frequently. Serve on split buns. If desired, serve with red onion slices and dill pickle slices. Makes 6 servings.

*For shredded chicken, use a purchased deli-roasted chicken. Pull the meat from the chicken, discarding skin and bones. Use two forks to pull chicken into shreds. Or use leftover cooked chicken breast.

Barbecue Sauce: In a medium sauccpan heat 1 tablespoon olive oil over medium heat. Add ¼ cup finely chopped onion; cook for 3 to 5 minutes or until tender, stirring occasionally. Add one 8-ounce can tomato sauce, 2 tablespoons tomato paste, 1 tablespoon Dijon-style mustard, 1 tablespoon Worcestershire sauce, and 1 teaspoon honey. Bring to boiling; reduce heat. Simmer, uncovered, about 5 minutes or until desired consistency. Season to taste with salt and black pepper.

Pulled Chicken Sandwiches

START TO FINISH: 25 minutes

NUTRITION FACTS per serving:

- -

CALORIES 254
TOTAL FAT 8 g (2 g sat. fat)
CHOLESTEROL 42 mg
PROTEIN 19 g
CARBOHYDRATE 27 g
FIBER 1 g
SODIUM 539 mg

EXCHANGES 2 Starch, 2 Lean Meat

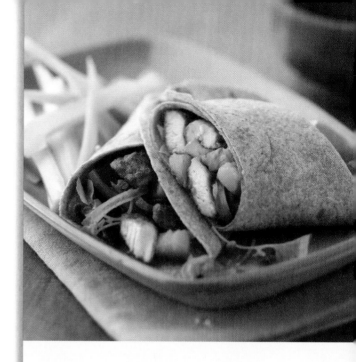

12 ounces skinless, boneless chicken breast halves, cut into ¼-inch-thick slices
1   tablespoon curry powder
1   teaspoon ground coriander
¼   teaspoon salt
¼   teaspoon black pepper
1   tablespoon olive oil
1   cup thinly sliced red onion
1   cup chopped mango
2   cups shredded romaine
1   cup watercress, tough stems removed
2   tablespoons lemon juice
2   teaspoons olive oil
6   7- to 8-inch whole wheat flour tortillas

Curried Chicken-Mango Wraps

1 In a medium bowl combine chicken, curry powder, coriander, salt, and pepper. Cover and marinate in the refrigerator for 30 minutes.

2 In a large skillet heat 1 tablespoon olive oil over medium heat. Add chicken and red onion; cook and stir for 4 to 6 minutes or until chicken is tender and no longer pink. Add mango; cook and stir until heated through.

3 Meanwhile, in a medium bowl combine romaine and watercress. Drizzle with lemon juice and 2 teaspoons olive oil; toss gently to coat.

4 To serve, divide the chicken mixture and the romaine mixture among tortillas. Roll up tortillas. Makes 6 servings.

PREP: 25 minutes

MARINATE: 30 minutes

NUTRITION FACTS per serving:

CALORIES 260
TOTAL FAT 8 g (2 g sat. fat)
CHOLESTEROL 33 mg
PROTEIN 22 g
CARBOHYDRATE 23 g
FIBER 12 g
SODIUM 459 mg

EXCHANGES 1.5 Starch, 2.5 Very Lean Meat, 1 Vegetable, 1 Fat

COOK'S TIP

Watercress is a mustard green that adds savory spicy flavor and vitamins A, C, and K. Thoroughly wash and pat dry watercress before storing it in a plastic bag in the refrigerator.

1 tablespoon olive oil

1 teaspoon lemon juice

¼ teaspoon paprika

Dash salt

Dash black pepper

2 small skinless, boneless chicken breast halves (8 to 12 ounces total)

2 large whole wheat pita bread rounds

1 7-ounce container hummus

¾ cup coarsely chopped plum tomato

½ cup thinly sliced cucumber

⅓ cup plain low-fat yogurt

Chicken and Hummus Pitas

PREP: 20 minutes

BROIL: 12 minutes

NUTRITION FACTS per serving:

CALORIES 289
TOTAL FAT 10 g (2 g sat. fat)
CHOLESTEROL 34 mg
PROTEIN 20 g
CARBOHYDRATE 31 g
FIBER 5 g
SODIUM 380 mg

EXCHANGES 1.5 Starch, 0.5 Other Carbohydrates, 2 Very Lean Meat, 1 Fat

1 Preheat broiler. In a small bowl combine oil, lemon juice, paprika, salt, and pepper. Place chicken on the unheated rack of a broiler pan. Brush all sides of the chicken breast halves with the oil mixture. Broil 4 to 5 inches from heat for 12 to 15 minutes or until chicken is no longer pink (170°F), turning once halfway through broiling. Cool slightly; cut into strips.

2 Cut pita rounds in half crosswise; open pita halves to make pockets. Spread hummus inside pita pockets. Stuff pockets with chicken strips, tomato, cucumber, and yogurt.
Makes 4 servings.

NUTRITION NOTE

While striving to include more beans in your diet, remember, they can be added to many dishes in a variety of forms, such as the hummus in this recipe. The main ingredient in hummus is garbanzo beans, which contain manganese, folate, protein, fiber, and iron.

- ½ cup Black Bean-Smoked Chile Dip
- 4 7- or 8-inch whole wheat flour tortillas
- 12 ounces cooked skinless chicken or turkey breast, chopped (about 2⅓ cups)
- 4 cups shredded or torn romaine or whole fresh baby spinach leaves
- 1 cup coarsely snipped fresh cilantro
- ¼ cup purchased salsa

1 Spread Black Bean-Smoked Chile Dip on one side of each tortilla. Top with chicken, romaine, cilantro, and salsa. Roll up tortillas. If desired, secure with toothpicks. Makes 4 servings.

Black Bean-Smoked Chile Dip: In a small saucepan heat 1 tablespoon canola oil over medium heat. Add ¾ cup finely chopped onion, 1 teaspoon ground coriander, and 1 teaspoon ground cumin; cover and cook about 10 minutes or until very tender, stirring occasionally. Remove from heat; stir in ¼ cup snipped fresh cilantro. Transfer onion mixture to a blender or food processor. Add one 15-ounce can black beans, rinsed and drained; ½ cup water; 1 tablespoon lime juice; 1 teaspoon finely chopped chipotle chile pepper in adobo sauce;* and ⅛ teaspoon salt. Cover and blend or process until nearly smooth. Serve immediately or cover and chill for up to 3 days before serving. Makes 1⅔ cups.

*Because chile peppers contain volatile oils that can burn your skin and eyes, avoid direct contact with them as much as possible. When working with chile peppers, wear plastic or rubber gloves. If your bare hands do touch the peppers, wash your hands and nails well with soap and warm water.

Chicken and Black Bean Wraps

START TO FINISH: 10 minutes

NUTRITION FACTS per serving:

CALORIES 324
TOTAL FAT 8 g (2 g sat. fat)
CHOLESTEROL 72 mg
PROTEIN 38 g
CARBOHYDRATE 24 g
FIBER 14 g
SODIUM 600 mg

EXCHANGES 1.5 Starch, 4.5 Very Lean Meat, 1 Vegetable, 1 Fat

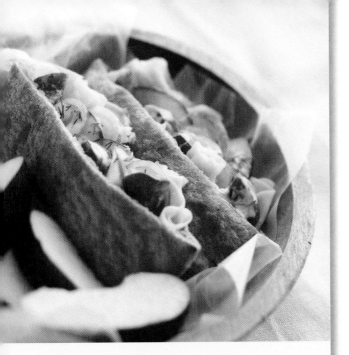

Deli Greek-Style Pitas

START TO FINISH: 20 minutes

NUTRITION FACTS per serving:

CALORIES 274
TOTAL FAT 4 g (1 g sat. fat)
CHOLESTEROL 40 mg
PROTEIN 18 g
CARBOHYDRATE 45 g
FIBER 6 g
SODIUM 1,204 mg

EXCHANGES 2.5 Starch, 2 Very Lean Meat, 0.5 Vegetable

NUTRITION NOTE

Cucumbers are more than 90 percent water, so feel free to munch on any extra cucumber that doesn't go in the pita. You'll be consuming very few calories while getting vitamin C and potassium.

¼ cup plain low-fat yogurt

2 teaspoons vinegar

1 teaspoon snipped fresh dill or ¼ teaspoon dried dill

½ teaspoon sugar

1 cup thinly sliced cucumber

½ of a small red onion, halved and thinly sliced

½ cup chopped plum tomato

4 6-inch whole wheat or white pita bread rounds

10 ounces thinly sliced deli cooked turkey, roast beef, or cooked chicken

1 In a medium bowl combine yogurt, vinegar, dill, and sugar. Add cucumber, red onion, and tomato. Toss gently to coat. Set aside.

2 Cut pita rounds in half crosswise; open pita halves to make pockets. Line pita pockets with turkey. Spoon the cucumber mixture into pita pockets. Makes 4 servings.

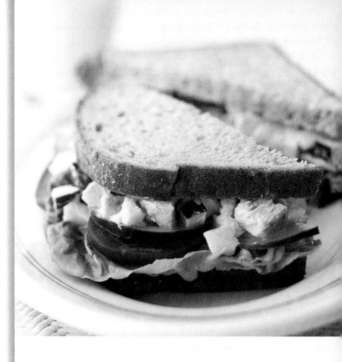

- 1 cup chopped cooked chicken (5 ounces)
- ⅓ cup chopped cored apple or finely chopped celery
- 1 hard-cooked egg, peeled and chopped
- 2 tablespoons plain low-fat yogurt
- 2 tablespoons light mayonnaise or salad dressing

    Salt

    Black pepper

- 8 slices whole wheat bread
- 4 leaf lettuce or romaine leaves
- 1 medium tomato, thinly sliced
- ½ of a small cucumber, thinly sliced (about ¾ cup)

1 In a medium bowl stir together chicken, apple, and egg. Add yogurt and mayonnaise; stir to combine. Season to taste with salt and pepper.*

2 Top half of the bread slices with a lettuce leaf each. Then add tomato slices, cucumber slices, and some of the chicken mixture to each. Add one of the remaining bread slices to each stack. Cut each sandwich in half. Makes 4 servings.

*If desired, cover and chill the chicken mixture for up to 4 hours before using.

Chicken Salad Sandwiches

START TO FINISH: 25 minutes

NUTRITION FACTS per serving:

CALORIES 248
TOTAL FAT 7 g (2 g sat. fat)
CHOLESTEROL 86 mg
PROTEIN 18 g
CARBOHYDRATE 28 g
FIBER 5 g
SODIUM 447 mg

EXCHANGES 1.5 Starch, 2 Very Lean Meat, 1 Vegetable, 0.5 Fat

NUTRITION NOTE

To cook chicken with the least amount of added calories and for perfectly moist meat, poach it in water. Put chicken in a small saucepan with just enough water to cover, bring to a rolling boil for 2 minutes, remove from heat. Let stand for 20 minutes. Or purchase refrigerated cooked chicken breast from the grocery store to save time.

Tuna Salad Pockets

START TO FINISH: 20 minutes

NUTRITION FACTS per serving:

CALORIES 272
TOTAL FAT 10 g (2 g sat. fat)
CHOLESTEROL 36 mg
PROTEIN 24 g
CARBOHYDRATE 22 g
FIBER 3 g
SODIUM 659 mg

EXCHANGES 1 Starch, 2.5 Very Lean Meat, 2 Vegetable, 2 Fat

1	12-ounce can solid white tuna (water pack), drained and broken into chunks
¼	cup finely chopped red onion
¼	cup thinly sliced celery
¼	cup shredded carrot
1	tablespoon capers, rinsed and drained
2	tablespoons olive oil
2	tablespoons lime juice
1	tablespoon Dijon-style mustard
1	tablespoon champagne vinegar or white wine vinegar
1½	cups torn mixed salad greens
2	large whole wheat pita bread rounds

1 In a medium bowl combine tuna, red onion, celery, carrot, and capers; set aside. For vinaigrette, in a small screw-top jar combine olive oil, lime juice, mustard, and vinegar. Cover and shake well to combine. Pour vinaigrette over tuna mixture; toss gently to combine. Add greens; toss gently to combine.

2 Cut pita rounds in half crosswise; open pita halves to make pockets. Fill pockets with tuna mixture. Makes 4 servings.

COOK'S TIP

Capers or caper buds, the buds of the caper flower, are salted and pickled. They are extremely salty, so be careful about adding seasoning when using capers.

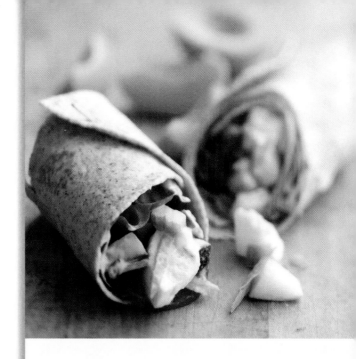

3 hard-cooked eggs, peeled and chopped

½ cup chopped cucumber

½ cup chopped zucchini or yellow summer squash

¼ cup chopped red onion

¼ cup shredded carrot

2 tablespoons fat-free mayonnaise dressing or light mayonnaise or salad dressing

1 tablespoon Dijon-style mustard

2 teaspoons fat-free milk

½ teaspoon snipped fresh basil or ¼ teaspoon dried basil, crushed

   Dash paprika

3 leaf lettuce leaves

3 10-inch whole grain, spinach, or vegetable flour tortillas

1 plum tomato, thinly sliced

1 In a large bowl combine eggs, cucumber, zucchini, red onion, and carrot. For dressing, in a small bowl stir together mayonnaise, mustard, milk, basil, and paprika. Pour dressing over egg mixture; toss gently to coat.

2 For each wrap, place a lettuce leaf on a tortilla. Top with tomato slices, slightly off center. Spoon egg mixture on tomato slices. Fold in two opposite sides of the tortilla; roll up from the bottom. Diagonally cut tortilla roll-ups in quarters. Makes 6 servings.

Egg and Vegetable Salad Wraps

START TO FINISH: 30 minutes

NUTRITION FACTS per serving:

CALORIES 161
TOTAL FAT 5 g (1 g sat. fat)
CHOLESTEROL 107 mg
PROTEIN 7 g
CARBOHYDRATE 21 g
FIBER 4 g
SODIUM 402 mg

EXCHANGES 1.5 Starch, 0.5 Very Lean Meat, 0.5 Vegetable, 0.5 Fat

Veggie Salad in a Pocket

PREP: 20 minutes

CHILL: 2 to 24 hours

NUTRITION FACTS per serving:

CALORIES 166
TOTAL FAT 2 g (0 g sat. fat)
CHOLESTEROL 0 mg
PROTEIN 7 g
CARBOHYDRATE 31 g
FIBER 6 g
SODIUM 599 mg

EXCHANGES 1 Starch, 0.5 Other Carbohydrates, 1 Vegetable

1   cup chopped yellow summer squash and/or zucchini

¾   cup chopped broccoli

2   plum tomatoes, seeded and chopped (about ⅔ cup)

8   pitted kalamata or ripe olives, chopped

2   tablespoons snipped fresh flat-leaf parsley or regular parsley

2   tablespoons bottled fat-free Italian salad dressing

2   6- to 7-inch whole wheat pita bread rounds or four 6- to 7-inch whole wheat flour tortillas

½   cup Spicy Navy Bean Hummus

1 In a medium bowl combine squash, broccoli, tomato, olives, and parsley; toss with salad dressing. Cover and chill for 2 to 24 hours.

2 If using pita bread, cut rounds in half crosswise; open pita halves to make pockets. Spread the inside of each pita bread pocket or one side of each tortilla with 2 tablespoons Spicy Navy Bean Hummus.

3 Spoon chilled vegetable mixture into pita pockets or onto tortillas. If using tortillas, fold or roll them. Makes 4 servings.

Spicy Navy Bean Hummus: In a food processor combine one 15- to 19-ounce can navy or cannellini beans (white kidney beans), rinsed and drained; ¼ cup bottled fat-free Italian salad dressing; and 1 tablespoon spicy brown mustard. Cover and process until smooth and spreadable. (Or mash beans with a potato masher or fork. Stir in salad dressing and mustard.) Transfer to an airtight storage container. Cover and chill for up to 1 week. Makes 1⅓ cups.

On the opener: Spinach and Lentil Salad with Toasted Walnuts *(see recipe, page 81)*

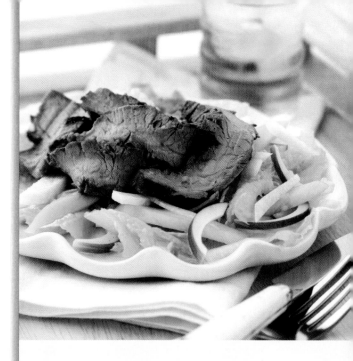

- 12 ounces beef flank steak or boneless beef top sirloin steak, cut 1 inch thick
- 1/8 teaspoon salt
- 1/8 teaspoon black pepper
- 1/3 cup lime juice
- 2 tablespoons olive oil
- 2 tablespoons snipped fresh cilantro
- 1 tablespoon honey
- 2 cloves garlic, minced
- 8 cups torn romaine
- 5 ounces jicama, peeled and cut into thin bite-size strips (1 cup)
- 1 medium mango, seeded, peeled, and sliced
- 1 small red onion, cut into thin wedges

1 Trim fat from steak. If using flank steak, score both sides of steak in a diamond pattern by making shallow diagonal cuts at 1-inch intervals. Sprinkle steak with salt and pepper.

2 For a charcoal grill, place steak on the rack of an uncovered grill directly over medium coals. Grill until medium doneness (160°F), turning once halfway through grilling time. Allow 17 to 21 minutes for flank steak or 18 to 22 minutes for top sirloin steak. (For a gas grill, preheat grill. Reduce heat to medium. Place steak on grill rack over heat. Cover and grill as above.) Thinly slice steak diagonally across the grain.

3 Meanwhile, for dressing, in a small bowl whisk together lime juice, oil, cilantro, honey, and garlic.

4 To serve, divide romaine among six serving plates. Top with steak slices, jicama, mango, and red onion. Drizzle dressing over salads. Makes 6 servings.

Broiler Directions: Preheat broiler. Place steak on the unheated rack of a broiler pan. Broil 3 to 4 inches from heat until medium doneness (160°F), turning once halfway through broiling time. Allow 15 to 18 minutes for flank steak or 20 to 22 minutes for sirloin steak.

Mango-Steak Salad with Lime Dressing

PREP: 25 minutes

GRILL: 17 minutes

NUTRITION FACTS per serving:

CALORIES 195
TOTAL FAT 9 g (2 g sat. fat)
CHOLESTEROL 23 mg
PROTEIN 14 g
CARBOHYDRATE 17 g
FIBER 3 g
SODIUM 87 mg

EXCHANGES 0.5 Fruit, 1.5 Lean Meat, 1.5 Vegetable, 1 Fat

Spinach and Basil Salad with Beef

START TO FINISH: 25 minutes

NUTRITION FACTS per serving:

- -

CALORIES 311
TOTAL FAT 15 g (3 g sat. fat)
CHOLESTEROL 49 mg
PROTEIN 30 g
CARBOHYDRATE 14 g
FIBER 4 g
SODIUM 92 mg

EXCHANGES 0.5 Fruit, 4 Lean Meat,
1.5 Vegetable, 0.5 Fat

NUTRITION NOTE

Oranges are known for high levels of the
antioxidant vitamin C, an important vitamin
for bones, teeth, and wound healing. Once
oranges are squeezed or cut, the level of
vitamin C diminishes quickly. Eat them
shortly after cutting or squeezing.

¼   cup pear nectar

2   tablespoons canola oil

2   tablespoons white wine vinegar

½   teaspoon Worcestershire sauce
      for chicken

⅛   teaspoon black pepper

4   cups fresh baby spinach

2   cups sliced fresh mushrooms

½   cup lightly packed fresh
      basil leaves

12   ounces sliced cooked beef sirloin
      steak, cut into thin strips*

2   medium oranges, peeled
      and sectioned

¼   cup sliced almonds, toasted

1 For dressing, in a screw-top jar combine pear
nectar, oil, vinegar, Worcestershire sauce, and
pepper. Cover and shake well.

2 In a bowl toss together spinach, mushrooms,
and basil leaves. Divide mixture among four
serving plates. Top with beef strips; add orange
sections. Drizzle with dressing and sprinkle with
almonds. Makes 4 servings.

*If you are cooking your own beef, start with
1 to 1¼ pounds boneless beef top sirloin steak,
cut 1 inch thick. Preheat broiler. Place steak on
the unheated rack of a broiler pan and broil 3 to
4 inches from heat to desired doneness, turning
once halfway through broiling. Allow
15 to 17 minutes for medium-rare doneness
(145°F) or 20 to 22 minutes for medium
doneness (160°F).

- 1 pound boneless beef top sirloin steak, cut 1 inch thick
- 1 cup reduced-calorie balsamic vinaigrette salad dressing
- ½ of a 1-pound loaf whole grain crusty bread, cut into 1-inch-thick slices
- 2 medium yellow, green, and/or red sweet peppers, quartered

  Nonstick cooking spray
- 2 cups cherry or grape tomatoes, halved if large
- 3 ounces part-skim mozzarella cheese, cubed
- 1 tablespoon snipped fresh mint

  Fresh mint leaves (optional)

1 Place steak in a large resealable plastic bag set in a shallow dish. Add ½ cup vinaigrette. Seal bag; turn to coat beef. Marinate in the refrigerator for 1 to 2 hours, turning bag occasionally.

2 Coat bread slices and pepper quarters with nonstick cooking spray. Set aside. Drain steak, discarding marinade.

3 For a charcoal grill, place steak, bread, and pepper quarters on the rack of an uncovered grill directly over medium coals. Grill bread for 3 to 4 minutes or until lightly browned, turning once. Grill peppers for 8 to 10 minutes or until crisp-tender, turning once halfway through grilling. Grill beef until desired doneness, turning once halfway through grilling. Allow 14 to 18 minutes for medium-rare doneness (145°F) or 18 to 22 minutes for medium doneness (160°F). Remove items from the grill as they are done. (For a gas grill, preheat grill. Reduce heat to medium. Place steak, bread, and pepper quarters on grill rack over heat. Cover and grill as above.)

4 To serve, cut bread into cubes. Cut pepper quarters into bite-size strips. Cut steak into bite-size strips. In a very large bowl toss together bread, peppers, steak, tomatoes, and mozzarella cheese. Stir the snipped mint into remaining ½ cup vinaigrette. Add to steak mixture; toss to coat. If desired, garnish with fresh mint leaves. Serve immediately. Makes 6 servings.

Grilled Beef Panzanella

PREP: 25 minutes **MARINATE:** 1 to 2 hours
GRILL: 14 minutes

NUTRITION FACTS per serving:

CALORIES 302
TOTAL FAT 11 g (3 g sat. fat)
CHOLESTEROL 55 mg
PROTEIN 27 g
CARBOHYDRATE 24 g
FIBER 5 g
SODIUM 722 mg

EXCHANGES 1.5 Starch, 3 Lean Meat, 0.5 Vegetable

12 ounces pork tenderloin

⅛ teaspoon salt

⅛ teaspoon black pepper

2 tablespoons honey mustard

6 cups torn romaine and/or
   fresh spinach

2 cups fresh or canned pineapple
   chunks and/or sliced fresh
   nectarines or peaches

   Cracked black pepper (optional)

1 recipe Ginger-Pineapple Dressing

Roast Pork Salad with Ginger-Pineapple Dressing

PREP: 25 minutes   **ROAST:** 25 minutes
OVEN: 425°F

NUTRITION FACTS per serving:

CALORIES 240
TOTAL FAT 8 g (2 g sat. fat)
CHOLESTEROL 60 mg
PROTEIN 19 g
CARBOHYDRATE 22 g
FIBER 3 g
SODIUM 219 mg

EXCHANGES 1 Fruit, 2.5 Very Lean Meat,
1 Vegetable, 1.5 Fat

1 Preheat oven to 425°F. Trim fat from pork tenderloin; sprinkle pork with salt and ground black pepper. Place pork tenderloin on a rack in a shallow roasting pan. Roast for 20 minutes.

2 Spoon honey mustard on pork tenderloin. Roast for 5 to 10 minutes more or until an instant-read thermometer inserted in the thickest part of the tenderloin registers 160°F.

3 To serve, thinly slice pork tenderloin. On four serving plates arrange romaine, pork, and fruit. If desired, sprinkle salads with cracked black pepper. Stir Ginger-Pineapple Dressing; drizzle onto salads. Makes 4 servings.

Make-Ahead Directions: Make Ginger-Pineapple Dressing; cover and chill for up to 24 hours.

Ginger-Pineapple Dressing: In a small bowl combine ¼ cup low-fat mayonnaise dressing, ¼ cup unsweetened pineapple juice or orange juice, 1 tablespoon honey mustard, and 1 teaspoon grated fresh ginger. Cover; chill until serving time.

1 small cantaloupe, halved, peeled, and seeded

4 cups torn romaine

8 ounces lean cooked ham, cut into bite-size strips (about 1½ cups)

1 small cucumber, sliced

1 cup torn fresh spinach

2 green onions, thinly sliced

¼ cup unsweetened pineapple juice

1 tablespoon white wine vinegar

1 tablespoon canola oil

1½ teaspoons snipped fresh mint or ½ teaspoon dried mint, crushed

¼ cup sliced almonds, toasted (optional)

1 Coarsely chop one-quarter of the melon; slice remaining melon. In a large bowl combine chopped melon, romaine, ham, cucumber, spinach, and green onion.

2 In a screw-top jar combine pineapple juice, white wine vinegar, oil, and mint. Cover and shake well.

3 Arrange melon slices on four serving plates. Drizzle dressing over greens mixture; toss lightly to coat. Divide greens mixture among plates with melon slices. If desired, sprinkle with almonds. Makes 4 servings.

COOK'S TIP

When choosing any type of melon, pick those that feel heavy for their size and have no cracks or bruises. When cantaloupe is ripe, the area between the webbing will be light gold.

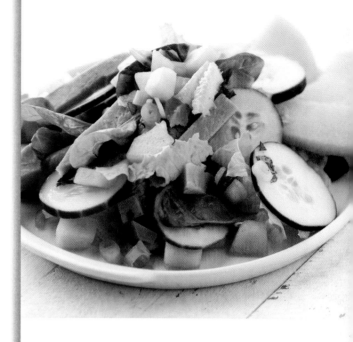

Ham and Cantaloupe Salad

START TO FINISH: 25 minutes

NUTRITION FACTS per serving:

CALORIES 155
TOTAL FAT 5 g (1 g sat. fat)
CHOLESTEROL 27 mg
PROTEIN 12 g
CARBOHYDRATE 16 g
FIBER 3 g
SODIUM 655 mg

EXCHANGES 0.5 Fruit, 2 Lean Meat, 1.5 Vegetable

Caesar Salad with Grilled Portobello Mushrooms

PREP: 25 minutes **BAKE:** 10 minutes
GRILL: 12 minutes **OVEN:** 350°F

NUTRITION FACTS per serving:

CALORIES 304
TOTAL FAT 13 g (3 g sat. fat)
CHOLESTEROL 79 mg
PROTEIN 32 g
CARBOHYDRATE 16 g
FIBER 4 g
SODIUM 612 mg

EXCHANGES 0.5 Starch, 4 Very Lean Meat, 2 Vegetable, 2 Fat

2	fresh portobello mushrooms (about 4 ounces each)
1	pound skinless, boneless chicken breast halves
	Nonstick cooking spray
¼	teaspoon salt
¼	teaspoon black pepper
1	tablespoon lemon juice
1	tablespoon red wine vinegar
2	teaspoons Dijon-style mustard
1	teaspoon Worcestershire sauce
1	clove garlic, minced
⅛	teaspoon black pepper
½	cup light mayonnaise or salad dressing
8	cups torn romaine
1	recipe Whole Wheat Croutons or ½ cup packaged whole wheat croutons
2	tablespoons shredded Parmesan cheese

1 Wipe mushrooms clean with a damp cloth. Remove stems and gills from mushrooms. Lightly coat both sides of mushrooms and chicken breast halves with nonstick cooking spray; sprinkle chicken with salt and ¼ teaspoon pepper.

2 For a charcoal grill, place mushrooms and chicken on the rack of an uncovered grill directly over medium coals. Grill mushrooms for 10 to 12 minutes or until tender. Grill chicken for 12 to 15 minutes or until no longer pink (170°F), turning once halfway through grilling. (For a gas grill, preheat grill. Reduce heat to medium. Place mushrooms and chicken on grill rack over heat. Cover and grill as above.)

3 Meanwhile, for dressing, in a small bowl combine lemon juice, red wine vinegar, Dijon-style mustard, Worcestershire sauce, garlic, and ⅛ teaspoon pepper. Whisk in mayonnaise.

4 Divide lettuce among four serving plates. Slice grilled mushrooms and chicken. Arrange on lettuce. Spoon dressing over salads. Sprinkle with Whole Wheat Croutons and Parmesan cheese. Makes 4 servings.

Whole Wheat Croutons: Preheat oven to 350°F. Cut 2 slices whole wheat bread into ½- to 1-inch pieces. Spread pieces in an even layer in a shallow baking pan. Lightly coat bread cubes with nonstick cooking spray; toss to turn pieces. Spread evenly and lightly coat again with nonstick cooking spray. Bake about 10 minutes or until bread cubes are lightly browned and crisp. Cool completely.

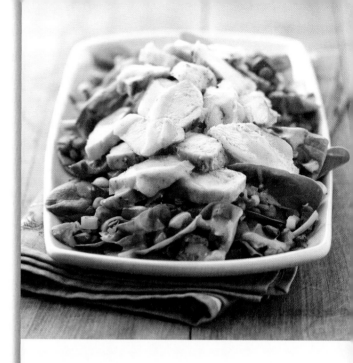

1 cup water

½ cup dry brown or French lentils, rinsed and drained

½ cup chopped red sweet pepper

⅓ cup chopped green onion

¼ cup snipped fresh flat-leaf parsley

2 tablespoons chopped walnuts, toasted

6 cups torn mixed salad greens

12 ounces cooked chicken breast, sliced

1 recipe Red Wine Vinaigrette

1 In a small saucepan combine water and lentils. Bring to boiling; reduce heat. Cover and simmer for 20 to 25 minutes or until lentils are tender and most of the liquid is absorbed. Drain lentils and place in a medium bowl. Stir in sweet pepper, green onion, parsley, and walnuts.

2 Place salad greens on a serving platter. Top with lentil mixture and chicken. Drizzle with Red Wine Vinaigrette. Makes 4 servings.

Red Wine Vinaigrette: In a small bowl combine 2 tablespoons red wine vinegar and 1 tablespoon finely chopped shallot. Let stand for 5 minutes. Whisk in 1½ teaspoons Dijon-style mustard. Add 2 tablespoons olive oil in a thin steady stream, whisking constantly until combined. Stir in ⅛ teaspoon salt and ⅛ teaspoon black pepper. Makes about ⅓ cup.

Spinach and Lentil Salad with Toasted Walnuts

PREP: 20 minutes

COOK: 20 minutes

NUTRITION FACTS per serving:

CALORIES 336
TOTAL FAT 13 g (2 g sat. fat)
CHOLESTEROL 72 mg
PROTEIN 35 g
CARBOHYDRATE 20 g
FIBER 9 g
SODIUM 192 mg

EXCHANGES 1 Starch, 4 Very Lean Meat, 1.5 Vegetable, 2 Fat

6 cups cut-up romaine or napa cabbage

2 cups chopped cooked chicken breast (about 10 ounces)

1 small apple, cored and cut into chunks

½ cup green and/or red seedless grapes, halved

3 tablespoons water

2 tablespoons reduced-fat peanut butter

2 teaspoons reduced-sodium soy sauce

¼ teaspoon ground ginger

1 On four serving plates stack romaine, chicken, apple, and grapes.

2 For dressing, in a small bowl whisk together the water, peanut butter, soy sauce, and ginger; drizzle over arranged salads.
Makes 4 servings.

Apple-Grape Chicken Salad

START TO FINISH: 30 minutes

NUTRITION FACTS per serving:
- -

CALORIES 205
TOTAL FAT 6 g (1 g sat. fat)
CHOLESTEROL 60 mg
PROTEIN 25 g
CARBOHYDRATE 14 g
FIBER 3 g
SODIUM 218 mg

EXCHANGES 0.5 Fruit, 3 Very Lean Meat, 1.5 Vegetable, 0.5 Fat

3 tablespoons canola oil

½ teaspoon finely shredded lime peel

2 tablespoons lime juice

1 tablespoon water

8 cups torn butterhead lettuce (Boston or Bibb)

2 medium mangoes, seeded, peeled, and thinly sliced

12 ounces cooked smoked turkey or chicken breast, cut into bite-size pieces

¼ cup chopped green onion

2 tablespoons snipped fresh cilantro

Lime wedges (optional)

1 For lime vinaigrette, in a screw-top jar combine oil, lime peel, lime juice, and water. Cover and shake well.

2 Divide lettuce among four salad plates. Arrange mangoes, smoked turkey, and green onion on lettuce. Sprinkle individual servings with cilantro and drizzle with lime vinaigrette. If desired, serve salads with lime wedges. Makes 4 servings.

Make-Ahead Directions: Prepare lime vinaigrette as above in step 1. Cover and chill for up to 4 hours. Shake the dressing before drizzling over salad.

COOK'S TIP

The tough skin of mangoes is not intended to be eaten. For some people the skin causes an allergic reaction.

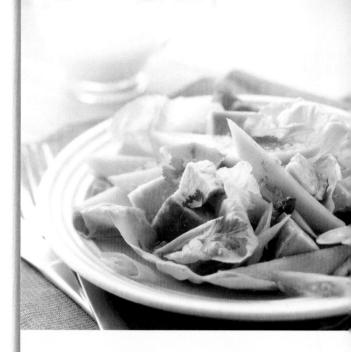

Mango Salad with Turkey

START TO FINISH: 30 minutes

NUTRITION FACTS per serving:

CALORIES 256
TOTAL FAT 12 g (1 g sat. fat)
CHOLESTEROL 37 mg
PROTEIN 19 g
CARBOHYDRATE 23 g
FIBER 3 g
SODIUM 1,031 mg

EXCHANGES 0.5 Fruit, 3 Very Lean Meat, 2 Vegetable, 2 Fat

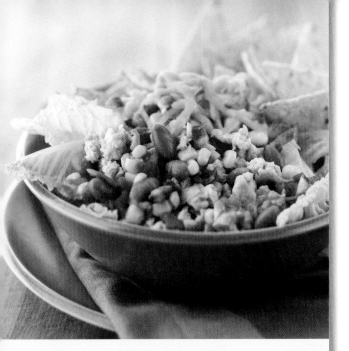

Nonstick cooking spray

12 ounces ground uncooked turkey breast

1 15-ounce can pinto beans, rinsed and drained (optional)

1 cup loose-pack frozen whole kernel corn

1 cup purchased salsa

¼ cup water

4 to 6 cups shredded romaine

¼ cup shredded reduced-fat cheddar cheese (1 ounce)

2 ounces purchased baked tortilla chips

Turkey Taco Salad

START TO FINISH: 25 minutes

NUTRITION FACTS per serving:
- -

CALORIES 228
TOTAL FAT 4 g (1 g sat. fat)
CHOLESTEROL 39 mg
PROTEIN 26 g
CARBOHYDRATE 27 g
FIBER 4 g
SODIUM 611 mg

EXCHANGES 1.5 Starch, 3 Very Lean Meat, 1 Vegetable

1 Lightly coat an unheated large nonstick skillet with nonstick cooking spray. Preheat over medium heat. Add ground turkey to hot skillet; cook about 5 minutes or until no longer pink. Drain off fat. Stir in beans (if desired), corn, salsa, and water. Bring to boiling; reduce heat. Cover and simmer for 2 to 3 minutes to blend flavors.

2 Line four salad bowls or serving plates with romaine. Top with hot turkey mixture. Sprinkle with cheese. Serve with tortilla chips. Makes 4 servings.

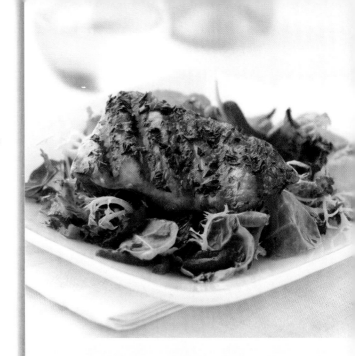

- 3 tablespoons water
- 2 tablespoons balsamic vinegar
- 1 tablespoon powdered fruit pectin
- 2 tablespoons snipped fresh oregano, thyme, and/or basil or 2 teaspoons dried oregano, thyme, and/or basil, crushed
- 1 tablespoon lime juice
- 1 tablespoon honey
- ½ teaspoon salt
- 4 fresh or frozen skinless salmon fillets, cut 1 inch thick (1 to 1¼ pounds total)
  Nonstick cooking spray
- 6 cups torn mixed salad greens
- ¾ cup bottled roasted red sweet peppers, drained and cut into thin strips

1 For dressing, in a screw-top jar combine water, balsamic vinegar, pectin, half of the fresh or dried herb, lime juice, honey, and ¼ teaspoon salt. Cover and shake well. Chill for 30 minutes to 3 days.

2 Thaw salmon, if frozen. Rinse salmon; pat dry with paper towels. Coat salmon on all sides with nonstick cooking spray. Sprinkle salmon with remaining fresh or dried herbs and remaining ¼ teaspoon salt. For a charcoal grill, place salmon on the greased rack of an uncovered grill directly over medium coals. Grill for 8 to 12 minutes or until salmon flakes easily when tested with a fork, turning once halfway through grilling. (For a gas grill, preheat grill. Reduce heat to medium. Place salmon on greased grill rack over heat. Cover and grill as above.)

3 Divide salad greens and roasted red peppers among four serving plates. Top with salmon. Shake dressing; drizzle over salads. Makes 4 servings.

Herbed Salmon with Greens

PREP: 20 minutes   **CHILL:** 30 minutes to 3 days
GRILL: 8 minutes

NUTRITION FACTS per serving:

CALORIES 255
TOTAL FAT 13 g (3 g sat. fat)
CHOLESTEROL 67 mg
PROTEIN 24 g
CARBOHYDRATE 11 g
FIBER 2 g
SODIUM 371 mg

EXCHANGES 3 Lean Meat, 1.5 Vegetable, 1 Fat

Shrimply Delicious Salad

PREP: 30 minutes   **MARINATE:** 1 hour
GRILL: 5 minutes

NUTRITION FACTS per serving:

CALORIES 331
TOTAL FAT 13 g (1 g sat. fat)
CHOLESTEROL 172 mg
PROTEIN 27 g
CARBOHYDRATE 30 g
FIBER 4 g
SODIUM 192 mg

EXCHANGES 1 Fruit, 3 Very Lean Meat,
2.5 Vegetable, 2 Fat

16   ounces fresh or frozen peeled, deveined large shrimp (leave tails intact if desired)
¼   cup orange juice
¼   cup lime juice
¾   to 1 teaspoon bottled hot pepper sauce
2   tablespoons canola oil
1   tablespoon sugar
2   teaspoons red wine vinegar
1   teaspoon toasted sesame oil
8   cups torn mixed salad greens
2   11-ounce cans mandarin orange sections, drained
2   medium red, green, and/or yellow sweet peppers, cut into bite-size strips
½   cup thinly sliced red onion
2   tablespoons sesame seeds, toasted

1 If using wooden skewers, soak skewers in warm water for 30 minutes.

2 Thaw shrimp, if frozen. Rinse shrimp; pat dry with paper towels. In a screw-top jar combine orange juice, lime juice, and hot pepper sauce. Cover and shake well. Place ¼ cup of the juice mixture in a medium bowl. Add shrimp and toss to coat. Cover and marinate in the refrigerator for 1 hour.

3 For dressing, add canola oil, sugar, red wine vinegar, and toasted sesame oil to remaining juice mixture in screw-top jar. Cover and shake well; set aside.

4 Drain shrimp, discarding marinade. Thread shrimp onto skewers, leaving a ¼-inch space between shrimp.

5 For a charcoal grill, place skewers on the greased rack of an uncovered grill directly over medium coals. Grill for 5 to 8 minutes or until shrimp are opaque, turning once halfway through grilling. (For a gas grill, preheat grill. Reduce heat to medium. Place skewers on grill rack over heat. Cover and grill as above.)

6 In a large bowl combine salad greens, orange sections, sweet peppers, and red onion. Add dressing; toss gently to coat. Divide among four serving plates. Arrange shrimp on greens mixture. Sprinkle with sesame seeds. Makes 4 servings.

- 3 medium red potatoes (about 1 pound)
- ½ cup light mayonnaise or salad dressing
- ½ cup plain fat-free yogurt
- 1 tablespoon snipped fresh dill or 1 teaspoon dried dill
- 1 tablespoon fat-free milk
- ½ teaspoon finely shredded lemon peel
- ¼ teaspoon salt
- 1 clove garlic, minced
- 1 cup chopped cucumber
- ¼ cup sliced green onion
- ¼ cup coarsely chopped radishes
- 1 9-ounce can chunk white tuna (water pack), drained and broken into chunks
- 2 hard-cooked eggs, chopped
- 12 leaves savoy cabbage or napa cabbage
- Fresh dill sprigs (optional)

1 Scrub potatoes; cut into ½-inch cubes. In a covered medium saucepan cook potatoes in a small amount of boiling water for 10 to 12 minutes or just until tender. Drain and cool slightly.

2 Meanwhile, in a large bowl stir together mayonnaise, yogurt, snipped dill, milk, lemon peel, salt, and garlic. Stir in cucumber, green onion, and radishes. Add cooked potatoes, tuna, and chopped eggs; toss gently to coat. Cover and chill for 4 to 6 hours.

3 To serve, line six serving bowls with cabbage leaves. Gently stir tuna mixture; spoon on cabbage. If desired, garnish with fresh dill. Makes 6 servings.

Dilled Tuna and Potato Salad

PREP: 25 minutes

CHILL: 4 to 6 hours

NUTRITION FACTS per serving:

CALORIES 243
TOTAL FAT 10 g (2 g sat. fat)
CHOLESTEROL 96 mg
PROTEIN 18 g
CARBOHYDRATE 22 g
FIBER 5 g
SODIUM 461 mg

EXCHANGES 1 Starch, 2 Very Lean Meat, 1.5 Vegetable, 1.5 Fat

4 ounces fresh green beans

5 cups packaged European-style torn mixed salad greens

1 6-ounce can chunk white tuna (water pack), drained and broken into chunks

4 medium tomatoes, quartered

2 hard-cooked eggs, quartered

¾ cup pitted ripe olives

½ cup snipped fresh flat-leaf parsley

3 green onions, cut into ½-inch-long pieces

4 anchovy fillets, drained, rinsed, and patted dry (optional)

1 recipe Niçoise Dressing

Salad Niçoise

START TO FINISH: 35 minutes

NUTRITION FACTS per serving:

CALORIES 232
TOTAL FAT 14 g (3 g sat. fat)
CHOLESTEROL 124 mg
PROTEIN 16 g
CARBOHYDRATE 12 g
FIBER 5 g
SODIUM 595 mg

EXCHANGES 1.5 Lean Meat, 2.5 Vegetable, 2 Fat

NUTRITION NOTE

Choose water-packed over oil-packed tuna. Water-packed tuna contains less fat than oil-packed and offers more healthful omega-3 fatty acids.

1 Leave beans whole or snap in half. In a covered medium saucepan cook green beans in a small amount of lightly salted boiling water about 5 minutes or just until tender. Drain and place in ice water until chilled; drain well. If desired, cover and chill for 2 to 24 hours.

2 In four salad bowls arrange greens, green beans, tuna, tomatoes, eggs, and olives. Sprinkle with parsley and green onion. If desired, top with anchovy fillets. Drizzle Niçoise Dressing over salads. Makes 4 servings.

Niçoise Dressing: In a small bowl combine 2 tablespoons olive oil, 2 tablespoons white wine vinegar, ½ teaspoon Dijon-style mustard, ¼ teaspoon salt, and ⅛ teaspoon black pepper. Whisk together until combined.

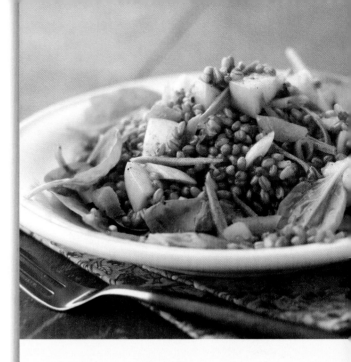

2½ cups water

1 cup wheat berries, rinsed

2 tablespoons lemon juice

2 tablespoons canola oil

1 tablespoon maple-flavored syrup

¼ teaspoon ground cinnamon

¼ teaspoon salt

¼ teaspoon black pepper

1 medium apple, cored, peeled, and sliced

1 large carrot, shredded

2 green onions, sliced

6 cups fresh baby spinach

¼ cup snipped dried apricots

1 In a small saucepan bring water to boiling. Add wheat berries to boiling water. Return to boiling; reduce heat. Cover and simmer for 40 to 50 minutes or until tender. Drain and transfer to a large bowl. Let cool for 1 hour.

2 In a small bowl whisk together lemon juice, oil, syrup, cinnamon, salt, and pepper. Drizzle dressing over cooled wheat berries. Add apple, carrot, and green onion; toss to coat. Serve wheat berry mixture with baby spinach; sprinkle with dried apricots. Makes 4 servings.

Wheat Berry Salad

PREP: 20 minutes **COOK:** 40 minutes

COOL: 1 hour

NUTRITION FACTS per serving:

CALORIES 284
TOTAL FAT 8 g (1 g sat. fat)
CHOLESTEROL 0 mg
PROTEIN 8 g
CARBOHYDRATE 50 g
FIBER 12 g
SODIUM 217 mg

EXCHANGES 2 Starch, 0.5 Fruit, 2 Vegetable, 1.5 Fat

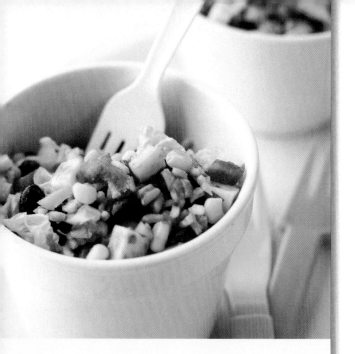

2 cups chopped romaine lettuce

2 cups cooked brown rice, chilled

1 15-ounce can black beans, rinsed and drained

2 cups chopped tomato

1 cup chopped green, yellow, and/or red sweet pepper

1 cup loose-pack frozen whole kernel corn, thawed

2 green onions, thinly sliced

2 tablespoons snipped fresh cilantro

1 cup purchased picante sauce or salsa

4 ounces Monterey Jack cheese with jalapeño chile peppers, cut into ¼-inch cubes (optional)

½ cup light dairy sour cream

Salsa, Black Bean, and Rice Salad

START TO FINISH: 25 minutes

NUTRITION FACTS per serving:
- -

CALORIES 201
TOTAL FAT 3 g (1 g sat. fat)
CHOLESTEROL 6 mg
PROTEIN 9 g
CARBOHYDRATE 39 g
FIBER 7 g
SODIUM 469 mg

EXCHANGES 2 Starch, 1 Vegetable

1 In a large bowl stir together lettuce, chilled rice, black beans, tomato, sweet pepper, corn, green onion, and cilantro; add picante sauce or salsa. Toss to coat. If desired, stir in cheese. Serve with sour cream. Makes 6 servings.

On the opener: Roasted Tomato-Vegetable Soup (*see recipe, page 103*)

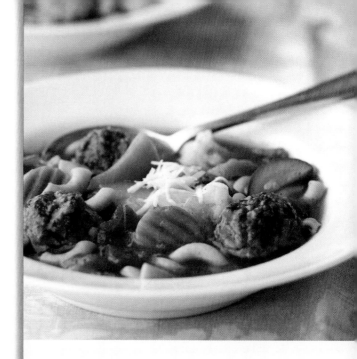

2¼ cups water

1 14½-ounce can diced tomatoes with onion and garlic, undrained

1 cup lower-sodium beef broth

½ teaspoon dried Italian seasoning, crushed

½ cup dried multigrain or whole wheat elbow macaroni

2 cups loose-pack frozen Italian-blend vegetables

½ of a 16-ounce package frozen bite-size Italian-style cooked meatballs (16)

2 tablespoons shredded or grated Parmesan cheese (optional)

1 In a large saucepan stir together water, undrained tomatoes, beef broth, and Italian seasoning. Bring to boiling. Add uncooked pasta and frozen vegetables. Return to boiling; reduce heat. Cover and simmer about 10 minutes or until pasta and vegetables are tender.

2 Meanwhile, place meatballs in a medium microwave-safe bowl. Microwave, uncovered, on 100% power (high) for 2½ to 3 minutes or until heated through. Drain meatballs; pat dry with paper towels. If desired, halve meatballs. Stir meatballs into soup mixture.

3 If desired, sprinkle individual servings with Parmesan cheese.
Makes 4 (1¾-cup) servings.

Italian Meatball Soup

START TO FINISH: 25 minutes

NUTRITION FACTS per serving:

- -

CALORIES 268
TOTAL FAT 13 g (6 g sat. fat)
CHOLESTEROL 37 mg
PROTEIN 14 g
CARBOHYDRATE 22 g
FIBER 5 g
SODIUM 1,052 mg

EXCHANGES 1 Starch, 1.5 High-Fat Meat, 1.5 Vegetable

2 pounds boneless beef chuck roast
  Nonstick cooking spray

12 ounces tiny new potatoes, quartered

4 medium carrots, cut into ½-inch pieces

1 medium onion, cut into wedges

1 10¾-ounce can reduced-fat and reduced-sodium condensed cream of mushroom soup

1 cup lower-sodium beef broth

1 teaspoon dried marjoram or dried thyme, crushed

2 cups loose-pack frozen cut green beans (9 ounces)

Super-Simple Beef Stew

PREP: 30 minutes

COOK: 8 to 9 hours (low) or

4 to 4½ hours (high); plus 30 minutes (high)

NUTRITION FACTS per serving:

CALORIES 317
TOTAL FAT 9 g (3 g sat. fat)
CHOLESTEROL 92 mg
PROTEIN 35 g
CARBOHYDRATE 22 g
FIBER 4 g
SODIUM 396 mg

EXCHANGES 1 Starch, 4 Lean Meat, 1 Vegetable

1 Trim fat from beef; cut beef into 1-inch cubes. Coat an unheated large skillet with nonstick cooking spray. Preheat over medium-high heat. Add half of the beef cubes. Cook and stir until browned; remove from skillet. Add remaining beef cubes; cook and stir until browned. Drain off fat from beef.

2 Place beef in a 3½- or 4-quart slow cooker. Add potatoes, carrots, onion, cream of mushroom soup, beef broth, and marjoram. Stir to combine. Cover and cook on low-heat setting for 8 to 9 hours or on high-heat setting for 4 to 4½ hours.

3 If using low-heat setting, turn to high-heat setting. Stir in green beans. Cover and cook about 30 minutes more or just until green beans are tender. Makes 6 (1⅓-cup) servings.

Nonstick cooking spray

8 ounces extra-lean ground beef, uncooked ground chicken breast, or uncooked ground turkey breast

1 cup chopped onion

1½ teaspoons ground cumin

2 14½-ounce cans stewed tomatoes, undrained, cut up

1 15-ounce can red beans, rinsed and drained

1½ cups coarsely chopped red and/or yellow sweet pepper

½ cup water

2 to 3 teaspoons chopped canned chipotle chile peppers in adobo sauce*

1 tablespoon snipped fresh oregano

¼ cup shredded reduced-fat cheddar cheese

Lime wedges (optional)

Baked tortilla chips (optional)

1 Lightly coat an unheated large saucepan with nonstick cooking spray. Preheat over medium heat. Add ground beef and onion; cook until browned. If necessary, drain off fat. Stir cumin into beef mixture in skillet; cook and stir for 1 minute more. Add undrained tomatoes, red beans, sweet pepper, water, and chile peppers. Bring to boiling; reduce heat. Cover and simmer for 5 minutes. Stir in oregano.

2 Spoon chili into serving bowls. Sprinkle individual servings with cheese. If desired, serve with lime wedges and tortilla chips. Makes 4 (1½-cup) servings.

*Because chile peppers contain volatile oils that can burn your skin and eyes, avoid direct contact with them as much as possible. When working with chile peppers, wear plastic or rubber gloves. If your bare hands do touch the peppers, wash your hands and nails well with soap and warm water.

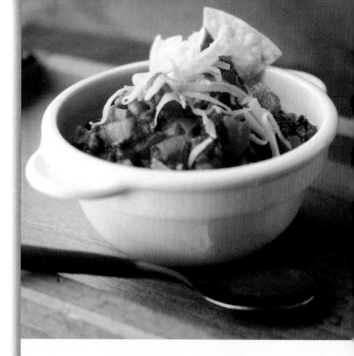

Chipotle Chili with Beans

START TO FINISH: 25 minutes

NUTRITION FACTS per serving:

CALORIES 398
TOTAL FAT 14 g (6 g sat. fat)
CHOLESTEROL 57 mg
PROTEIN 27 g
CARBOHYDRATE 40 g
FIBER 10 g
SODIUM 1,030 mg

EXCHANGES 2.5 Starch, 2.5 Lean Meat, 0.5 Vegetable, 1 Fat

COOK'S TIP

Chipotles in adobo sauce are smoked jalapeño peppers stewed in tomatoes, garlic, vinegar, salt, and spices. One pepper goes a long way, so don't overdo it.

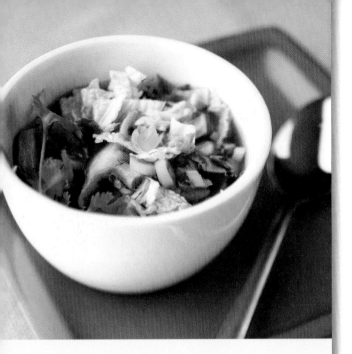

Asian Pork Soup

START TO FINISH: 25 minutes

NUTRITION FACTS per serving:

CALORIES 160
TOTAL FAT 6 g (1 g sat. fat)
CHOLESTEROL 31 mg
PROTEIN 16 g
CARBOHYDRATE 10 g
FIBER 1 g
SODIUM 691 mg

EXCHANGES 2 Lean Meat, 0.5 Vegetable

1	tablespoon canola oil
12	ounces lean boneless pork, cut into thin bite-size strips
2	cups sliced fresh shiitake mushrooms
2	cloves garlic, minced
3	14-ounce cans reduced-sodium chicken broth
2	tablespoons dry sherry
2	tablespoons reduced-sodium soy sauce
2	teaspoons grated fresh ginger or ½ teaspoon ground ginger
¼	teaspoon crushed red pepper
2	cups shredded napa cabbage
1	green onion, thinly sliced
	Fresh cilantro sprigs (optional)

1 In a large saucepan heat oil over medium heat. Add pork; cook and stir for 2 to 3 minutes or until pork is slightly pink in center. Remove from pan; set aside. Add mushrooms and garlic to saucepan; cook until tender.

2 Stir in chicken broth, sherry, soy sauce, ginger, and crushed red pepper. Bring to boiling. Stir in pork, napa cabbage, and green onion; heat through. If desired, garnish individual servings with cilantro. Makes 6 (about 1-cup) servings.

COOK'S TIP

To clean mushrooms, wipe them with a damp paper towel. Avoid washing/rinsing them under running water, which causes them to absorb excess liquid.

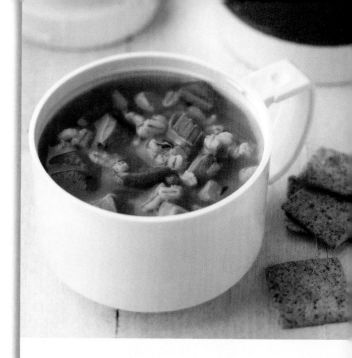

- 1 tablespoon olive oil
- 2 cups chopped onion
- 6 cloves garlic, minced
- 1 tablespoon snipped fresh rosemary or 1 teaspoon dried rosemary, crushed
- 6 ounces cooked ham, chopped (about 1 cup)
- 1 cup sliced celery
- ¾ cup regular barley (not quick-cooking), rinsed
- 5 cups reduced-sodium chicken broth
- 3 cups water
- 1½ cups sliced carrot
- 2 teaspoons snipped fresh marjoram or ½ teaspoon dried marjoram, crushed
- 2 teaspoons snipped fresh oregano or ½ teaspoon dried oregano, crushed
- 1 tablespoon lemon juice
- 2 tablespoons shredded Parmesan cheese (optional)

  Cracked or freshly ground black pepper (optional)

1 In a 4- to 6-quart Dutch oven heat oil over medium heat. Add onion; cook about 5 minutes or until tender, stirring occasionally. Add garlic and rosemary; cook and stir for 1 minute. Add ham, celery, and uncooked barley; cook for 4 minutes, stirring occasionally.

2 Add chicken broth and water. Bring to boiling; reduce heat. Cover and simmer for 30 minutes. Stir in carrot, marjoram, and oregano. Cover and simmer for 15 to 20 minutes more or until carrot and barley are tender.

3 Stir in lemon juice. If desired, sprinkle individual servings with Parmesan cheese and black pepper. Makes 6 (1¾-cup) servings.

Ham and Barley Soup

PREP: 30 minutes
COOK: 45 minutes

NUTRITION FACTS per serving:

CALORIES 182
TOTAL FAT 4 g (1 g sat. fat)
CHOLESTEROL 13 mg
PROTEIN 12 g
CARBOHYDRATE 27 g
FIBER 6 g
SODIUM 985 mg

EXCHANGES 1.5 Starch, 1 Lean Meat, 0.5 Vegetable

2 teaspoons olive oil

12 ounces skinless, boneless chicken
breast halves, cut
into ¾-inch pieces

3 cloves garlic, minced

3 cups sliced fresh mushrooms
(about 8 ounces)

2 14-ounce cans reduced-sodium
chicken broth

1 ¾ cups water

1 9-ounce package refrigerated
cheese-filled tortellini

2 medium carrots, cut into thin
bite-size strips

2 cups torn fresh baby spinach

1 tablespoon snipped fresh tarragon

Chicken-Tortellini Soup

START TO FINISH: 40 minutes

NUTRITION FACTS per serving:

CALORIES 265
TOTAL FAT 6 g (2 g sat. fat)
CHOLESTEROL 53 mg
PROTEIN 24 g
CARBOHYDRATE 30 g
FIBER 3 g
SODIUM 618 mg

EXCHANGES 2 Starch, 2 Very Lean Meat,
1 Vegetable, 0.5 Fat

1 In a 4- to 6-quart Dutch oven heat olive oil over medium-high heat. Add chicken and garlic; cook and stir about 4 minutes or until outsides of chicken pieces are no longer pink. Using a slotted spoon, remove chicken from Dutch oven. Add mushrooms to the same Dutch oven. Cook about 5 minutes or just until tender, stirring frequently. Carefully add chicken broth and water; bring to boiling.

2 Add tortellini, carrot strips, and partially cooked chicken to broth mixture. Return to boiling; reduce heat. Cover and simmer for 7 to 9 minutes or until tortellini are tender, stirring occasionally. Stir in spinach and tarragon. Makes 6 (1⅓-cup) servings.

- 2 14-ounce cans reduced-sodium chicken broth
- 2 cups loose-pack frozen yellow, green, and red peppers and onion stir-fry vegetables
- 1 14½-ounce can Mexican-style stewed tomatoes, undrained
- 2 cups chopped cooked chicken breast (10 ounces)
- 2 cups packaged baked tortilla chips
- Chopped avocado (optional)

1 In a large saucepan combine chicken broth, frozen vegetables, and undrained tomatoes. Bring to boiling; reduce heat. Cover and simmer for 3 to 5 minutes or until vegetables are tender. Stir in chicken; heat through.

2 Ladle soup into warm soup bowls. Serve individual servings with tortilla chips. If desired, top with avocado. Makes 4 (about 1½-cup) servings.

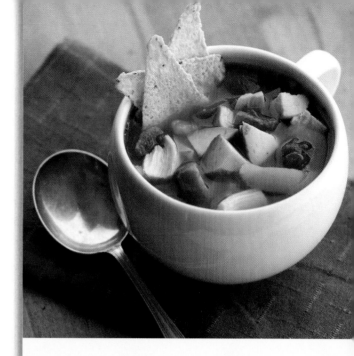

Chicken Tortilla Soup

START TO FINISH: 20 minutes

NUTRITION FACTS per serving:

- -

CALORIES 287
TOTAL FAT 4 g (1 g sat. fat)
CHOLESTEROL 60 mg
PROTEIN 29 g
CARBOHYDRATE 32 g
FIBER 4 g
SODIUM 870 mg

EXCHANGES 2 Starch, 3 Very Lean Meat, 1 Vegetable

Hot 'n' Spicy Fish Soup

START TO FINISH: 35 minutes

NUTRITION FACTS per serving:
- -

CALORIES 270
TOTAL FAT 9 g (1 g sat. fat)
CHOLESTEROL 54 mg
PROTEIN 37 g
CARBOHYDRATE 10 g
FIBER 2 g
SODIUM 393 mg

EXCHANGES 0.5 Starch, 5 Very Lean Meat, 1 Vegetable, 1 Fat

12	ounces fresh or frozen halibut steaks, cut 1 inch thick
2	teaspoons canola oil
¼	teaspoon cumin seeds
1	medium onion, chopped
2	to 3 teaspoons grated fresh ginger
1	fresh serrano chile pepper, seeded and finely chopped*
2	medium plum tomatoes, chopped
¾	cup water
½	teaspoon ground coriander
¼	teaspoon ground turmeric
¼	teaspoon salt

1 Thaw fish, if frozen. Rinse fish; pat dry with paper towels. Remove and discard skin and bones. Cut fish into 1-inch pieces; set aside.

2 In a medium saucepan heat oil over medium heat. Add cumin seeds; cook and stir about 1 minute or until toasted. Add onion; cook and stir for 4 to 5 minutes or until tender. Add ginger and chile pepper; cook and stir for 1 minute more. Add chopped tomato; cook and stir for 2 to 3 minutes more or until tomatoes have softened. Stir in water, coriander, turmeric, and salt. Bring just to boiling; reduce heat. Stir in fish pieces.

3 Cover and cook about 5 minutes or just until fish pieces flake easily when tested with a fork. Serve immediately. Makes 2 (1-cup) servings.

*Because chile peppers contain volatile oils that can burn your skin and eyes, avoid direct contact with them as much as possible. When working with chile peppers, wear plastic or rubber gloves. If your bare hands do touch the peppers, wash your hands and nails well with soap and warm water.

Nonstick cooking spray

- 2 leeks, thinly sliced (⅔ cup)
- 2 cloves garlic, minced
- 1 small sweet potato, peeled and chopped (1 cup)
- 2 cups peeled, chopped assorted root vegetables (such as parsnips, turnips, rutabagas, and/or carrots)
- 1 14-ounce can reduced-sodium chicken broth
- 1 12-ounce can evaporated fat-free milk
- ¼ teaspoon fennel seeds, crushed
- ⅛ teaspoon black pepper

1 Lightly coat an unheated medium saucepan with nonstick cooking spray. Preheat over medium heat. Add leeks and garlic; cook and stir until tender. Add sweet potato, assorted root vegetables, and chicken broth. Bring to boiling; reduce heat. Cover and simmer about 20 minutes or until vegetables are tender.

2 Stir in evaporated milk, fennel seeds, and pepper. Heat through but do not boil. Makes 4 (1-cup) servings.

Root Vegetable Chowder

PREP: 30 minutes

COOK: 20 minutes

NUTRITION FACTS per serving:

CALORIES 161
TOTAL FAT 0 g (0 g sat. fat)
CHOLESTEROL 3 mg
PROTEIN 10 g
CARBOHYDRATE 31 g
FIBER 4 g
SODIUM 388 mg

EXCHANGES 1.5 Starch, 0.5 Milk, 0.5 Vegetable

Indian Vegetable Soup

PREP: 30 minutes

COOK: 9 to 10 hours (low)
or 4½ to 5 hours (high)

NUTRITION FACTS per serving:

- -

CALORIES 186
TOTAL FAT 1 g (0 g sat. fat)
CHOLESTEROL 0 mg
PROTEIN 7 g
CARBOHYDRATE 39 g
FIBER 9 g
SODIUM 837 mg

EXCHANGES 2 Starch, 1.5 Vegetable

1 medium eggplant, cut into ½-inch cubes (5 to 6 cups)
2 14-ounce cans vegetable broth
1 pound tiny new potatoes, cut into 1-inch pieces
2 cups chopped tomatoes or one 14½-ounce can no-salt-added diced tomatoes, undrained
1 15-ounce can garbanzo beans (chickpeas), rinsed and drained
2 teaspoons grated fresh ginger or ½ teaspoon ground ginger
1½ teaspoons curry powder
1 teaspoon ground coriander
¼ teaspoon salt
¼ teaspoon black pepper
2 tablespoons snipped fresh cilantro (optional)

1 In a 5- to 6-quart slow cooker combine eggplant, vegetable broth, potatoes, tomatoes, garbanzo beans, ginger, curry powder, coriander, salt, and pepper.

2 Cover and cook on low-heat setting for 9 to 10 hours or on high-heat setting for 4½ to 5 hours. If desired, sprinkle individual servings with cilantro. Makes 6 (1½-cup) servings.

COOK'S TIP

Choose eggplants that are firm and heavy for their size. The skin should be smooth and shiny and free of discoloration, scars, and bruises, which usually indicate that the flesh has been damaged.

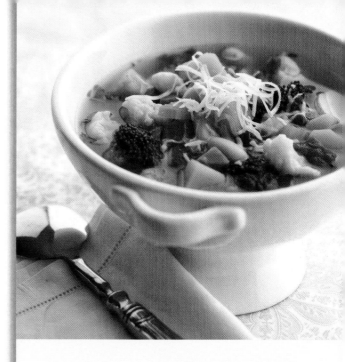

1	tablespoon olive oil
½	cup chopped onion
½	cup chopped celery
½	cup chopped carrot
2	cloves garlic, minced
3	14-ounce cans reduced-sodium chicken broth
2	cups peeled, seeded, and coarsely chopped butternut squash
1	14½-ounce can fire-roasted diced tomatoes, undrained
1	15- to 19-ounce can cannellini beans (white kidney beans), rinsed and drained
1	small zucchini, halved lengthwise and sliced
1	cup broccoli and/or cauliflower florets
1	tablespoon snipped fresh oregano or 1 teaspoon dried oregano, crushed
¼	teaspoon salt
¼	teaspoon freshly ground black pepper
	Freshly shredded Parmesan cheese (optional)

1 In a 4-quart Dutch oven heat oil over medium heat. Add onion, celery, carrot, and garlic; cook and stir for 5 minutes.

2 Stir in chicken broth, squash, and undrained tomatoes. Bring to boiling; reduce heat. Cover and simmer for 20 minutes. Add cannellini beans, zucchini, broccoli, oregano, salt, and pepper; cook for 5 minutes more. If desired, sprinkle individual servings with Parmesan cheese. Makes 6 servings.

Slow Cooker Directions: Omit olive oil. In a 3½- to 4-quart slow cooker combine onion, celery, carrot, garlic, chicken broth, squash, undrained tomatoes, cannellini beans, and dried oregano (if using). Cover and cook on low-heat setting for 7 to 8 hours or on high-heat setting for 3½ to 4 hours. If using low-heat setting, turn to high-heat setting. Add zucchini, broccoli, fresh oregano (if using), salt, and pepper. Cover and cook for 30 minutes more. Serve as above.

Roasted Tomato-Vegetable Soup

PREP: 35 minutes

COOK: 25 minutes

NUTRITION FACTS per serving:

CALORIES 131
TOTAL FAT 3 g (0 g sat. fat)
CHOLESTEROL 0 mg
PROTEIN 9 g
CARBOHYDRATE 24 g
FIBER 5 g
SODIUM 855 mg

EXCHANGES 1 Starch, 0.5 Very Lean Meat, 1.5 Vegetable

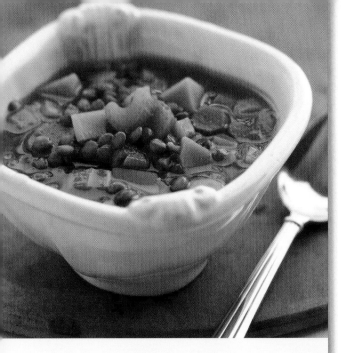

1 cup dry brown lentils

2 14-ounce cans vegetable broth

1 pound butternut squash, halved, seeded, peeled, and cut into ¾-inch pieces

1½ cups water

2 medium carrots, chopped

2 stalks celery, sliced

1 medium onion, chopped

2 cloves garlic, minced

1 teaspoon garam masala

1 Rinse and drain lentils. In a 3½- or 4-quart slow cooker combine lentils, vegetable broth, squash, water, carrot, celery, onion, garlic, and garam masala.

2 Cover and cook on low-heat setting for 8 to 9 hours or on high-heat setting for 4 to 4½ hours. Makes 4 (1¾-cup) servings.

COOK'S TIP

A staple in Indian cooking, garam masala lends warm, exotic flavors to your dish. Look for it in the spice aisle of your grocery store or at a local Indian market.

Squash and Lentil Soup

PREP: 25 minutes

COOK: 8 to 9 hours (low)

or 4 to 4½ hours (high)

NUTRITION FACTS per serving:

CALORIES 260
TOTAL FAT 1 g (0 g sat. fat)
CHOLESTEROL 0 mg
PROTEIN 14 g
CARBOHYDRATE 51 g
FIBER 19 g
SODIUM 824 mg

EXCHANGES 3 Starch, 1 Vegetable

NUTRITION NOTE

Boost iron intake with lentils. Unlike red meat, also a source of iron, lentils are low in fat and calories.

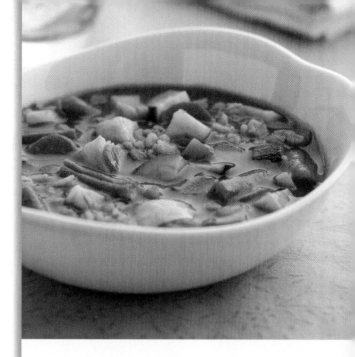

1   14-ounce can vegetable broth

1¾ cups water

¾   cup quick-cooking barley

¾   cup thinly sliced carrot*

1   teaspoon dried thyme, crushed

⅛   teaspoon black pepper

1   19-ounce can ready-to-serve
    tomato-basil soup

2   cups coarsely chopped zucchini*
    and/or yellow summer squash

1   cup loose-pack frozen cut
    green beans*

1 In a large saucepan combine vegetable broth, water, uncooked barley, carrot, thyme, and pepper. Bring to boiling; reduce heat. Cover and simmer for 10 minutes, stirring occasionally.

2 Stir in tomato-basil soup, zucchini, and green beans. Return to boiling; reduce heat. Cover and simmer for 8 to 10 minutes more or until vegetables and barley are tender, stirring occasionally. Makes 4 (1¾-cup) servings.

*You can substitute one 16-ounce package of your favorite frozen vegetable blend for the carrot, zucchini, and green beans, adding it with the tomato-basil soup.

COOK'S TIP

Over time spices and herbs lose color, flavor, and aroma. Store them in a cool, dry place away from light, heat, moisture, and oxygen. Replace ground spices after six months and whole spices after one year.

Tomato-Barley Soup with Garden Vegetables

PREP: 15 minutes

COOK: 18 minutes

NUTRITION FACTS per serving:

CALORIES 243
TOTAL FAT 3 g (0 g sat. fat)
CHOLESTEROL 0 mg
PROTEIN 7 g
CARBOHYDRATE 49 g
FIBER 9 g
SODIUM 988 mg

EXCHANGES 2.5 Starch, 1.5 Vegetable

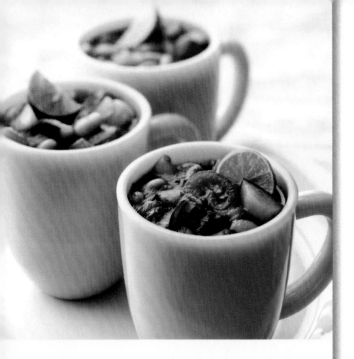

Zesty Gazpacho

PREP: 30 minutes

CHILL: 2 to 24 hours

NUTRITION FACTS per serving:

- -

CALORIES 152
TOTAL FAT 1 g (0 g sat. fat)
CHOLESTEROL 0 mg
PROTEIN 11 g
CARBOHYDRATE 35 g
FIBER 10 g
SODIUM 861 mg

EXCHANGES 1 Starch, 3.5 Vegetable

1   19-ounce can cannellini beans (white kidney beans), rinsed and drained

1   14½-ounce can Italian- or Mexican-style stewed tomatoes, undrained, cut up

2   cups tiny red pear-shape tomatoes, halved, and/or cherry tomatoes, halved or quartered

1¼ cups vegetable juice

1   cup lower-sodium beef broth

1   cup coarsely chopped seeded cucumber

½   cup coarsely chopped yellow and/or red sweet pepper

¼   cup coarsely chopped red onion

¼   cup snipped fresh cilantro

3   tablespoons lime juice or lemon juice

2   cloves garlic, minced

¼   to ½ teaspoon bottled hot pepper sauce

    Lime wedges (optional)

1 In a large bowl combine cannellini beans, undrained stewed tomatoes, fresh tomatoes, vegetable juice, beef broth, cucumber, sweet pepper, red onion, cilantro, lime juice, garlic, and hot pepper sauce. Cover and chill for 2 to 24 hours. If desired, serve individual servings with lime wedges. Makes 4 (2-cup) servings.

Chapter 7

Beef, Veal & Lamb

On the opener: Beef-Broccoli Stir-Fry *(see recipe, page 111)*

- 8 cloves garlic, peeled
- 1 teaspoon salt
- 1 tablespoon chili powder
- 1 tablespoon five-spice powder
- 2 teaspoons ground ginger
- 1 teaspoon black pepper
- 2 1-pound boneless beef top sirloin steaks, cut 1 inch thick

1 On a cutting board, chop garlic with salt; press with the side of a large knife to form a chunky paste. In a small bowl combine garlic paste, chili powder, five-spice powder, ginger, and pepper; set aside.

2 Sprinkle garlic mixture on all sides of the steaks; rub in with your fingers. Place steaks in a large resealable plastic bag; seal bag. Chill for 2 hours.

3 For a charcoal grill, place steaks on the rack of an uncovered grill directly over medium coals. Grill until desired doneness, turning once halfway through grilling. Allow 14 to 18 minutes for medium-rare doneness (145°F) or 18 to 22 minutes for medium doneness (160°F). (For a gas grill, preheat grill. Reduce heat to medium. Place steaks on grill rack over heat. Cover and grill as above.) Makes 8 servings.

Spicy Sirloin Steaks

PREP: 20 minutes   **CHILL:** 2 hours
GRILL: 14 minutes

NUTRITION FACTS per serving:
- -

CALORIES 153
TOTAL FAT 4 g (1 g sat. fat)
CHOLESTEROL 53 mg
PROTEIN 25 g
CARBOHYDRATE 3 g
FIBER 1 g
SODIUM 362 mg

EXCHANGES 3.5 Very Lean Meat

1 6-ounce carton plain fat-free or low-fat yogurt

¼ cup coarsely shredded unpeeled cucumber

1 tablespoon finely chopped red onion

1 tablespoon snipped fresh mint

¼ teaspoon sugar

¼ teaspoon salt

⅛ teaspoon black pepper

1 pound boneless beef sirloin steak, cut 1-inch thick

½ teaspoon Greek seasoning

Beef with Cucumber Raita

PREP: 20 minutes

GRILL: 15 minutes

NUTRITION FACTS per serving:

CALORIES 176
TOTAL FAT 5 g (2 g sat. fat)
CHOLESTEROL 48 mg
PROTEIN 28 g
CARBOHYDRATE 4 g
FIBER 0 g
SODIUM 252 mg

EXCHANGES 4 Very Lean Meat, 1 Fat

1 For raita, in a small bowl combine yogurt, cucumber, red onion, snipped mint, sugar, salt, and pepper; set aside.

2 Trim fat from steak. Sprinkle steak with Greek seasoning. For a charcoal grill, place steak on the rack of an uncovered grill directly over medium coals. Grill until desired doneness, turning once halfway through grilling. Allow 15 to 17 minutes for medium-rare doneness (145°F) or 20 to 22 minutes for medium doneness (160°F). (For a gas grill, preheat grill. Reduce heat to medium. Place steak on grill rack over heat. Cover and grill as above.)

3 Thinly slice steak across the grain. Serve sliced steak with raita. Makes 4 servings.

NUTRITION NOTE

Keep the peel on cucumbers to give food bright color and more fiber and minerals than peeled cucumbers.

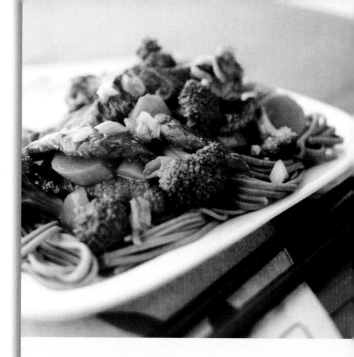

- ¾ cup lower-sodium beef broth
- 2 tablespoons reduced-sodium soy sauce
- 1 tablespoon rice vinegar or white vinegar
- 2 teaspoons cornstarch
- 2 teaspoons grated fresh ginger or ½ teaspoon ground ginger
- 2 cloves garlic, minced
- ¼ teaspoon crushed red pepper
- 1 pound broccoli
- 12 ounces boneless beef top sirloin steak
- 2 teaspoons canola oil
- 2 medium carrots, sliced
- 4 green onions, sliced
- 6 ounces dried soba (buckwheat noodles) or multigrain spaghetti, cooked according to package directions

1 For sauce, in a small bowl combine beef broth, soy sauce, vinegar, cornstarch, ginger, garlic, and crushed red pepper; set aside.

2 Cut broccoli florets from stems. If desired, peel stems. Cut stems into ¼-inch-thick slices. Set aside. Trim fat from meat. Cut meat across the grain into thin slices; set aside.

3 In a wok or large skillet heat 1 teaspoon of oil over medium-high heat. Add broccoli and carrot. Cook and stir for 5 to 6 minutes or until crisp-tender; remove from wok or skillet.

4 Add remaining 1 teaspoon oil to hot wok or skillet. Add beef. Cook and stir for 2 to 3 minutes or until desired doneness. Push meat from center of wok or skillet. Stir sauce; add to wok or skillet. Cook and stir until thickened and bubbly. Return vegetables to wok or skillet; add green onion. Stir to coat all ingredients with sauce. Cook and stir until heated through.

5 Serve beef mixture over hot cooked soba or spaghetti. Makes 4 servings.

Beef-Broccoli Stir-Fry

START TO FINISH: 30 minutes

NUTRITION FACTS per serving:

CALORIES 351
TOTAL FAT 7 g (2 g sat. fat)
CHOLESTEROL 40 mg
PROTEIN 30 g
CARBOHYDRATE 46 g
FIBER 6 g
SODIUM 793 mg

EXCHANGES 2 Starch, 3 Very Lean Meat, 2 Vegetable, 1 Fat

1 pound boneless beef round steak
Nonstick cooking spray

2 cups sliced fresh mushrooms

2 medium onions, chopped

1 medium green sweet pepper, seeded and chopped

1 stalk celery, chopped

1 14½-ounce can diced tomatoes with basil, garlic, and oregano, undrained

2 tablespoons water

⅛ to ¼ teaspoon crushed red pepper

6 ounces dried whole wheat or multigrain pasta, cooked according to package directions
Snipped fresh parsley (optional)

2 tablespoons grated Parmesan cheese

Italian Beef Skillet

PREP: 30 minutes

COOK: 1¼ hours

NUTRITION FACTS per serving:

CALORIES 269
TOTAL FAT 5 g (2 g sat. fat)
CHOLESTEROL 51 mg
PROTEIN 24 g
CARBOHYDRATE 32 g
FIBER 3 g
SODIUM 431 mg

EXCHANGES 1.5 Starch, 2.5 Very Lean Meat, 1.5 Vegetable, 0.5 Fat

1 Trim fat from meat. Cut meat into six serving-size pieces. Lightly coat an unheated large nonstick skillet with nonstick cooking spray. Preheat over medium heat. Add meat and cook until brown, turning to brown evenly. Remove meat from skillet; set aside.

2 Add mushrooms, onion, sweet pepper, and celery to skillet. Cook about 5 minutes or until vegetables are nearly tender, stirring occasionally. Stir in undrained tomatoes, water, and crushed red pepper. Return meat to skillet, spooning vegetable mixture over meat. Bring to boiling; reduce heat. Cover and simmer about 1¼ hours or until meat is tender, stirring occasionally.

3 Place steak on hot cooked pasta. Spoon vegetable mixture over steak. If desired, sprinkle with parsley. Serve with Parmesan cheese. Makes 6 servings.

COOK'S TIP

Braising or slow-cooking meat in a small amount of liquid for a long time is an ideal method for cooking slightly tough cuts. It tenderizes the meat and develops great flavor.

1   2-pound boneless beef round steak, cut ¾ to 1 inch thick

½   teaspoon salt

¼   teaspoon black pepper

1   14½-ounce can Cajun-, Mexican-, or Italian-style stewed tomatoes, undrained

⅓   cup tomato paste

½   teaspoon bottled hot pepper sauce (optional)

1   16-ounce package frozen yellow, green, and red peppers and onion stir-fry vegetables

4   cups hot cooked whole wheat pasta (optional)

1 Trim fat from steak. Cut steak into six serving-size pieces. Sprinkle meat with salt and black pepper. Place in a 3½- or 4-quart slow cooker. In a medium bowl combine undrained tomatoes, tomato paste, and, if desired, hot pepper sauce. Pour over meat in cooker. Top with frozen vegetables.

2 Cover and cook on low-heat setting for 9 to 10 hours or on high-heat setting for 4½ to 5 hours. If desired, serve with hot cooked pasta. Makes 6 servings.

So-Easy Pepper Steak

PREP: 15 minutes

COOK: 9 to 10 hours (low) or 4½ to 5 hours (high)

NUTRITION FACTS per serving:

CALORIES 257
TOTAL FAT 6 g (2 g sat. fat)
CHOLESTEROL 83 mg
PROTEIN 37 g
CARBOHYDRATE 12 g
FIBER 3 g
SODIUM 655 mg

EXCHANGES 4.5 Very Lean Meat, 2 Vegetable, 1 Fat

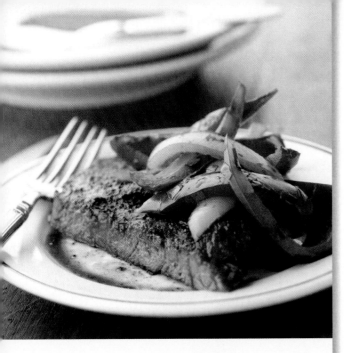

2   10- to 12-ounce beef ribeye steaks,
    cut 1 inch thick
1½ teaspoons paprika
1½ teaspoons garlic salt
1   teaspoon dried thyme, crushed
1   teaspoon dried oregano, crushed
½   teaspoon lemon-pepper seasoning
¼   to ½ teaspoon cayenne pepper
1   recipe Grilled Peppers

1 Trim fat from steaks. In a small bowl combine paprika, garlic salt, thyme, oregano, lemon-pepper seasoning, and cayenne pepper. Evenly sprinkle paprika mixture over steaks; rub in with your fingers. Cover steaks; chill for 1 hour. Meanwhile, prepare Grilled Peppers.

2 For a charcoal grill, place steaks on the rack of an uncovered grill directly over medium coals. Grill for 10 to 12 minutes for medium-rare doneness (145°F) or 12 to 15 minutes for medium doneness (160°F), turning once halfway through grilling. (For a gas grill, preheat grill. Reduce heat to medium. Place steaks on grill rack over heat. Cover and grill as above.)

3 Cut each steak in half. Serve with Grilled Peppers. Makes 4 servings.

Grilled Peppers: Seed and quarter 3 green, red, yellow, and/or orange sweet peppers. For a charcoal grill, place pepper quarters on the rack of an uncovered grill directly over medium coals. Grill for 12 to 15 minutes or until peppers are crisp-tender and lightly browned, turning once halfway through grilling. (For a gas grill, preheat grill. Reduce heat to medium. Place pepper quarters on grill rack over heat. Cover and grill as above.) Remove peppers from grill; cool slightly. Cut peppers into wide strips. Place peppers in bowl. Add 1 tablespoon snipped fresh basil or 1 teaspoon dried basil, crushed, and 1 tablespoon balsamic vinegar; toss well. Serve immediately or cool to room temperature.

Peppered Ribeye Steaks with Grilled Sweet Peppers

PREP: 20 minutes   **CHILL:** 1 hour
GRILL: 10 minutes

NUTRITION FACTS per serving:

CALORIES 249
TOTAL FAT 11 g (4 g sat. fat)
CHOLESTEROL 83 mg
PROTEIN 30 g
CARBOHYDRATE 6 g
FIBER 2 g
SODIUM 764 mg

EXCHANGES 4 Lean Meat, 1 Vegetable

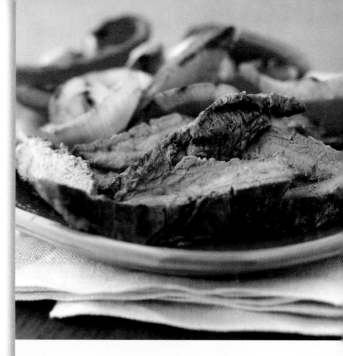

1   1-pound beef flank steak
⅓   cup orange juice
¼   cup snipped fresh cilantro
2   tablespoons red wine vinegar
1   tablespoon olive oil
4   cloves garlic, minced
2   teaspoons ground cumin
1   teaspoon ground coriander
¼   teaspoon salt
¼   teaspoon crushed red pepper
2   red and/or green sweet peppers, halved, stemmed, and seeded
1   red onion, cut into ½-inch-thick slices

Spicy Cilantro Flank Steak

PREP: 25 minutes   **MARINATE:** 4 to 6 hours
GRILL: 17 minutes

NUTRITION FACTS per serving:

CALORIES 244
TOTAL FAT 11 g (3 g sat. fat)
CHOLESTEROL 47 mg
PROTEIN 26 g
CARBOHYDRATE 10 g
FIBER 2 g
SODIUM 209 mg

EXCHANGES 3.5 Lean Meat, 1 Vegetable, 0.5 Fat

1 Trim fat from steak. Score both sides of steak in a diamond pattern by making shallow diagonal cuts at 1-inch intervals. Place steak in a resealable plastic bag set in a shallow dish.

2 For marinade, in a small bowl stir together orange juice, cilantro, vinegar, oil, garlic, cumin, coriander, salt, and crushed red pepper. Pour over steak. Seal bag; turn to coat steak. Marinate in the refrigerator for 4 to 6 hours, turning bag occasionally.

3 Drain steak, reserving marinade. Brush sweet peppers and onion with reserved marinade; discard any remaining marinade. Set vegetables aside. For a charcoal grill, place steak on the rack of an uncovered grill directly over medium coals. Grill for 8 minutes. Turn steak. Place vegetables, cut sides down, on grill rack with steak. Grill steak and vegetables for 9 to 13 minutes or until steak is medium doneness (160°F) and vegetables are crisp-tender, turning vegetables occasionally to brown evenly. (For a gas grill, preheat grill. Reduce heat to medium. Place steak, then vegetables on grill rack over heat. Cover and grill as above.)

4 To serve, thinly slice steak across the grain and cut sweet peppers into strips. Serve with grilled onion. Makes 4 servings.

COOK'S TIP
Store onions up to one month in a cool, dry place in a container such as a wire basket so air can circulate around them.

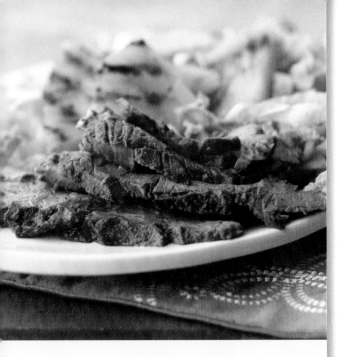

1   pound beef flank steak

2   tablespoons reduced-sodium soy sauce

1   tablespoon sweet rice wine (mirin)

1   tablespoon lemon juice

4   cloves garlic, minced

2   teaspoons five-spice powder

2   teaspoons ground coriander

1   teaspoon toasted sesame oil

¼   teaspoon fennel seeds, crushed

⅛   teaspoon cayenne pepper

½   of a cored and peeled fresh pineapple, cut crosswise into 4 slices

2   cups shredded napa cabbage

Five-Spice Steak

PREP: 20 minutes

MARINATE: 30 minutes to 4 hours

GRILL: 17 minutes

NUTRITION FACTS per serving:

CALORIES 231
TOTAL FAT 8 g (3 g sat. fat)
CHOLESTEROL 47 mg
PROTEIN 26 g
CARBOHYDRATE 13 g
FIBER 2 g
SODIUM 381 mg

EXCHANGES 0.5 Fruit, 3.5 Lean Meat, 0.5 Vegetable

1 Trim fat from steak. Score both sides of steak in a diamond pattern by making shallow diagonal cuts at 1-inch intervals. Place steak in a large resealable plastic bag set in a shallow dish.

2 For marinade, in a small bowl combine soy sauce, sweet rice wine, lemon juice, garlic, five-spice powder, coriander, toasted sesame oil, fennel seeds, and cayenne pepper. Pour marinade over steak. Seal bag; turn to coat steak. Marinate in the refrigerator for 30 minutes to 4 hours, turning bag occasionally.

3 Drain steak, discarding marinade. For a charcoal grill, place steak on the rack of an uncovered grill directly over medium coals. Grill for 17 to 21 minutes or until medium doneness (160°F), turning once halfway through grilling. Add pineapple slices to grill with steak for the last 5 minutes of grilling; turn pineapple after 2 to 3 minutes and remove pineapple when it is lightly browned. (For a gas grill, preheat grill. Reduce heat to medium. Place steak on grill rack over heat. Cover and grill as above, adding pineapple slices as directed.)

4 To serve, thinly slice steak across the grain. Serve with pineapple and cabbage. Makes 4 servings.

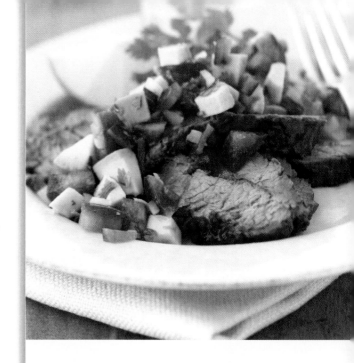

1	pound beef flank steak
¼	cup water
¼	cup lime juice
6	cloves garlic, minced
2	tablespoons snipped fresh cilantro
2	teaspoons snipped fresh oregano or ½ teaspoon dried oregano, crushed
¼	teaspoon chipotle chili powder or regular chili powder
1	recipe Avocado-Poblano Pico de Gallo
¼	teaspoon salt
⅛	teaspoon black pepper
	Lime wedges and/or fresh cilantro (optional)

1 Trim fat from steak. Score both sides of steak in a diamond pattern by making shallow diagonal cuts at 1-inch intervals. Place steak in a resealable plastic bag set in a shallow dish.

2 For marinade, in a small bowl stir together water, lime juice, garlic, cilantro, oregano, and chili powder. Pour marinade over steak in bag. Seal bag; turn to coat steak. Marinate in the refrigerator for 1 to 2 hours, turning bag occasionally.

3 Prepare Avocado-Poblano Pico de Gallo. Drain steak, reserving marinade. Sprinkle steak with salt and black pepper. For a charcoal grill, place steak on the rack of an uncovered grill directly over medium coals. Grill for 17 to 21 minutes or until medium doneness (160°F), turning once and brushing with the reserved marinade halfway through grilling. Discard any remaining marinade. (For a gas grill, preheat grill. Reduce heat to medium. Place steak on grill rack over heat. Cover and grill as above.)

4 To serve, thinly slice beef across the grain; divide among four serving plates. Top with Avocado-Poblano Pico de Gallo. If desired, garnish with lime wedges and/or cilantro. Makes 4 servings.

Avocado-Poblano Pico de Gallo: Preheat broiler. Arrange 1 fresh poblano chile pepper* or 1 sweet pepper on a foil-lined baking sheet. Broil 4 to 5 inches from heat for 8 to 10 minutes or until skin is bubbly and blackened, turning occasionally. Carefully bring the foil up and around the pepper to enclose. Let stand about 15 minutes or until cool enough to handle. Using a paring knife, pull off the skin gently and slowly. Discard skin. Remove pepper stem, seeds, and membranes; chop the pepper.

Lime-Marinated Flank Steak

PREP: 35 minutes **MARINATE:** 1 to 2 hours
GRILL: 17 minutes

NUTRITION FACTS per serving:

CALORIES 212
TOTAL FAT 9 g (3 g sat. fat)
CHOLESTEROL 47 mg
PROTEIN 27 g
CARBOHYDRATE 8 g
FIBER 2 g
SODIUM 282 mg

EXCHANGES 3.5 Lean Meat, 0.5 Vegetable

In a medium bowl combine chopped pepper; 1 small tomato, chopped; 3 tablespoons finely chopped red onion; 1 tablespoon snipped fresh cilantro; ¼ teaspoon finely shredded lime peel; 1½ teaspoons lime juice; and ⅛ teaspoon salt. Stir in ½ of a small avocado, halved, seeded, peeled, and chopped. Makes about 1½ cups.

*Because chile peppers contain volatile oils that can burn your skin and eyes, avoid direct contact with them as much as possible. When working with chile peppers, wear plastic or rubber gloves. If your bare hands do touch the peppers, wash your hands and nails well with soap and warm water.

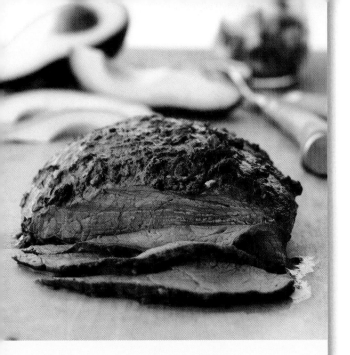

1 tablespoon finely chopped canned chipotle chile peppers in adobo sauce*

1 tablespoon snipped fresh oregano or 1 teaspoon dried oregano, crushed

1 tablespoon olive oil

1 teaspoon ground cumin

½ teaspoon salt

2 cloves garlic, minced

1 1½- to 2-pound boneless beef tri-tip roast (bottom sirloin)

Avocado slices (optional)

Purchased pico de gallo (optional)

Southwestern Tri-Tip Roast

PREP: 15 minutes **CHILL:** 6 to 24 hours
ROAST: 30 minutes **STAND:** 15 minutes
OVEN: 425°F

NUTRITION FACTS per serving:

CALORIES 156
TOTAL FAT 7 g (2 g sat. fat)
CHOLESTEROL 45 mg
PROTEIN 20 g
CARBOHYDRATE 1 g
FIBER 0 g
SODIUM 260 mg

EXCHANGES 3 Lean Meat

1 For rub, combine chile peppers, oregano, oil, cumin, salt, and garlic. Spread on surface of roast, rubbing in with glove-covered hands. Cover and chill for 6 to 24 hours.

2 Preheat oven to 425°F. Place roast on a rack in a shallow roasting pan. Insert an oven-going meat thermometer into center of roast. For medium-rare doneness, roast for 30 to 35 minutes or until meat thermometer registers 140°F. Cover with foil and let stand for 15 minutes. The temperature of the meat after standing should be 145°F. (For medium doneness, roast for 40 to 45 minutes or until meat thermometer registers 155°F. Cover and let stand for 15 minutes. The temperature of the meat after standing should be 160°F.)

3 Thinly slice roast across the grain. If desired, serve with avocado and pico de gallo. Makes 6 servings.

*Because chile peppers contain volatile oils that can burn your skin and eyes, avoid direct contact with them as much as possible. When working with chile peppers, wear plastic or rubber gloves. If your bare hands do touch the peppers, wash your hands and nails well with soap and warm water.

6	ounces lean ground beef or lamb
¼	cup finely chopped onion
2	cloves garlic, minced
1	8-ounce can tomato sauce
1	teaspoon snipped fresh rosemary or ¼ teaspoon dried rosemary, crushed
2	6-inch whole wheat or white pita bread rounds
½	cup shredded reduced-fat mozzarella cheese (2 ounces)
½	cup shredded fresh spinach
1	medium tomato, seeded and chopped
¼	cup crumbled reduced-fat feta cheese (1 ounce)
12	pitted kalamata or ripe olives, quartered

Greek Pita Pizzas

START TO FINISH: 35 minutes

OVEN: 400°F

1 Preheat oven to 400°F. In a medium nonstick skillet cook ground beef, onion, and garlic until meat is browned; drain off fat. Stir tomato sauce and rosemary into meat mixture in skillet. Bring to boiling; reduce heat. Simmer, uncovered, for 2 minutes.

2 Carefully split pita bread rounds in half horizontally; place pita halves, rough sides up, in a single layer on a large baking sheet. Bake for 3 to 4 minutes or until lightly toasted.

3 Top toasted pita bread with meat mixture; sprinkle with mozzarella cheese. Bake for 2 to 3 minutes more or until cheese is melted. Remove from oven. Top with spinach, tomato, feta cheese, and olives; serve immediately. Makes 4 servings.

NUTRITION FACTS per serving:

CALORIES 256
TOTAL FAT 10 g (4 g sat. fat)
CHOLESTEROL 40 mg
PROTEIN 18 g
CARBOHYDRATE 25 g
FIBER 5 g
SODIUM 842 mg

EXCHANGES 1.5 Starch, 1.5 Lean Meat, 0.5 Vegetable, 1 Fat

COOK'S TIP

Uncooked ground beef can be stored in the freezer for 6 to 12 months and in the refrigerator for 2 or 3 days. Leftover cooked beef should be stored in the refrigerator no more than 3 or 4 days.

Burgers with Dill Sauce

PREP: 20 minutes

BROIL: 12 minutes

NUTRITION FACTS per serving:

CALORIES 234
TOTAL FAT 12 g (5 g sat. fat)
CHOLESTEROL 75 mg
PROTEIN 25 g
CARBOHYDRATE 6 g
FIBER 1 g
SODIUM 474 mg

EXCHANGES 3.5 Lean Meat, 0.5 Vegetable, 0.5 Fat

¼ cup finely chopped onion

¼ cup snipped fresh parsley or ½ teaspoon dried dill

2 cloves garlic, minced

½ teaspoon salt

1 pound lean ground beef

⅓ cup plain low-fat yogurt

1 tablespoon stone-ground mustard or Dijon-style mustard

1 tablespoon snipped fresh dill or 1 teaspoon dried dill

1 teaspoon balsamic vinegar

¼ cup chopped seeded cucumber

Cucumber slices (optional)

Tomato slices (optional)

Red onion slices (optional)

Fresh spinach leaves (optional)

1 Preheat broiler. In a large bowl combine chopped onion, parsley, garlic, and salt. Add beef; mix well. Shape into four ¾-inch-thick patties.

2 Place patties on the unheated rack of a broiler pan. Broil 3 to 4 inches from heat for 12 to 14 minutes or until done (160°F),* turning once halfway through broiling.

3 Meanwhile, for sauce, in a small bowl combine yogurt, mustard, dill, and balsamic vinegar. Stir in chopped cucumber. Spoon sauce over burgers. If desired, serve with cucumber slices, tomato slices, red onion slices, and spinach. Makes 4 servings.

*The internal color of a burger is not a reliable doneness indicator. A beef patty cooked to 160°F is safe, regardless of color. To measure the doneness of a patty, insert an instant-read thermometer through the side of the patty to a depth of 2 to 3 inches.

COOK'S TIP

Dill loses its fragrance quickly when heated. When you cook with it, be sure to add it at the end of the cooking time.

1 lemon

6 ounces dried whole wheat orzo
   (about 1 cup)

1 cup cherry tomatoes, halved

¼ cup capers, rinsed and drained

2 teaspoons snipped fresh rosemary
   or ½ teaspoon dried rosemary,
   crushed

1 tablespoon olive oil

1 pound veal scaloppine
   (about ¼ inch thick)

¼ teaspoon salt

¼ teaspoon black pepper

¼ cup dry white wine or lower-
   sodium beef broth

1 tablespoon snipped fresh
   flat-leaf parsley

   Fresh rosemary sprigs (optional)

   Lemon wedges (optional)

Veal Piccata

START TO FINISH: 25 minutes

NUTRITION FACTS per serving:

CALORIES 329
TOTAL FAT 7 g (1 g sat. fat)
CHOLESTEROL 89 mg
PROTEIN 30 g
CARBOHYDRATE 35 g
FIBER 9 g
SODIUM 481 mg

EXCHANGES 2 Starch, 3 Lean Meat,
0.5 Vegetable

1 Finely shred peel from the lemon. Squeeze juice from lemon; set peel and juice aside separately. Cook orzo in lightly salted boiling water according to package directions; drain. Stir in half of the lemon peel, half of the lemon juice, cherry tomatoes, half of the capers, and snipped or dried rosemary. Cover and let stand until serving time.

2 Meanwhile, in a very large skillet heat oil over medium-high heat. Sprinkle veal with salt and pepper. Add veal to skillet. Cook about 4 minutes or until no longer pink, turning veal occasionally to brown evenly. Transfer veal to a serving platter; cover and keep warm.

3 Add remaining lemon peel, remaining lemon juice, remaining capers, and white wine to the skillet. Bring to boiling, scraping the browned bits from the bottom of the pan.

4 Pour wine mixture over veal. Serve with cooked orzo. Sprinkle orzo mixture with parsley. If desired, garnish with rosemary sprigs and serve with lemon wedges. Makes 4 servings.

COOK'S TIP

Orzo is a rice-shape pasta, generally found in the pasta aisle of grocery stores. If you have trouble finding the whole wheat variety, look for it at health or specialty markets or ask your grocer to carry it.

8 lamb rib chops, cut about 1 inch thick (2 to 2½ pounds total)

4 cloves garlic, minced

1½ teaspoons fennel seeds, crushed

1½ teaspoons ground cumin

½ teaspoon ground coriander

½ teaspoon salt

½ teaspoon cracked black pepper

1 Trim fat from lamb chops; set chops aside. In a small bowl combine garlic, fennel seeds, cumin, coriander, salt, and pepper. Sprinkle evenly over all sides of lamb chops; rub in with your fingers. Place lamb chops on a plate; cover with plastic wrap. Chill for 30 minutes to 24 hours.

2 For a charcoal grill, place lamb chops on the rack of an uncovered grill directly over medium coals. Grill until desired doneness, turning once halfway through grilling. Allow 12 to 14 minutes for medium-rare doneness (145°F) or 15 to 17 minutes for medium doneness (160°F). (For a gas grill, preheat grill. Reduce heat to medium. Place chops on grill rack over heat. Cover and grill as above.) Makes 4 servings.

Garlic-Fennel Lamb Chops

PREP: 15 minutes

CHILL: 30 minutes to 24 hours

GRILL: 12 minutes

NUTRITION FACTS per serving:

CALORIES 249
TOTAL FAT 8 g (3 g sat. fat)
CHOLESTEROL 119 mg
PROTEIN 39 g
CARBOHYDRATE 2 g
FIBER 1 g
SODIUM 384 mg

EXCHANGES 5.5 Very Lean Meat, 1 Fat

NUTRITION NOTE

Lamb has less fat marbling than other meats; most visible fat is on the outer edges of the cuts. To reduce saturated fat and cholesterol, trim the fat.

8 lamb loin chops, cut 1 inch thick (about 2 pounds total)

1 tablespoon snipped fresh thyme or 1 teaspoon dried thyme, crushed

¼ teaspoon salt

¼ teaspoon black pepper

3 medium tomatoes, chopped

1 medium cucumber, chopped

1 medium yellow sweet pepper, seeded and chopped

½ of a medium red onion, chopped

1 teaspoon snipped fresh oregano or ½ teaspoon dried oregano, crushed

2 tablespoons balsamic vinegar

1 tablespoon olive oil

Fresh romaine leaves (optional)

Lamb Chops with Fresh Greek Salad

PREP: 25 minutes

GRILL: 12 minutes

NUTRITION FACTS per serving:

CALORIES 325
TOTAL FAT 12 g (4 g sat. fat)
CHOLESTEROL 119 mg
PROTEIN 43 g
CARBOHYDRATE 13 g
FIBER 2 g
SODIUM 245 mg

EXCHANGES 5.5 Very Lean Meat, 2 Vegetable, 2 Fat

1 Trim fat from chops. Sprinkle chops with 2 teaspoons fresh thyme or ¾ teaspoon dried thyme, ⅛ teaspoon salt, and ⅛ teaspoon black pepper. For a charcoal grill, place chops on the rack of an uncovered grill directly over medium coals. Grill until desired doneness, turning once halfway through grilling. Allow 12 to 14 minutes for medium-rare doneness (145°F) or 15 to 17 minutes for medium doneness (160°F). (For a gas grill, preheat grill. Reduce heat to medium. Place chops on grill rack over heat. Cover and grill as above.)

2 Meanwhile, for salad, in a large bowl combine tomato, cucumber, sweet pepper, red onion, oregano, remaining 1 teaspoon fresh thyme or ¼ teaspoon dried thyme, and remaining ⅛ teaspoon salt and ⅛ teaspoon black pepper. Drizzle with balsamic vinegar and oil. Toss gently to combine. If desired, spoon onto romaine leaves.

3 Serve grilled lamb chops with salad. Makes 4 servings.

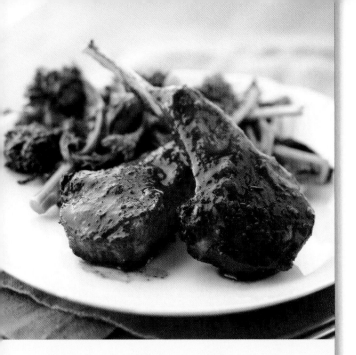

Spicy Apricot Lamb Chops

PREP: 20 minutes

BROIL: 10 minutes

NUTRITION FACTS per serving:

CALORIES 335
TOTAL FAT 12 g (4 g sat. fat)
CHOLESTEROL 119 mg chol
PROTEIN 42 g
CARBOHYDRATE 14 g
FIBER 4 g
SODIUM 376 mg

EXCHANGES 0.5 Other Carbohydrates, 5.5 Very Lean Meat, 1 Vegetable, 2 Fat

NUTRITION NOTE

Lamb is a great source of protein, vitamin B$_{12}$, zinc, niacin, iron, and riboflavin. It also contains all eight of the essential amino acids.

2	pounds broccoli rabe
8	lamb rib chops, cut 1 inch thick (about 2 pounds total)
1	tablespoon packed brown sugar
1	teaspoon garlic salt
1	teaspoon chili powder
1	teaspoon paprika
½	teaspoon dried oregano, crushed
¼	teaspoon ground cinnamon
¼	teaspoon ground allspice
¼	teaspoon black pepper
¼	cup low-sugar apricot preserves
1	tablespoon olive oil

1 Preheat broiler. Wash broccoli rabe; remove and discard woody stems. Coarsely chop the leafy greens; set aside.

2 Trim fat from chops. In a small bowl combine brown sugar, garlic salt, chili powder, paprika, oregano, cinnamon, allspice, and pepper. Set aside 1 teaspoon of the spice mixture. Sprinkle remaining spice mixture on all sides of the chops; rub in with your fingers.

3 Place chops on the unheated rack of a broiler pan. Broil 4 to 5 inches from the heat for 10 to 15 minutes or until done (160°F), turning meat and brushing with preserves halfway through broiling.

4 Meanwhile, in a very large skillet heat oil over medium-high heat. Add 1 teaspoon reserved spice mixture. Cook and stir for 1 minute. Add broccoli rabe. Using tongs, toss and cook for 4 to 6 minutes or until broccoli rabe is crisp-tender.

5 Serve lamb chops with broccoli rabe mixture. Makes 4 servings.

Chapter 8

Pork

On the opener: Apple-Glazed Tenderloin (see recipe, page 129)

- 1 1-pound pork tenderloin
- ¼ cup balsamic vinegar
- 2 tablespoons olive oil
- 1 tablespoon snipped fresh rosemary or ½ teaspoon dried rosemary, crushed
- 2 cloves garlic, minced
- ¾ teaspoon black pepper
- ⅛ teaspoon salt
- 1 recipe Balsamic Glaze

1 Place tenderloin in large resealable plastic bag set in a shallow dish. For marinade, in a small bowl combine balsamic vinegar, oil, rosemary, garlic, pepper, and salt. Pour over tenderloin. Seal bag; turn to coat tenderloin. Marinate in the refrigerator for 1 hour, turning bag occasionally.

2 Remove tenderloin from marinade, discarding marinade. For a charcoal grill, arrange hot coals around a drip pan. Test for medium-hot heat above the pan. Place tenderloin on grill rack over drip pan. Cover and grill for 30 to 35 minutes or until an instant-read thermometer inserted into the thickest part of the tenderloin registers 155°F. (For a gas grill, preheat grill. Reduce heat to medium-high. Adjust for indirect cooking. Place tenderloin on grill rack over burner that is off. Grill as above.)

3 Brush tenderloin on all sides with Balsamic Glaze. Grill for 1 minute more. Remove from grill. Cover tightly with foil; let stand for 15 minutes before slicing. The temperature of the meat after standing should be 160°F. Makes 4 servings.

Balsamic Glaze: In a small saucepan bring ½ cup balsamic vinegar to boiling. Reduce heat; boil gently for 5 minutes. Makes about ¼ cup.

Balsamic Pork Tenderloin

PREP: 20 minutes **MARINATE:** 1 hour
GRILL: 31 minutes **STAND:** 15 minutes

NUTRITION FACTS per serving:

CALORIES 189
TOTAL FAT 7 g (2 g sat. fat)
CHOLESTEROL 73 mg
PROTEIN 24 g
CARBOHYDRATE 5 g
FIBER 0 g
SODIUM 81 mg

EXCHANGES 3.5 Very Lean Meat, 1.5 Fat

COOK'S TIP

When selecting pork, choose a pale pink cut that has little marbling. The fat that is present should be white, not yellow, or you will not be getting the freshest product.

1 pound boneless pork loin

¼ cup bottled plum sauce

1 tablespoon reduced-sodium soy sauce

1 tablespoon lime juice

2 teaspoons honey

⅛ teaspoon ground ginger

½ of a cored peeled pineapple, cut into 1½-inch chunks

1 medium red sweet pepper, seeded and cut into 1-inch pieces

Pork and Pineapple Kabobs

PREP: 25 minutes **MARINATE:** 30 to 60 minutes

GRILL: 18 minutes

NUTRITION FACTS per serving:

CALORIES 218
TOTAL FAT 5 g (2 g sat. fat)
CHOLESTEROL 71 mg
PROTEIN 25 g
CARBOHYDRATE 18 g
FIBER 2 g
SODIUM 244 mg

EXCHANGES 0.5 Other Carbohydrates, 0.5 Fruit, 3.5 Very Lean Meat, 0.5 Fat

1 Trim fat from pork; cut pork into 1½-inch cubes. Place pork cubes in a large resealable plastic bag set in a shallow dish. For marinade, in a small bowl whisk together plum sauce, soy sauce, lime juice, honey, and ginger. Pour marinade over pork cubes in bag. Seal bag; turn to coat pork cubes. Marinate in the refrigerator for 30 to 60 minutes, turning bag occasionally.

2 Drain pork, discarding marinade. On two or three 10- to 12-inch metal skewers, thread pork cubes, leaving a ¼-inch space between cubes. On two more 10- to 12-inch metal skewers, alternately thread pineapple and sweet pepper pieces, leaving a ¼-inch space between pieces.

3 For a charcoal grill, place skewers on the rack of an uncovered grill directly over medium coals. Grill for 8 to 10 minutes for pineapple and sweet pepper or until pineapple is lightly browned and 18 to 20 minutes for pork or until no pink remains, turning skewers to brown evenly. (For a gas grill, preheat grill. Reduce heat to medium. Place skewers on grill rack over heat. Cover and grill as above.)

4 Serve pork with pineapple and sweet pepper. Makes 4 servings.

COOK'S TIP

To peel a pineapple, begin by cutting off the crown and the bottom. With the pineapple upright, cut in strips, following the contour of the fruit, to remove the skin.

- 2 cups apple or hickory wood chips
- 1 1-pound pork tenderloin
- ½ teaspoon coarsely ground black pepper
- ¼ teaspoon salt
- 2 tablespoons apple jelly, melted
- ¼ teaspoon ground cinnamon
- 1 recipe Apple-Onion Spice Packet (optional)

1 At least 1 hour before grilling, soak wood chips in enough water to cover. Drain chips before using. Trim fat from tenderloin. Sprinkle tenderloin with pepper and salt. In a small bowl stir together apple jelly and cinnamon; set aside.

2 For a charcoal grill, arrange medium-hot coals around a drip pan. Pour 1 inch of water into the drip pan. Test for medium heat above the pan. Sprinkle wood chips over the coals. Place tenderloin on grill rack over the drip pan. Place Apple-Onion Spice Packet (if using) directly over the coals. Cover and grill the pork for 35 to 40 minutes or until an instant-read thermometer inserted in the thickest part of the tenderloin registers 155°F. Brush tenderloin with the apple jelly mixture for the last 10 minutes of grilling. If using spice packet, turn packet after 10 minutes and continue grilling for 10 minutes more. Remove packet from grill and let stand while pork continues to cook. (For a gas grill, preheat grill. Reduce heat to medium. Adjust for indirect cooking. Place tenderloin over burner that is off and spice packet [if using] on grill rack over burner that is on. Cover and grill as above.)

3 Remove from grill. Cover tightly with foil; let stand for 15 minutes. The temperature of meat after standing should be 160°F. If using Apple-Onion Spice Packet, serve with pork. Makes 4 servings.

Apple-Onion Spice Packet: Fold a 36×18-inch piece of heavy foil in half to make an 18-inch square; set aside. Core 2 medium cooking apples; cut into thin wedges. Cut 1 medium sweet onion (such as Vidalia, Walla Walla, or Maui) into thin wedges. Place apple and onion wedges in the center of the foil. Top with 2 tablespoons apple jelly and sprinkle with ¼ teaspoon ground cinnamon. Bring up two opposite edges of the foil square and seal with a double fold. Fold remaining edges to enclose apple and onion, leaving space for steam to build.

Apple-Glazed Tenderloin

PREP: 20 minutes **SOAK:** 1 hour
GRILL: 35 minutes **STAND:** 15 minutes

NUTRITION FACTS per serving:

CALORIES 189
TOTAL FAT 6 g (2 g sat. fat)
CHOLESTEROL 62 mg
PROTEIN 25 g
CARBOHYDRATE 8 g
FIBER 0 g
SODIUM 200 mg

EXCHANGES 0.5 Other Carbohydrates, 3.5 Lean Meat

NUTRITION NOTE

When a craving for pork hits, pork tenderloin is a good choice. It's one of the lowest fat cuts of meat available, and very little of the fat is saturated.

Sesame Pork Tenderloin

PREP: 25 minutes   **ROAST:** 25 minutes
STAND: 10 minutes   **OVEN:** 425°F

NUTRITION FACTS per serving:

CALORIES 167
TOTAL FAT 6 g (1 g sat. fat)
CHOLESTEROL 55 mg
PROTEIN 21 g
CARBOHYDRATE 8 g
FIBER 3 g
SODIUM 365 mg

EXCHANGES 3 Lean Meat, 1 Vegetable

2   tablespoons bottled chili sauce or
     1 tablespoon Asian chili sauce
1   tablespoon reduced-sodium
     teriyaki sauce
2   cloves garlic, minced
½   teaspoon grated fresh ginger
     or ⅛ teaspoon ground ginger
1   12- to 16-ounce pork tenderloin
1   teaspoon sesame seeds
2   teaspoons olive oil
⅛   teaspoon salt
⅛   teaspoon black pepper
4   cups packaged shredded broccoli
     (broccoli slaw mix)

1 Preheat oven to 425°F. For sauce, in a small bowl stir together chili sauce, teriyaki sauce, half of the garlic, and ginger.

2 Place tenderloin on a rack in a shallow roasting pan. Spread half of the sauce on tenderloin. Roast, uncovered, for 15 minutes. Spread remaining sauce on tenderloin; sprinkle tenderloin with sesame seeds. Roast, uncovered, for 10 to 20 minutes more or until an instant-read thermometer inserted in the thickest part of the tenderloin registers 155°F.

3 Remove from oven. Cover tightly with foil; let stand for 10 minutes before serving. The temperature of the meat after standing should be 160°F.

4 Meanwhile, in a 4-quart Dutch oven heat oil over medium heat. Add remaining garlic, salt, and pepper; cook and stir for 15 seconds. Add broccoli. Cook and toss for 1 to 2 minutes or until broccoli is heated through.

5 To serve, slice tenderloin and serve with broccoli. Makes 4 servings.

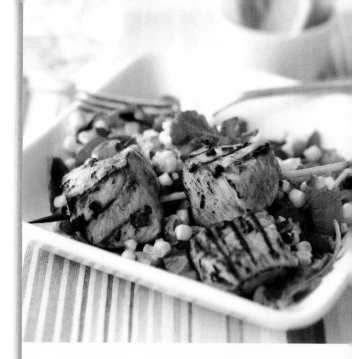

1 pound boneless pork loin

⅓ cup lime juice

2 tablespoons honey

1 fresh jalapeño chile pepper, seeded and finely chopped*

¼ cup snipped fresh cilantro

½ teaspoon salt

3 fresh ears of corn or 1½ cups loose-pack frozen whole kernel corn, thawed

2 cups coarsely chopped fresh arugula or spinach

1 medium red sweet pepper, seeded and chopped

1 Trim fat from pork; cut pork into 1½-inch cubes. Place pork cubes in a large resealable plastic bag set in a shallow dish. For marinade, in a small bowl whisk together lime juice and honey. Stir in chile pepper, cilantro, and salt. Add ¼ cup of the lime juice mixture to pork cubes in bag. Seal bag; turn to coat pork cubes. Marinate in the refrigerator for 1 hour, turning bag occasionally.

2 Drain pork, discarding marinade. Thread pork onto eight 8-inch skewers,** leaving a ¼-inch space between cubes. For a charcoal grill, place skewers on the rack of an uncovered grill directly over medium coals. Grill for 18 to 20 minutes or until no pink remains, turning skewers to brown evenly. (For a gas grill, preheat grill. Reduce heat to medium. Place skewers on grill rack over heat. Cover and grill as above.)

3 Meanwhile, if using fresh corn, carefully cut corn kernels off the cobs. For corn salad, in a medium bowl combine corn kernels, arugula, and sweet pepper. Add remaining lime juice mixture; toss to coat. Serve pork with corn salad. Makes 4 servings.

*Because chile peppers contain volatile oils that can burn your skin and eyes, avoid direct contact with them as much as possible. When working with chile peppers, wear plastic or rubber gloves. If your bare hands do touch the peppers, wash your hands and nails well with soap and warm water.

**If using wooden skewers, soak in enough water to cover for 30 minutes.

Pork Kabobs with Corn Salad

PREP: 20 minutes   **MARINATE:** 1 hour
GRILL: 18 minutes

NUTRITION FACTS per serving:

CALORIES 286
TOTAL FAT 10 g (3 g sat. fat)
CHOLESTEROL 73 mg
PROTEIN 25 g
CARBOHYDRATE 26 g
FIBER 3 g
SODIUM 384 mg

EXCHANGES 1.5 Starch, 3 Lean Meat, 0.5 Vegetable

COOK'S TIP

Store chile peppers, such as jalapeño peppers, unwashed and wrapped in paper towels in a plastic bag in the refrigerator for up to 10 days.

Margarita-Glazed Pork Chops

PREP: 10 minutes

GRILL: 7 minutes

NUTRITION FACTS per serving:

CALORIES 184
TOTAL FAT 3 g (1 g sat. fat)
CHOLESTEROL 62 mg
PROTEIN 26 g
CARBOHYDRATE 8 g
FIBER 0 g
SODIUM 211 mg

EXCHANGES 0.5 Other Carbohydrates,
3.5 Very Lean Meat

4   boneless pork top loin chops, cut ¾-inch thick (1 to 1½ pounds total)

⅓   cup low-sugar orange marmalade

1   fresh jalapeño chile pepper, seeded and finely chopped*

2   tablespoons tequila or lime juice

½   teaspoon grated fresh ginger or ¼ teaspoon ground ginger

¼   cup snipped fresh cilantro

1 Trim fat from pork. For glaze, in a small bowl stir together orange marmalade, chile pepper, tequila, and ginger.

2 For a charcoal grill, place chops on the rack of an uncovered grill directly over medium coals. Grill for 7 to 9 minutes or until no pink remains (160°F) and juices run clear, turning once halfway through grilling and spooning glaze over chops frequently during the last 2 minutes of grilling. (For a gas grill, preheat grill. Reduce heat to medium. Place chops on grill rack over heat. Cover and grill as above.)

3 To serve, sprinkle pork chops with cilantro. Makes 4 servings.

*Because chile peppers contain volatile oils that can burn your skin and eyes, avoid direct contact with them as much as possible. When working with chile peppers, wear plastic or rubber gloves. If your bare hands do touch the peppers, wash your hands and nails well with soap and warm water.

4	boneless or bone-in pork loin chops, cut ½ inch thick (1 to 1½ pounds total)
¼	teaspoon salt
¼	teaspoon freshly ground black pepper
1	tablespoon finely snipped fresh rosemary or 1 teaspoon dried rosemary, crushed
3	cloves garlic, minced

1 Preheat oven to 425°F. Sprinkle all sides of chops with salt and pepper; set aside. In a small bowl combine rosemary and garlic. Sprinkle rosemary mixture evenly over all sides of the chops; rub in with your fingers.

2 Place chops on a rack in a shallow roasting pan. Roast chops for 10 minutes. Reduce oven temperature to 350°F and continue roasting about 25 minutes or until no pink remains (160°F) and juices run clear. Makes 4 servings.

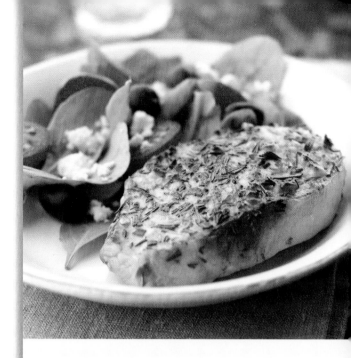

Mediterranean Pork Chops

PREP: 10 minutes   **ROAST:** 35 minutes
OVEN: 425°F/350°F

NUTRITION FACTS per serving:

CALORIES 161
TOTAL FAT 5 g (2 g sat. fat)
CHOLESTEROL 62 mg
PROTEIN 25 g
CARBOHYDRATE 1 g
FIBER 0 g
SODIUM 192 mg

EXCHANGES 3.5 Very Lean Meat, 1 Fat

Sassy Pork Chops

PREP: 25 minutes

COOK: 6 to 7 hours (low) or 3 to 3½ hours (high)

NUTRITION FACTS per serving:

CALORIES 215
TOTAL FAT 7 g (1 g sat. fat)
CHOLESTEROL 78 mg
PROTEIN 33 g
CARBOHYDRATE 4 g
FIBER 1 g
SODIUM 363 mg

EXCHANGES 4 Lean Meat, 1 Vegetable

NUTRITION NOTE

Sweet peppers, also called bell peppers, are excellent sources of vitamin C, a potent antioxidant. It's better to eat these peppers raw because cooking quickly destroys the vitamin C.

2 medium red, green, and/or yellow sweet peppers, cut into strips*
1 cup thinly sliced celery
½ cup chopped onion
8 bone-in pork loin chops, cut ¾ inch thick (about 3 pounds)
½ teaspoon garlic salt
¼ teaspoon black pepper
2 tablespoons canola oil
¼ cup reduced-sodium chicken broth
¼ cup orange juice
1 tablespoon chopped canned chipotle chile peppers in adobo sauce**
½ teaspoon dried oregano, crushed

1 In a 4- to 5-quart slow cooker combine sweet pepper, celery, and onion; set aside. Season chops with garlic salt and black pepper. In a 12-inch skillet heat oil over medium heat. Add chops, half at a time; cook until brown on both sides. Add chops to slow cooker. In a small bowl combine chicken broth, orange juice, chile peppers, and oregano. Pour broth mixture over mixture in cooker.

2 Cover and cook on low-heat setting for 6 to 7 hours or on high-heat setting for 3 to 3½ hours. Using a slotted spoon, transfer chops and vegetables to a serving platter; discard cooking liquid. Makes 8 servings.

*To add more color to this dish, use three small peppers of different colors.

**Because chile peppers contain volatile oils that can burn your skin and eyes, avoid direct contact with them as much as possible. When working with chile peppers, wear plastic or rubber gloves. If your bare hands do touch the peppers, wash your hands and nails well with soap and warm water.

- 4   bone-in pork rib chops, cut ¾ inch thick (about 1¾ pounds total)
- ¼   cup lime juice
- 1   tablespoon chili powder
- 1   tablespoon olive oil
- 2   cloves garlic, minced
- 2   teaspoons ground cumin
- 1   teaspoon ground cinnamon
- ½   teaspoon bottled hot pepper sauce
- ¼   teaspoon salt
     Lettuce leaves (optional)
     Sliced mango (optional)
     Sliced fresh chile pepper* (optional)

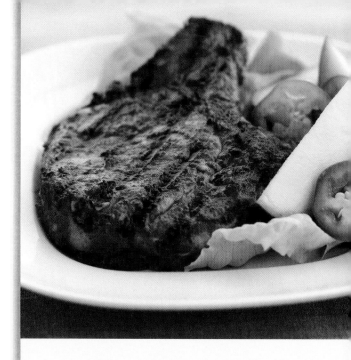

1 Trim fat from chops. Place chops in a resealable plastic bag set in a shallow dish. For marinade, in a small bowl stir together lime juice, chili powder, oil, garlic, cumin, cinnamon, hot pepper sauce, and salt; pour over chops. Seal bag; turn to coat chops. Marinate in the refrigerator for 4 to 24 hours, turning bag occasionally.

2 Drain chops, discarding marinade. For a charcoal grill, place chops on the rack of an uncovered grill directly over medium coals. Grill for 11 to 14 minutes or until juices run clear (160°F), turning once. (For a gas grill, preheat grill. Reduce heat to medium. Place chops on grill rack over heat. Cover and grill as above.) If desired, garnish with lettuce leaves, mango, and chile pepper. Makes 4 servings.

*Because chile peppers contain volatile oils that can burn your skin and eyes, avoid direct contact with them as much as possible. When working with chile peppers, wear plastic or rubber gloves. If your bare hands do touch the peppers, wash your hands and nails well with soap and warm water.

Spicy Grilled Pork Chops

PREP: 15 minutes   **MARINATE:** 4 to 24 hours
GRILL: 11 minutes

NUTRITION FACTS per serving:

CALORIES 196
TOTAL FAT 9 g (2 g sat. fat)
CHOLESTEROL 61 mg
PROTEIN 25 g
CARBOHYDRATE 3 g
FIBER 1 g
SODIUM 159 mg

EXCHANGES 3.5 Lean Meat

Nonstick cooking spray

1⅓	cups water
½	cup yellow cornmeal
½	cup cold water
½	teaspoon salt
8	ounces ground pork
½	cup chopped green and/or red sweet pepper
1	tablespoon chili powder
1	14½-ounce can diced tomatoes with onion and garlic, drained
1	11-ounce can whole kernel corn, drained
2	tablespoons tomato paste
½	cup shredded reduced-fat cheddar cheese (2 ounces)
2	tablespoons snipped fresh cilantro

Tamale Pie

PREP: 35 minutes   **COOK:** 10 minutes
BAKE: 30 minutes   **OVEN:** 350°F

NUTRITION FACTS per serving:

CALORIES 246
TOTAL FAT 11 g (4 g sat. fat)
CHOLESTEROL 34 mg
PROTEIN 12 g
CARBOHYDRATE 26 g
FIBER 4 g
SODIUM 812 mg

EXCHANGES 1.5 Starch, 1 Medium-Fat Meat, 1 Vegetable, 1 Fat

1 Preheat oven to 350°F. Lightly coat a 2-quart square baking dish with nonstick cooking spray; set aside. In a small saucepan bring 1⅓ cups water to boiling. Meanwhile, in a small bowl stir together cornmeal, ½ cup cold water, and ¼ teaspoon salt. Slowly add the cornmeal mixture to boiling water, stirring constantly. Cook and stir until mixture returns to boiling; reduce heat. Cook over low heat about 10 minutes or until mixture is very thick, stirring frequently.

2 Spoon hot cornmeal mixture into the prepared baking dish. Cover and chill while preparing filling.

3 For filling, in a large skillet cook pork and sweet pepper until meat is brown. Drain off fat. Stir chili powder and remaining ¼ teaspoon salt into meat mixture in skillet; cook for 1 minute. Stir in drained tomatoes, corn, and tomato paste. Spoon the meat mixture on chilled cornmeal mixture in baking dish.

4 Bake, uncovered, about 30 minutes or until heated through. Sprinkle with cheese and cilantro. Makes 6 servings.

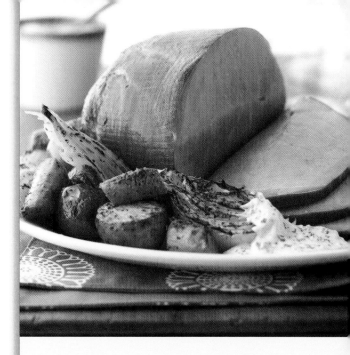

1	pound tiny new potatoes, halved
4	large carrots, cut into 1-inch pieces
1	large fennel bulb, trimmed and cut in ½-inch-thick wedges, or 1 medium onion, cut in ½-inch-thick wedges
1	tablespoon olive oil
½	teaspoon dried dill
½	teaspoon cracked black pepper
1	2- to 3-pound cooked boneless ham
1	8-ounce carton light dairy sour cream
¼	cup fat-free milk
2	tablespoons country Dijon-style mustard
1	tablespoon prepared horseradish

1 Preheat oven to 425°F. In a large bowl combine potatoes, carrot pieces, and fennel; add oil, ¼ teaspoon dill, and cracked black pepper. Arrange vegetables in a shallow roasting pan. Roast for 20 minutes.

2 Reduce oven temperature to 325°F. Push vegetables to sides of pan. Place a meat rack in center of pan; place ham on rack. Roast for 1 to 1¼ hours or until ham is hot (140°F) and vegetables are tender, stirring vegetables once.

3 Meanwhile, in a small bowl combine remaining ¼ teaspoon dill, sour cream, milk, mustard, and horseradish.

4 To serve, transfer ham and vegetables to a serving platter. Serve with sour cream mixture. Makes 8 servings.

COOK'S TIP

Most potatoes should be stored in dark, cool, well-ventilated areas for no more than two weeks. New potatoes should be used within three days of purchase.

Roasted Ham and Vegetables with Horseradish Sauce

PREP: 20 minutes   **ROAST:** 1 hour 20 minutes
OVEN: 425°F/325°F

NUTRITION FACTS per serving:

CALORIES 318
TOTAL FAT 15 g (5 g sat. fat)
CHOLESTEROL 75 mg
PROTEIN 22 g
CARBOHYDRATE 24 g
FIBER 5 g
SODIUM 1,650 mg

EXCHANGES 1.5 Starch, 2 Medium-Fat Meat, 1 Vegetable, 1 Fat

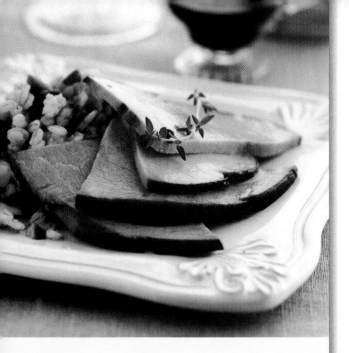

1½- to 2-pound cooked boneless ham

1 recipe Pomegranate Glaze

2 teaspoons canola oil or olive oil

½ cup finely chopped shallot or onion

2 cups reduced-sodium chicken broth

1¼ cups quick-cooking barley

2 teaspoons snipped fresh thyme or ½ teaspoon dried thyme, crushed

¼ cup coarsely chopped pistachio nuts

¼ cup coarsely chopped dried cranberries or cherries

Fresh thyme sprigs (optional)

Pomegranate-Glazed Ham with Pistachio Barley

PREP: 20 minutes **BAKE:** 1¼ hours
OVEN: 325°F

NUTRITION FACTS per serving:

CALORIES 423
TOTAL FAT 15 g (4 g sat. fat)
CHOLESTEROL 65 mg
PROTEIN 26 g
CARBOHYDRATE 48 g
FIBER 9 g
SODIUM 1,680 mg

EXCHANGES 3 Starch, 2.5 Medium-Fat Meat

1 Preheat oven to 325°F. Line a shallow baking pan with foil; set aside. Score ham in a diamond pattern by making shallow diagonal cuts at 1-inch intervals. Place ham on a rack in prepared pan. Insert an oven-going meat thermometer into center of ham. Bake, uncovered, about 1¼ hours or until thermometer registers 140°F, brushing with ¼ cup Pomegranate Glaze during the last 20 minutes of baking.

2 Meanwhile, in a medium saucepan heat oil over medium-high heat. Add shallot; cook until tender. Add chicken broth, barley, and dried thyme (if using). Bring to boiling; reduce heat. Cover and simmer for 10 to 12 minutes or until most of the liquid is absorbed and barley is tender. Stir in snipped fresh thyme (if using), pistachio nuts, and dried cranberries.

3 Slice ham and serve with barley mixture. If desired, garnish with fresh thyme sprigs. Pass the remaining Pomegranate Glaze. Makes 6 servings.

Pomegranate Glaze: In a small saucepan combine ¾ cup pomegranate juice or cranberry juice, ¼ cup balsamic vinegar, and 2 teaspoons cornstarch. Cook and stir over medium heat until thickened and bubbly. Cook and stir for 2 minutes more.

On the opener: Apricot Chicken Kabobs *(see recipe, page 143)*

Nonstick cooking spray

1 cup finely crushed multigrain tortilla chips

½ teaspoon dried oregano, crushed

¼ teaspoon ground cumin

¼ teaspoon black pepper

1 egg

4 skinless, boneless chicken breast halves (about 1¼ pounds total)

Shredded romaine (optional)

Purchased salsa (optional)

Avocado slices (optional)

1 Preheat oven to 375°F. Coat a 15×10×1-inch baking pan with nonstick cooking spray; set aside. In a shallow dish combine tortilla chips, oregano, cumin, and pepper. Place egg in another shallow dish; beat lightly. Dip chicken in beaten egg, then coat with tortilla chip mixture.

2 Arrange chicken in prepared baking pan. Bake about 25 minutes or until chicken is no longer pink (170°F). If desired, serve chicken on a bed of shredded romaine with salsa and avocado slices. Makes 4 servings.

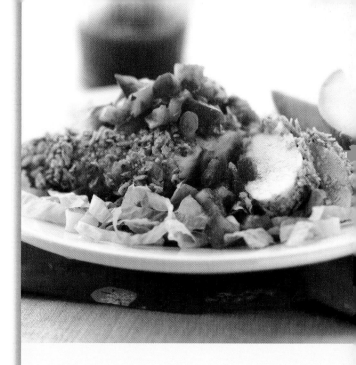

Tortilla-Crusted Chicken

PREP: 10 minutes   **BAKE:** 25 minutes
OVEN: 375°F

NUTRITION FACTS per serving:

CALORIES 230
TOTAL FAT 6 g (1 g sat. fat)
CHOLESTEROL 135 mg
PROTEIN 35 g
CARBOHYDRATE 7 g
FIBER 1 g
SODIUM 143 mg

EXCHANGES 0.5 Starch, 4.5 Very Lean Meat, 1 Fat

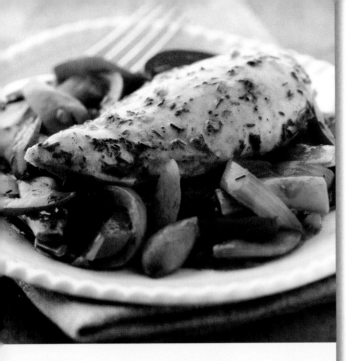

1 medium onion, cut into thin wedges

1 tablespoon quick-cooking tapioca, crushed

6 bone-in chicken breast halves (3½ to 4 pounds total), skinned

1 teaspoon dried rosemary, crushed

1 teaspoon dried thyme, crushed

½ teaspoon salt

¼ teaspoon black pepper

¼ cup balsamic vinegar

2 tablespoons chicken broth

1 9-ounce package frozen Italian green beans

1 medium red sweet pepper, seeded and cut into bite-size strips

Herbed Balsamic Chicken

PREP: 20 minutes

COOK: 4½ hours (low) or 2 hours (high); plus 30 minutes (high)

NUTRITION FACTS per serving:

CALORIES 234
TOTAL FAT 2 g (1 g sat. fat)
CHOLESTEROL 100 mg
PROTEIN 41 g
CARBOHYDRATE 10 g
FIBER 2 g
SODIUM 308 mg

EXCHANGES 5.5 Very Lean Meat, 1 Vegetable

1 Place onion in a 3½- or 4-quart slow cooker. Sprinkle with tapioca. Add chicken. Sprinkle with rosemary, thyme, salt, and black pepper. Pour balsamic vinegar and chicken broth over all.

2 Cover and cook on low-heat setting for 4½ hours or on high-heat setting for 2 hours.

3 If using low-heat setting, turn to high-heat setting. Add green beans and sweet pepper. Cover and cook for 30 minutes more.

4 Using a slotted spoon, transfer chicken and vegetables to a serving platter. Spoon some of the sauce over chicken and vegetables. Pass remaining sauce. Makes 6 servings.

- 1 pound skinless, boneless chicken breasts, cut into 1-inch pieces
- 1½ teaspoons Jamaican jerk seasoning
- 1 cup fresh sugar snap peas or pea pods, strings and tips removed
- 1 cup fresh or canned pineapple chunks
- 1 medium red sweet pepper, seeded and cut into 1-inch pieces
- ¼ cup apricot spreadable fruit

1 Sprinkle chicken with half of the jerk seasoning; toss gently to coat. Cut any large pea pods in half crosswise.

2 On metal skewers, alternately thread chicken, sugar snap peas, pineapple, and sweet pepper, leaving a ¼-inch space between pieces.

3 For sauce, in a small saucepan combine remaining jerk seasoning and spreadable fruit. Cook and stir just until spreadable fruit is melted; set aside.

4 For a charcoal grill, place kabobs on the rack of an uncovered grill directly over medium coals. Grill for 8 to 12 minutes or until chicken is no longer pink and vegetables are crisp-tender, turning once and brushing occasionally with sauce during the last 3 minutes of grilling. (For a gas grill, preheat grill. Reduce heat to medium. Place kabobs on grill rack over heat. Cover and grill as above.) Makes 4 servings.

Apricot Chicken Kabobs

PREP: 20 minutes

GRILL: 8 minutes

NUTRITION FACTS per serving:

CALORIES 199
TOTAL FAT 2 g (0 g sat. fat)
CHOLESTEROL 66 mg
PROTEIN 27 g
CARBOHYDRATE 20 g
FIBER 2 g
SODIUM 173 mg

EXCHANGES 1 Starch, 3 Very Lean Meat, 0.5 Vegetable

Tarragon Chicken Linguine

START TO FINISH: 25 minutes

NUTRITION FACTS per serving:
- -

CALORIES 285
TOTAL FAT 4 g (1 g sat. fat)
CHOLESTEROL 49 mg
PROTEIN 28 g
CARBOHYDRATE 36 g
FIBER 1 g
SODIUM 214 mg

EXCHANGES 2 Starch, 3 Very Lean Meat, 0.5 Vegetable

6	ounces dried whole wheat linguine or fettuccine
2	cups broccoli florets
½	cup reduced-sodium chicken broth
2	teaspoons cornstarch
¼	teaspoon lemon-pepper seasoning or black pepper
12	ounces skinless, boneless chicken breasts, cut into bite-size strips
2	teaspoons olive oil or cooking oil
1	tablespoon snipped fresh tarragon or dill or ½ teaspoon dried tarragon or dill, crushed

1 Cook pasta according to package directions, adding broccoli for the last 4 minutes of cooking. Drain. Return to hot pan; cover and keep warm.

2 In a small bowl combine chicken broth, cornstarch, and seasoning; set aside.

3 In a large nonstick skillet cook chicken in hot oil about 4 minutes or until no longer pink, stirring often.

4 Stir cornstarch mixture; add to skillet. Cook and stir until thickened. Stir in tarragon; cook for 2 minutes more. Serve over hot cooked pasta. Makes 4 servings.

COOK'S TIP

Defrost chicken in the refrigerator, in cold water, or in the microwave. It's safest to plan ahead and thaw meat in the refrigerator. Boneless chicken breasts usually defrost overnight in the refrigerator. Never defrost meat at room temperature.

4 teaspoons canola oil

1 medium red onion, halved lengthwise and sliced

¼ of a medium fresh pineapple, peeled, cored, and cut into bite-size pieces

¾ cup zucchini cut into thin bite-size strips

¾ cup trimmed fresh pea pods

12 ounces skinless, boneless chicken breasts, cut into thin bite-size strips

3 tablespoons bottled stir-fry sauce

Cooked brown rice (optional)

1 In a wok or very large skillet heat 2 teaspoons oil over medium-high heat. Add red onion; cook and stir for 2 minutes. Add pineapple pieces, zucchini, and pea pods. Cook and stir for 2 minutes more. Remove mixture from wok.

2 Add remaining 2 teaspoons oil to hot wok. Add chicken. Cook and stir for 2 to 3 minutes or until chicken is tender and no longer pink. Return onion mixture to wok. Add stir-fry sauce. Cook and stir about 1 minute or until heated through. If desired, serve with brown rice. Makes 4 servings.

Pineapple-Chicken Stir-Fry

START TO FINISH: 30 minutes

NUTRITION FACTS per serving:

- -

CALORIES 187
TOTAL FAT 6 g (1 g sat. fat)
CHOLESTEROL 49 mg
PROTEIN 21 g
CARBOHYDRATE 11 g
FIBER 1 g
SODIUM 450 mg

EXCHANGES 0.5 Fruit, 3 Very Lean Meat, 0.5 Vegetable, 1 Fat

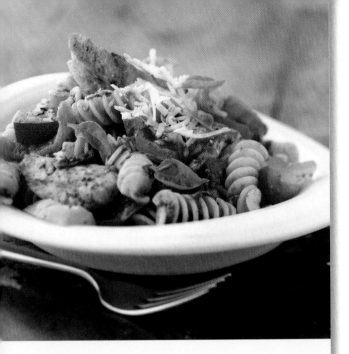

8 ounces dried whole wheat or multigrain rotini pasta (about 3¼ cups)

1 16-ounce package frozen yellow, green, and red peppers and onions stir-fry vegetables

Nonstick cooking spray

12 ounces skinless, boneless chicken breasts, cut into bite-size pieces

4 cloves garlic, minced

1 cup chopped plum tomato

⅓ cup purchased dried tomato pesto

¼ cup snipped fresh basil

¼ cup finely shredded Parmesan cheese (1 ounce)

Fresh basil leaves (optional)

Pasta and Sweet Peppers

START TO FINISH: 25 minutes

NUTRITION FACTS per serving:

- -

CALORIES 296
TOTAL FAT 7 g (2 g sat. fat)
CHOLESTEROL 36 mg
PROTEIN 22 g
CARBOHYDRATE 37 g
FIBER 4 g
SODIUM 199 mg

EXCHANGES 2 Starch, 2 Very Lean Meat, 1 Vegetable, 1 Fat

1 In a 4-quart Dutch oven cook pasta according to package directions, adding stir-fry vegetables for the last 2 minutes of cooking.* Drain well; return to hot Dutch oven. Cover and keep warm.

2 Meanwhile, coat an unheated large nonstick skillet with nonstick cooking spray. Preheat over medium-high heat. Add chicken and garlic to hot skillet. Cook and stir for 3 to 4 minutes or until chicken is no longer pink.

3 Add chicken mixture to cooked pasta mixture along with tomato, pesto, and snipped basil. Toss to coat. Sprinkle with Parmesan cheese. If desired, garnish with fresh basil. Makes 6 servings.

*Slowly add vegetables to pasta to prevent the water from cooling down too quickly. If water does stop boiling, return it to boiling, then begin timing for 2 minutes.

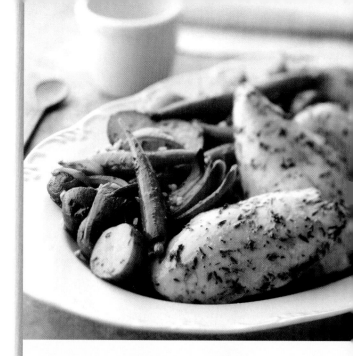

12 ounces tiny whole new potatoes, halved

1 cup baby carrots

1 medium red onion, cut into thin wedges

⅓ cup orange juice

6 cloves garlic, minced

1 tablespoon olive oil

1½ teaspoons dried thyme, crushed

¼ teaspoon salt

4 bone-in chicken breast halves (about 3 pounds total), skinned

1 Preheat oven to 375°F. Place potatoes, carrots, red onion, orange juice, garlic, oil, thyme, and salt in a large resealable plastic bag. Seal bag; turn several times to combine.

2 Using a slotted spoon, transfer vegetables to a shallow roasting pan (reserve bag and juices). Cover and bake for 10 minutes. Meanwhile, add chicken to bag with orange juice mixture. Seal bag; turn to coat chicken. Transfer chicken to roasting pan with vegetables. Bake, uncovered, for 55 to 65 minutes or until chicken is no longer pink (170°F) and vegetables are tender. Makes 4 servings.

Thyme and Garlic Chicken

PREP: 20 minutes   **BAKE:** 65 minutes
OVEN: 375°F

NUTRITION FACTS per serving:

CALORIES 378
TOTAL FAT 6 g (1 g sat. fat)
CHOLESTEROL 128 mg
PROTEIN 53 g
CARBOHYDRATE 24 g
FIBER 3 g
SODIUM 288 mg

EXCHANGES 1 Starch, 7 Very Lean Meat, 1 Vegetable, 0.5 Fat

NUTRITION NOTE

This hearty recipe features tiny new potatoes, which are packed with complex carbohydrates, vitamin C, fiber, potassium, and minerals.

1 16-ounce package loose-pack frozen broccoli, baby carrots, and water chestnuts
2 tablespoons quick-cooking tapioca
1 pound skinless, boneless chicken breasts or thighs, cut into 1-inch pieces
¾ cup reduced-sodium chicken broth
3 tablespoons low-sugar orange marmalade
2 tablespoons bottled teriyaki sauce
1 teaspoon dry mustard
½ teaspoon ground ginger
2 cups hot cooked brown rice

Teriyaki Chicken with Orange Sauce

PREP: 15 minutes
COOK: 4 to 5 hours (low) or
2 to 2½ hours (high)

NUTRITION FACTS per serving:

CALORIES 320
TOTAL FAT 2 g (1 g sat. fat)
CHOLESTEROL 66 mg
PROTEIN 32 g
CARBOHYDRATE 40 g
FIBER 5 g
SODIUM 532 mg

EXCHANGES 2 Starch, 3.5 Very Lean Meat, 1 Vegetable

1 Place frozen vegetables in a 3½- or 4-quart slow cooker. Sprinkle tapioca over vegetables. Stir to combine. Place chicken pieces on vegetable mixture.

2 For sauce, in a small bowl combine chicken broth, orange marmalade, teriyaki sauce, dry mustard, and ginger. Pour sauce over chicken pieces.

3 Cover and cook on low-heat setting for 4 to 5 hours or on high-heat setting for 2 to 2½ hours. Serve with hot cooked brown rice. Makes 4 servings.

COOK'S TIP

Meals prepared in the slow cooker during summer months will keep your kitchen cool and give you time to do other things while your meal cooks.

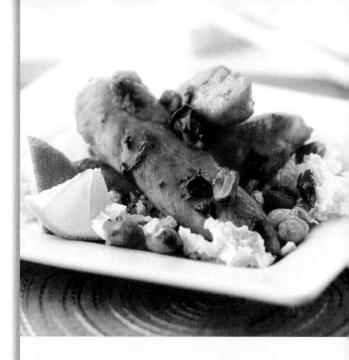

2   teaspoons peanut oil or canola oil
1   pound chicken breast tenderloins
¼   cup dry-roasted peanuts
1   tablespoon reduced-sodium
     soy sauce
1   tablespoon rice vinegar
2   teaspoons toasted sesame oil
½   cup fresh cilantro leaves
4   cups sliced napa cabbage
     Lime wedges

1 In a large heavy skillet heat oil over medium-high heat. Add chicken; cook and stir for 3 minutes. Add peanuts. Cook and stir about 3 minutes more or until chicken is no longer pink.

2 Add soy sauce, rice vinegar, and toasted sesame oil. Cook and stir for 2 minutes more. Remove from heat. Stir in cilantro leaves.

3 To serve, spoon chicken mixture over cabbage. Serve with lime wedges to squeeze over individual servings. Makes 4 servings.

COOK'S TIP

Napa cabbage is sometimes called Chinese cabbage. Commonly used in raw salads and slaws, it also can be used in any recipe that calls for cabbage.

Cilantro Chicken with Nuts

START TO FINISH: 25 minutes

NUTRITION FACTS per serving:

- -

CALORIES 239
TOTAL FAT 11 g (2 g sat. fat)
CHOLESTEROL 66 mg
PROTEIN 30 g
CARBOHYDRATE 6 g
FIBER 1 g
SODIUM 303 mg

EXCHANGES 4 Very Lean Meat, 1 Vegetable, 2 Fat

1 to 1¼ pounds chicken breast tenderloins

⅛ teaspoon salt

⅛ teaspoon black pepper

Nonstick cooking spray

1 14½-ounce can no-salt-added diced tomatoes, drained

¼ cup snipped fresh basil

1 9- to 10-ounce package fresh spinach

2 tablespoons shredded Parmesan cheese

Basil-Tomato Chicken Skillet

START TO FINISH: 25 minutes

NUTRITION FACTS per serving:

- -

CALORIES 171
TOTAL FAT 2 g (1 g sat. fat)
CHOLESTEROL 68 mg
PROTEIN 30 g
CARBOHYDRATE 7 g
FIBER 3 g
SODIUM 266 mg

EXCHANGES 4 Very Lean Meat, 1 Vegetable

NUTRITION NOTE

Vitamin K is found in large amounts in dark green leafy vegetables. Basil, although an herb, is no exception. It has a healthy dose of this vitamin that is important for blood clotting and bone mineralization.

1 Cut any large chicken breast tenderloins in half lengthwise. Sprinkle with salt and pepper. Coat an unheated 12-inch skillet with nonstick cooking spray. Preheat over medium-high heat. Add chicken; cook and stir about 5 minutes or until no longer pink.

2 Add tomatoes and basil to chicken in skillet; heat through. Remove from heat. Add spinach; toss until wilted. Divide among four serving plates. Sprinkle with cheese. Makes 4 servings.

- 1   9-ounce package frozen Italian-style green beans
- 1   cup fresh mushrooms, quartered
- 1   medium onion, cut into ¼-inch-thick slices
- 12   ounces skinless, boneless chicken thighs, cut into 1-inch pieces
- 1   14½-ounce can Italian-style stewed tomatoes, undrained
- 1   6-ounce can Italian-style tomato paste
- 1   teaspoon dried Italian seasoning, crushed
- 2   cloves garlic, minced
- 6   ounces spinach or whole wheat fettuccine, cooked according to package directions and drained
- 3   tablespoons finely shredded or grated Parmesan cheese

1 In a 3½- or 4-quart slow cooker combine green beans, mushrooms, and onion. Place chicken on vegetables.

2 In a small bowl combine undrained tomatoes, tomato paste, Italian seasoning, and garlic. Pour over chicken.

3 Cover and cook on low-heat setting for 5 to 6 hours or on high-heat setting for 2½ to 3 hours. Serve over hot cooked fettuccine. Sprinkle with Parmesan cheese. Makes 4 servings.

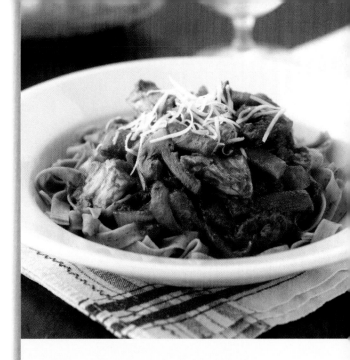

Italian Chicken and Pasta

PREP: 15 minutes

COOK: 5 to 6 hours (low) or 2½ to 3 hours (high)

NUTRITION FACTS per serving:

CALORIES 362
TOTAL FAT 7 g (2 g sat. fat)
CHOLESTEROL 111 mg
PROTEIN 28 g
CARBOHYDRATE 45 g
FIBER 6 g
SODIUM 801 mg

EXCHANGES 2.5 Starch, 2.5 Very Lean Meat, 1.5 Vegetable, 0.5 Fat

Oven-Fried Parmesan Chicken

PREP: 25 minutes   **BAKE:** 45 minutes
OVEN: 375°F

NUTRITION FACTS per serving:

CALORIES 219
TOTAL FAT 9 g (3 g sat. fat)
CHOLESTEROL 116 mg
PROTEIN 28 g
CARBOHYDRATE 5 g
FIBER 1 g
SODIUM 195 mg

EXCHANGES 4 Lean Meat

1	egg, lightly beaten
2	tablespoons fat-free milk
⅓	cup grated Parmesan cheese
⅓	cup fine dry bread crumbs
1	teaspoon dried oregano, crushed
½	teaspoon paprika
⅛	teaspoon black pepper
2½	pounds meaty chicken pieces (breast halves, thighs, and drumsticks), skinned
	Nonstick cooking spray
	Fresh oregano leaves (optional)

1 Preheat oven to 375°F. Grease a large shallow baking pan; set aside. In a small bowl combine egg and milk. In a shallow dish combine Parmesan cheese, bread crumbs, dried oregano, paprika, and pepper.

2 Dip chicken pieces into egg mixture; coat with crumb mixture. Arrange chicken pieces in prepared baking pan, making sure pieces do not touch. Coat tops of chicken pieces with nonstick cooking spray.

3 Bake for 45 to 55 minutes or until chicken is tender and no longer pink (170°F for breasts; 180°F for thighs and drumsticks). Do not turn chicken pieces during baking. If desired, sprinkle with fresh oregano. Makes 6 servings.

6	cloves garlic, minced
1	teaspoon smoked paprika or paprika
1	teaspoon black pepper
½	teaspoon salt
½	teaspoon onion powder
½	teaspoon dried thyme, crushed
¼	teaspoon dried sage, crushed
¼	teaspoon cayenne pepper
1	3½-pound whole roasting chicken
1	tablespoon olive oil
	Fresh thyme sprigs (optional)

1 Preheat oven to 450°F. In a small bowl combine garlic, paprika, black pepper, salt, onion powder, dried thyme, sage, and cayenne pepper.

2 Starting at the opening by the leg and thigh, carefully slide your fingertips between the breast and leg meat and the skin to loosen skin from meat. Rub half of the spice mixture between the breast and leg meat and skin. Rub remaining spice mixture on the outside of the chicken. Using 100%-cotton kitchen string, tie legs together. Twist wing tips under back.

3 Place chicken, breast side up, on a rack set in a shallow roasting pan. Brush oil on the outside of the chicken. Insert an oven-going meat thermometer into center of an inside thigh muscle. (The thermometer should not touch bone.)

4 Roast, uncovered, for 15 minutes. Reduce oven temperature to 350°F. Continue roasting about 1 hour more or until drumsticks move easily in their sockets and thermometer registers 180°F (to ensure thighs cook evenly, cut string after 40 minutes of roasting).

5 Remove chicken from oven. Cover chicken with foil and let stand for 10 minutes before carving. If desired, garnish with fresh thyme. While carving, carefully remove and discard chicken skin. Makes 6 servings.

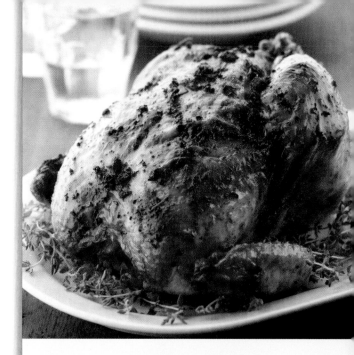

Spice-Rubbed Roasted Chicken

PREP: 20 minutes   **ROAST:** 1¼ hours
STAND: 10 minutes   **OVEN:** 450°F/350°F

NUTRITION FACTS per serving:

CALORIES 299
TOTAL FAT 13 g (3 g sat. fat)
CHOLESTEROL 127 mg
PROTEIN 42 g
CARBOHYDRATE 2 g
FIBER 0 g
SODIUM 318 mg

EXCHANGES 6 Lean Meat

Turkey and Wild Rice Pilaf

PREP: 25 minutes

COOK: 50 minutes

NUTRITION FACTS per serving:

CALORIES 277
TOTAL FAT 7 g (1 g sat. fat)
CHOLESTEROL 47 mg
PROTEIN 24 g
CARBOHYDRATE 33 g
FIBER 4 g
SODIUM 218 mg

EXCHANGES 1.5 Starch, 0.5 Fruit, 2.5 Very Lean Meat, 0.5 Vegetable, 0.5 Fat

NUTRITION NOTE

About half the fat of turkey and chicken breast meat is contained in the skin. To lower fat, skin the poultry before cooking.

1	tablespoon olive oil
1	cup sliced celery
1	medium onion, chopped
½	cup wild rice, rinsed and drained
½	cup regular brown rice
1	14-ounce can reduced-sodium chicken broth
¾	cup water
1	cup carrots cut into thin bite-size strips
2	medium red apples, cored and coarsely chopped
12	ounces cooked turkey breast or chicken breast,* cubed
¼	cup chopped walnuts, toasted

1 In a large skillet heat oil over medium heat. Add celery and onion; cook about 5 minutes or until tender, stirring occasionally. Add uncooked wild rice and brown rice; cook and stir for 2 minutes. Add chicken broth and water.

2 Bring to boiling; reduce heat. Cover and simmer for 40 minutes. Stir in carrots and chopped apples. Cover and cook for 3 to 5 minutes more or until rice and vegetables are tender.

3 Stir in cubed turkey; heat through. Top individual servings with walnuts. Makes 6 servings.

*For cooked turkey breast or chicken breast, place 1 pound turkey breast tenderloins, halved horizontally, or 1 pound skinless, boneless chicken breasts in a large skillet. Add 1½ cups water. Bring to boiling; reduce heat. Cover and simmer for 12 to 14 minutes or until turkey or chicken is no longer pink (170°F). Drain well.

1   pound turkey breast tenderloins
¾   cup lightly packed fresh cilantro sprigs or fresh basil leaves
3   tablespoons walnuts
2   tablespoons olive oil
2   tablespoons lime juice
1   clove garlic, minced
⅛   teaspoon salt
¼   teaspoon salt
¼   teaspoon black pepper
    Lime or lemon wedges (optional)

Turkey Tenderloins with Cilantro Pesto

PREP: 20 minutes

GRILL: 12 minutes

1 Split each turkey breast tenderloin in half horizontally; set aside. For pesto, in a blender or food processor combine cilantro or basil, walnuts, oil, lime juice, garlic, and ⅛ teaspoon salt. Cover and blend or process until nearly smooth. Cover and store in the refrigerator until ready to use or for up to 2 days.

2 Season turkey with ¼ teaspoon salt and pepper. For a charcoal grill, place turkey on the rack of an uncovered grill directly over medium coals. Grill for 7 minutes; turn. Brush lightly with half of the pesto. Grill for 5 to 8 minutes more or until no longer pink (170°F). (For a gas grill, preheat grill. Reduce heat to medium. Place turkey on grill rack. Cover and grill as above.)

3 Slice into serving-size pieces. Serve with remaining pesto. If desired, serve with lime wedges to squeeze over turkey. Makes 4 servings.

NUTRITION FACTS per serving:

CALORIES 228
TOTAL FAT 11 g (2 g sat. fat)
CHOLESTEROL 70 mg
PROTEIN 29 g
CARBOHYDRATE 2 g
FIBER 1 g
SODIUM 268 mg

EXCHANGES 4 Very Lean Meat, 2 Fat

COOK'S TIP

To keep cilantro fresh, wrap it in damp paper towels, place it in a plastic bag, and store it in the refrigerator for up to one week.

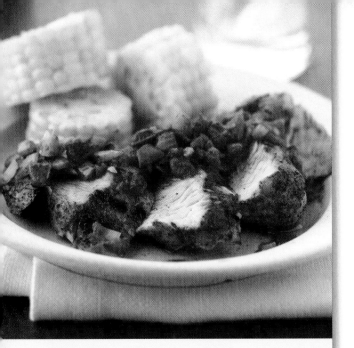

Grilled Turkey Mole

PREP: 30 minutes   **MARINATE:** 2 to 4 hours

GRILL: 8 minutes

NUTRITION FACTS per serving:

CALORIES 247
TOTAL FAT 5 g (1 g sat. fat)
CHOLESTEROL 105 mg
PROTEIN 44 g
CARBOHYDRATE 6 g
FIBER 2 g
SODIUM 223 mg

EXCHANGES 6 Very Lean Meat,
0.5 Vegetable, 0.5 Fat

COOK'S TIP

In a pinch, garlic powder can be substituted for fresh garlic cloves. Use ½ teaspoon of garlic powder to equal one clove.

---

2 turkey breast tenderloins
(about 1½ pounds total)
¼ cup lime juice
1 tablespoon chili powder
2 teaspoons bottled hot
pepper sauce
1 tablespoon canola oil
⅓ cup finely chopped onion
1 clove garlic, minced
1 large tomato, chopped
2 tablespoons canned diced green
chile peppers
1 teaspoon unsweetened
cocoa powder
1 teaspoon chili powder
⅛ teaspoon salt
Fat-free dairy sour cream
(optional)

1 Split each turkey breast tenderloin in half horizontally. Place turkey in a resealable plastic bag set in a shallow dish. For marinade, in a small bowl stir together lime juice, 1 tablespoon chili powder, and hot pepper sauce. Pour over turkey. Seal bag; turn to coat turkey. Marinate in the refrigerator for 2 to 4 hours, turning bag occasionally.

2 For mole sauce, in a small saucepan heat oil over medium heat. Add onion and garlic; cook and stir for 4 to 5 minutes or until onion is tender. Stir in tomato, chile peppers, cocoa powder, 1 teaspoon chili powder, and salt. Bring to boiling; reduce heat. Cover and simmer for 10 minutes. Remove from heat; set aside.

3 Drain turkey, discarding marinade. For a charcoal grill, place turkey on the lightly greased rack of an uncovered grill directly over medium coals. Grill for 8 to 10 minutes or until turkey is tender and no longer pink, turning once halfway through grilling. (For a gas grill, preheat grill. Reduce heat to medium. Place turkey on grill rack over heat. Cover and grill as above.) Serve turkey with mole sauce and, if desired, sour cream. Makes 4 servings.

On the opener: Almond-Herbed Salmon (*see recipe, page 159*)

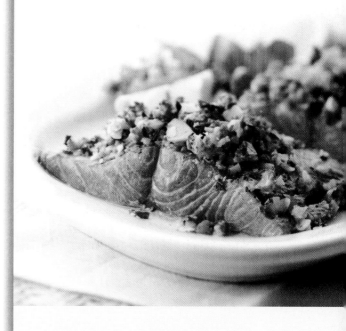

4 5-ounce fresh or frozen skinless salmon fillets, about 1 inch thick

Nonstick cooking spray

1 slice whole wheat bread, torn

¼ cup sliced almonds

2 tablespoons snipped fresh basil or 2 teaspoons dried basil, crushed

2 tablespoons chopped shallot

1 tablespoon snipped fresh parsley

½ teaspoon salt

1 clove garlic, minced

2 tablespoons lemon juice

¼ teaspoon black pepper

Fresh basil sprigs (optional)

Lemon wedges (optional)

1 Thaw fish, if frozen. Preheat oven to 400°F. Rinse fish; pat dry with paper towels. Set aside. Lightly coat a shallow baking pan with nonstick cooking spray; set aside. In a food processor or blender combine bread, almonds, snipped or dried basil, shallot, parsley, ¼ teaspoon salt, and garlic. Cover and process or blend until coarsely chopped.

2 Place fish in prepared baking pan; drizzle with lemon juice. Sprinkle with remaining ¼ teaspoon salt and pepper. Gently pat some of the bread crumb mixture on top of each fish fillet.

3 Bake, uncovered, for 10 to 12 minutes or until fish flakes easily when tested with a fork. If desired, garnish with fresh basil sprigs and serve with lemon wedges. Makes 4 servings.

Almond-Herbed Salmon

PREP: 20 minutes   **BAKE:** 10 minutes

OVEN: 400°F

NUTRITION FACTS per serving:

CALORIES 331
TOTAL FAT 19 g (3 g sat. fat)
CHOLESTEROL 83 mg
PROTEIN 31 g
CARBOHYDRATE 9 g
FIBER 2 g
SODIUM 416 mg

EXCHANGES 0.5 Starch, 4.5 Lean Meat, 1 Fat

NUTRITION NOTE

Salmon is loaded with omega-3 fatty acids, is low in saturated fat and cholesterol, and is a good source of protein.

Salmon with Tropical Rice

PREP: 15 minutes

BAKE: 4 minutes per ½-inch thickness

OVEN: 450°F

NUTRITION FACTS per serving:

CALORIES 366
TOTAL FAT 13 g (3 g sat. fat)
CHOLESTEROL 66 mg
PROTEIN 26 g
CARBOHYDRATE 35 g
FIBER 3 g
SODIUM 155 mg

EXCHANGES 2 Starch, 0.5 Fruit,
3 Lean Meat

1	1-pound fresh or frozen skinless salmon fillet
	Nonstick cooking spray
1	tablespoon coriander seeds, coarsely crushed*
1	tablespoon packed brown sugar
1	teaspoon lemon-pepper seasoning
2	cups hot cooked brown rice
1	medium mango, seeded, peeled, and chopped
1	tablespoon snipped fresh cilantro
1	teaspoon finely shredded lemon peel
	Lemon wedges (optional)
	Fresh cilantro sprigs (optional)

1 Thaw salmon, if frozen. Preheat oven to 450°F. Coat a shallow baking pan with nonstick cooking spray. Rinse fish; pat dry with paper towels. Measure thickness of fish. Place fish in the prepared baking pan.

2 In a small bowl stir together coriander seeds, brown sugar, and lemon-pepper seasoning. Sprinkle fish evenly with coriander seed mixture; use your fingers to press in slightly. Bake for 4 to 6 minutes per ½-inch thickness of fish or until fish flakes easily when tested with a fork.

3 Meanwhile, in a medium bowl stir together cooked rice, mango, snipped cilantro, and lemon peel. Serve fish on rice mixture. If desired, garnish with lemon wedges and cilantro sprigs. Makes 4 servings.

*You can substitute 1 tablespoon sesame seeds (toasted if desired) and ¼ teaspoon ground cumin for the crushed coriander seeds.

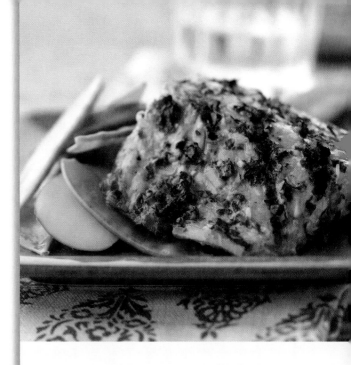

4	4- to 5-ounce fresh or frozen skinless salmon fillets, about ¾ inch thick
⅓	cup coarsely snipped fresh oregano
⅓	cup coarsely snipped fresh cilantro
¼	cup sliced green onion
1	tablespoon lemon juice
2	teaspoons olive oil
1	clove garlic
¼	teaspoon salt
⅛	teaspoon black pepper

1 Thaw fish, if frozen. Rinse fish; pat dry with paper towels. Set aside.

2 In a food processor combine oregano, cilantro, green onion, lemon juice, oil, garlic, salt, and pepper. Cover and process until finely chopped. (Or use a knife to finely chop the oregano, cilantro, green onion, and garlic. Transfer to a shallow bowl. Stir in lemon juice, oil, salt, and pepper.) Generously coat all sides of fish with the herb mixture.

3 For a charcoal grill, place fish on the rack of an uncovered grill directly over medium coals. Grill for 6 to 8 minutes or just until the salmon flakes easily when tested with a fork, turning once halfway through grilling. (For a gas grill, preheat grill. Reduce heat to medium. Place salmon on grill rack over heat. Cover and grill as above.) Makes 4 servings.

COOK'S TIP

Cook fresh fish such as salmon the same day of purchase if possible. If you have to wait, loosely wrap the fish in plastic wrap, store it in the coldest part of the refrigerator, and use it within two days.

Grilled Salmon with Herb Crust

PREP: 15 minutes

GRILL: 6 minutes

NUTRITION FACTS per serving:

CALORIES 236
TOTAL FAT 15 g (3 g sat. fat)
CHOLESTEROL 66 mg
PROTEIN 23 g
CARBOHYDRATE 2 g
FIBER 0 g
SODIUM 192 mg

EXCHANGES 3.5 Lean Meat, 0.5 Fat

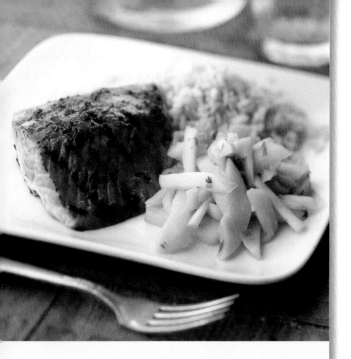

Salmon with Mango Salsa

PREP: 25 minutes **MARINATE:** 2 to 4 hours
GRILL: 14 minutes

NUTRITION FACTS per serving:

CALORIES 402
TOTAL FAT 19 g (4 g sat. fat)
CHOLESTEROL 100 mg
PROTEIN 35 g
CARBOHYDRATE 24 g
FIBER 2 g
SODIUM 541 mg

EXCHANGES 1.5 Starch, 4 Lean Meat,
0.5 Vegetable, 1 Fat

4	6-ounce fresh or frozen skinless salmon fillets, about 1 inch thick
2	tablespoons honey
1½	teaspoons finely shredded lime peel
¾	teaspoon salt
¼	teaspoon cayenne pepper
1	large mango, seeded, peeled, and cut into thin bite-size strips
½	of a medium cucumber, seeded and cut into thin bite-size strips
2	green onions, sliced
3	tablespoons lime juice
1	tablespoon snipped fresh cilantro or 2 teaspoons snipped fresh mint
1	small fresh jalapeño chile pepper, seeded and chopped*
1	clove garlic, minced

1 Thaw fish, if frozen. Rinse fish; pat dry. Place fish in a shallow dish. Drizzle with honey, spreading evenly. In a small bowl combine lime peel, ½ teaspoon salt, and cayenne pepper. Sprinkle evenly over fish. Cover and marinate in the refrigerator for 2 to 4 hours.

2 Meanwhile, for salsa, in a medium bowl combine mango, cucumber, green onion, lime juice, cilantro, chile pepper, garlic, and remaining ¼ teaspoon salt. Cover and chill until ready to serve.

3 For a charcoal grill, arrange medium-hot coals around a drip pan. Test for medium heat above the pan. Place fish on greased grill rack over drip pan. Cover and grill for 14 to 18 minutes or until fish begins to flake when tested with a fork, turning once halfway through grilling. (For a gas grill, preheat grill. Reduce heat to medium. Adjust for indirect cooking. Place fish on grill rack over burner that is off. Grill as above.)

4 Serve grilled salmon with salsa. Makes 4 servings.

*Because chile peppers contain volatile oils that can burn your skin and eyes, avoid direct contact with them as much as possible. When working with chile peppers, wear plastic or rubber gloves. If your bare hands do touch the peppers, wash your hands and nails well with soap and warm water.

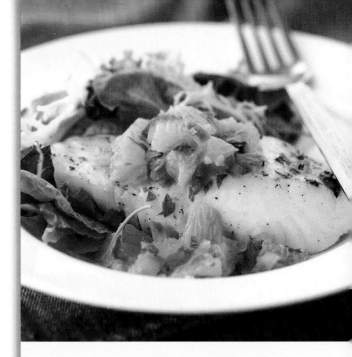

- 6 4-ounce fresh or frozen skinless halibut, cod, sole, or other whitefish fillets
- ¼ teaspoon salt
- ¼ teaspoon black pepper
- ⅓ cup orange juice
- ¼ cup finely chopped red onion or shallot
- 2 teaspoons white balsamic vinegar or regular balsamic vinegar
- 1 teaspoon snipped fresh tarragon or rosemary or ½ teaspoon dried tarragon or rosemary, crushed
- 1 teaspoon olive oil
- 1 clove garlic, minced
   Dash bottled hot pepper sauce
   Nonstick cooking spray
- 4 medium tangerines, peeled
- 2 tablespoons snipped fresh parsley
- 6 cups torn mixed salad greens (optional)

1 Thaw fish fillets, if frozen. Rinse fish; pat dry with paper towels. Sprinkle with salt and pepper. Measure thickness of fish; set aside.

2 Preheat broiler. In a small saucepan combine orange juice, red onion, balsamic vinegar, tarragon, oil, garlic, and hot pepper sauce. Bring to boiling; reduce heat. Simmer, uncovered, for 5 to 6 minutes or until reduced to about ⅓ cup. Remove from heat. Remove 2 tablespoons of the orange juice mixture; set both mixtures aside.

3 Coat the unheated rack of a broiler pan with nonstick cooking spray. Place fish fillets on rack. Brush both sides of each fish fillet with reserved 2 tablespoons orange juice mixture. Turn under any thin portions of fish to make uniform thickness. Broil 4 inches from heat for 4 to 6 minutes per ½-inch thickness of fish or until fish flakes easily when tested with a fork.

4 Meanwhile, for tangerine relish, separate tangerines into segments. Remove seeds and cut up segments. In a small bowl combine chopped tangerines, remaining orange juice mixture, and parsley.

5 To serve, divide greens, if using, among serving plates; top greens with fish. Spoon tangerine relish over fish. Makes 6 servings.

Broiled Fillets with Tangerine Relish

PREP: 25 minutes

BROIL: 4 minutes per ½-inch thickness

NUTRITION FACTS per serving:

CALORIES 175
TOTAL FAT 4 g (1 g sat. fat)
CHOLESTEROL 36 mg
PROTEIN 24 g
CARBOHYDRATE 11 g
FIBER 1 g
SODIUM 161 mg

EXCHANGES 0.5 Fruit, 3.5 Very Lean Meat, 0.5 Fat

NUTRITION NOTE

Red onions impart good flavor and bright color while supplying vitamin C, chromium, and flavonoids—which act as antioxidants.

1 pound fresh or frozen skinless fish fillets (sea bass, halibut, salmon, swordfish, or tuna), about 1 inch thick

3 tablespoons maple syrup

1 tablespoon balsamic vinegar

1 to 2 teaspoons Dijon-style mustard

1 recipe Spinach Saute

1 Thaw fish, if frozen. Preheat broiler. Rinse fish; pat dry with paper towels. If necessary, cut fish into four serving-size pieces. For glaze, in a small bowl whisk together syrup, balsamic vinegar, and mustard.

2 Place fish on the greased unheated rack of a broiler pan. Broil 4 inches from the heat for 8 to 12 minutes or until fish flakes easily when tested with a fork. Carefully turn once halfway through broiling and brush with glaze during the last 2 to 3 minutes of broiling.

3 Meanwhile, prepare Spinach Saute. Serve with fish. Makes 4 servings.

Spinach Saute: In a Dutch oven heat 1 tablespoon olive oil over medium-high heat. Add 1 pound fresh spinach; cook and stir for 1 to 2 minutes or just until spinach is wilted. Remove from heat. Stir in 3 tablespoons chopped toasted walnuts; 1 tablespoon Worcestershire sauce; ¼ teaspoon salt; and ⅛ teaspoon black pepper.

Maple-Balsamic Glazed Fish with Spinach Saute

PREP: 15 minutes

BROIL: 8 minutes

NUTRITION FACTS per serving:

CALORIES 250
TOTAL FAT 10 g (1 g sat. fat)
CHOLESTEROL 46 mg
PROTEIN 25 g
CARBOHYDRATE 17 g
FIBER 3 g
SODIUM 386 mg

EXCHANGES 0.5 Other Carbohydrates, 3 Very Lean Meat, 2 Vegetable, 1.5 Fat

- 1 pound fresh or frozen grouper fillets, ½ to ¾ inch thick
- ½ teaspoon salt
- ¼ teaspoon black pepper
- 2 tablespoons lemon juice
- 2 tablespoons olive oil
- 1 large zucchini, halved lengthwise and thinly sliced
- 1 large yellow sweet pepper, seeded and cut into bite-size strips
- 2 cloves garlic, minced
- 4 teaspoons snipped fresh marjoram or basil or 1 teaspoon dried marjoram or basil, crushed

1 Thaw fish, if frozen. Preheat oven to 450°F. Cut fish into four serving-size pieces. Rinse fish; pat dry with paper towels. Place fish in a 2-quart rectangular baking dish; sprinkle with ¼ teaspoon salt and ⅛ teaspoon black pepper. Set aside.

2 In a small bowl stir together lemon juice and 1 tablespoon oil. Drizzle over fish. Bake, uncovered, for 4 to 6 minutes per ½-inch thickness of fish or until fish flakes easily when tested with a fork.

3 Meanwhile, in a large skillet cook zucchini, sweet pepper, and garlic in remaining 1 tablespoon oil until crisp-tender. Stir in half of the marjoram, remaining ¼ teaspoon salt, and remaining ⅛ teaspoon black pepper. Sprinkle fish with remaining marjoram. Serve fish with vegetables. Makes 4 servings.

Grouper with Summer Vegetables

PREP: 20 minutes

BAKE: 4 minutes per ½-inch thickness

OVEN: 450°F

NUTRITION FACTS per serving:

CALORIES 195
TOTAL FAT 8 g (1 g sat. fat)
CHOLESTEROL 42 mg
PROTEIN 23 g
CARBOHYDRATE 7 g
FIBER 1 g
SODIUM 359 mg

EXCHANGES 3 Very Lean Meat, 1 Vegetable, 1.5 Fat

NUTRITION NOTE

Grouper is a lean fish that is low in calories and fat and delivers plenty of protein. Prepare it using cooking methods from baking and broiling to poaching or grilling.

1 pound fresh or frozen skinless fish fillets (cod, flounder, catfish, or trout)

¼ teaspoon salt

⅛ teaspoon black pepper

3 tablespoons lemon juice

4 medium plum tomatoes
Olive oil

1 19-ounce can cannellini beans (white kidney beans), rinsed and drained

1 tablespoon olive oil

1 clove garlic, minced

1 teaspoon snipped fresh rosemary or ¼ teaspoon dried rosemary, crushed

⅛ teaspoon salt
Lemon wedges
Fresh rosemary sprigs (optional)

Fish with Tomato and Cannellini Relish

START TO FINISH: 30 minutes

NUTRITION FACTS per serving:

- -

CALORIES 255
TOTAL FAT 8 g (1 g sat. fat)
CHOLESTEROL 48 mg
PROTEIN 32 g
CARBOHYDRATE 24 g
FIBER 8 g
SODIUM 492 mg

EXCHANGES 1.5 Starch, 3.5 Very Lean Meat, 1 Vegetable, 0.5 Fat

1 Thaw fish, if frozen. Rinse fish; pat dry with paper towels. Measure thickness of fish. Sprinkle fish with ¼ teaspoon salt and pepper; drizzle with 1 tablespoon lemon juice. Set aside.

2 Heat a nonstick or well-seasoned grill pan or skillet over medium heat until hot. Meanwhile, cut tomatoes in half lengthwise. Brush tomatoes lightly with oil. Add tomato halves, cut sides down, to grill pan or skillet. Cook for 6 to 8 minutes or until tomatoes are very tender, turning once. Remove tomatoes from pan; set aside to cool slightly.

3 Place fish fillets on grill pan. Cook for 4 to 6 minutes per ½-inch thickness of fish or until fish flakes easily when tested with a fork, turning once halfway through cooking.

4 Coarsely chop grilled tomatoes. In a medium serving bowl gently toss together tomatoes, remaining 2 tablespoons lemon juice, beans, 1 tablespoon oil, garlic, snipped or dried rosemary, and ⅛ teaspoon salt. Divide bean mixture among four dinner plates. Place fish on bean mixture. Serve with lemon wedges. If desired, garnish with fresh rosemary sprigs. Makes 4 servings.

- 1¼ pounds fresh or frozen cod or haddock fillets, ¾ to 1 inch thick
- ¼ teaspoon salt
- ⅛ teaspoon black pepper
- ¼ cup snipped fresh cilantro
- 1 tablespoon olive oil or canola oil
- 1 teaspoon shredded lime peel
- 1 tablespoon lime juice

1 Thaw fish, if frozen. Rinse fish; pat dry with paper towels. Cut fish into four serving-size pieces if necessary. Sprinkle with salt and pepper.

2 Place fish in a well-greased grill basket. Tuck under any thin edges. For a charcoal grill, place fish in grill basket on the rack of an uncovered grill directly over medium coals. Grill for 4 to 6 minutes per ½-inch thickness of fish or until fish flakes easily when tested with a fork, turning basket once. (For a gas grill, preheat grill. Reduce heat to medium. Place fish in grill basket on grill rack over heat. Cover and grill as above.)

3 Meanwhile, in a small bowl stir together cilantro, oil, lime peel, and lime juice. Spoon cilantro mixture over fish. Makes 4 servings.

COOK'S TIP

Grilled fish takes on tremendous flavor, but some fish, such as cod and haddock, are too delicate to cook directly on the grill. For these fish varieties, use grill baskets to turn without tearing or flaking it and to keep the fillets safely out of the fire.

Cilantro-Lime Grilled Fish

PREP: 10 minutes

GRILL: 4 minutes per ½-inch thickness

NUTRITION FACTS per serving:

CALORIES 148
TOTAL FAT 4 g (1 g sat. fat)
CHOLESTEROL 60 mg
PROTEIN 25 g
CARBOHYDRATE 1 g
FIBER 0 g
SODIUM 225 mg

EXCHANGES 3.5 Very Lean Meat, 0.5 Fat

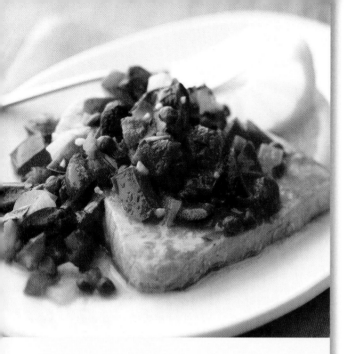

Italian Tuna Steak

START TO FINISH: 45 minutes

NUTRITION FACTS per serving:

CALORIES 237
TOTAL FAT 6 g (1 g sat. fat)
CHOLESTEROL 51 mg
PROTEIN 29 g
CARBOHYDRATE 13 g
FIBER 3 g
SODIUM 402 mg

EXCHANGES 3.5 Very Lean Meat,
2 Vegetable, 1 Fat

4	fresh or frozen tuna steaks, cut 1 inch thick (about 1 pound total)
1	tablespoon olive oil
1	small onion, chopped
2	cloves garlic, minced
2	pounds plum tomatoes, seeded and chopped, or one 28-ounce can diced tomatoes, drained
½	cup dry white wine
¼	to ½ teaspoon crushed red pepper
¼	cup pitted ripe olives, coarsely chopped
2	tablespoons capers, rinsed and drained
2	tablespoons snipped fresh basil or 2 teaspoons dried basil, crushed
1	tablespoon snipped fresh mint or 1 teaspoon dried mint, crushed
¼	teaspoon salt
⅛	teaspoon black pepper
	Lemon wedges

1 Thaw tuna, if frozen. Rinse tuna; pat dry with paper towels. Set aside.

2 In a very large skillet heat oil over medium heat. Add onion and garlic; cook until onion is tender. Stir in chopped tomatoes, wine, and crushed red pepper. Bring to boiling; reduce heat. Simmer, uncovered, for 7 minutes. Stir in olives, capers, and basil and mint; cook for 3 minutes more.

3 Sprinkle tuna with salt and black pepper. Add tuna to skillet on top of tomato mixture. Cover and cook over medium heat for 5 minutes. Uncover and cook for 10 to 15 minutes more or until tuna flakes easily when tested with a fork and is slightly pink in the center.

4 Transfer tuna to four serving plates. Spoon tomato mixture over tuna. Serve with lemon wedges. Makes 4 servings.

2	5- to 6-ounce fresh or frozen tuna or halibut steaks, cut 1 inch thick
¼	cup lime juice
2	tablespoons snipped fresh cilantro or parsley
1	tablespoon olive oil
2	cloves garlic, minced
¼	teaspoon coarsely ground black pepper
⅛	teaspoon cayenne pepper
8	6-inch corn tortillas
	Nonstick cooking spray
2	medium red and/or yellow sweet peppers, quartered and stems and membranes removed
1	cup purchased tomato salsa or tomatillo salsa

1 Thaw fish, if frozen. Rinse fish; pat dry with paper towels. Place fish in a large resealable plastic bag set in a shallow dish.

2 For marinade, in a small bowl stir together lime juice, cilantro, oil, garlic, black pepper, and cayenne pepper. Pour marinade over fish in bag. Seal bag; turn to coat fish. Marinate in the refrigerator for 30 minutes, turning bag occasionally.

3 Wrap tortillas tightly in foil. Drain fish, reserving marinade. Lightly coat the unheated rack of a broiler pan with nonstick cooking spray. Place fish on prepared broiler pan. Place sweet pepper quarters beside fish. Place wrapped tortillas alongside the broiler pan. Broil 4 to 5 inches from heat for 8 to 12 minutes or just until fish flakes easily when tested with a fork. Brush once with reserved marinade after 3 minutes of broiling and turn once halfway through broiling. Discard any remaining marinade. Broil sweet peppers about 8 minutes or until tender, turning occasionally. Broil tortillas about 8 minutes or until heated through, turning foil package once.

4 Using a fork, break fish into large chunks. Cut sweet peppers into ½-inch-wide strips. Immediately fill warm tortillas with fish and sweet pepper strips. Serve with salsa. Makes 4 servings.

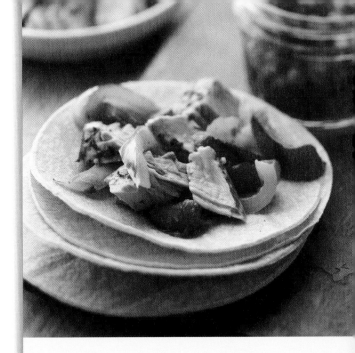

Broiled Tuna Fajitas

PREP: 20 minutes   **MARINATE:** 30 minutes
BROIL: 8 minutes

NUTRITION FACTS per serving:

CALORIES 285
TOTAL FAT 9 g (2 g sat. fat)
CHOLESTEROL 27 mg
PROTEIN 21 g
CARBOHYDRATE 33 g
FIBER 6 g
SODIUM 440 mg

EXCHANGES 2 Starch, 2 Very Lean Meat, 1 Vegetable, 1 Fat

12 fresh or frozen sea scallops
    (about 1¼ pounds total)

⅓ cup pitted kalamata olives,
    coarsely chopped

1 green onion, sliced

½ teaspoon finely shredded
    orange peel

2 teaspoons orange juice

¼ teaspoon anise seeds, crushed

⅛ teaspoon cayenne pepper

   Nonstick cooking spray

   Finely shredded orange peel
   (optional)

1 Thaw scallops, if frozen. Rinse scallops; pat dry with paper towels. Set aside.

2 For tapenade, in a small bowl combine olives, green onion, ½ teaspoon orange peel, orange juice, anise seeds, and cayenne pepper.

3 Coat an unheated large nonstick skillet with nonstick cooking spray. Preheat over medium-high heat. Add scallops to skillet; cook for 3 to 6 minutes or until scallops are opaque, turning once.

4 Serve scallops with tapenade. If desired, sprinkle with additional orange peel. Makes 4 servings.

Scallops with Anise-Orange Tapenade

START TO FINISH: 20 minutes

NUTRITION FACTS per serving:

- -

CALORIES 145
TOTAL FAT 3 g (0 g sat. fat)
CHOLESTEROL 47 mg
PROTEIN 24 g
CARBOHYDRATE 5 g
FIBER 1 g
SODIUM 353 mg

EXCHANGES 3.5 Very Lean Meat, 0.5 Fat

12　fresh or frozen sea scallops (about 1¼ pound total)

8　fresh or frozen jumbo shrimp (about 8 ounces total)

4　teaspoons olive oil

2　cups thin bite-size strips zucchini or sweet peppers

1½　cups thin bite-size strips carrot

1　cup sliced leek

¼　cup Dijon-style mustard

2　tablespoons dry white wine or water

2　teaspoons snipped fresh thyme or ½ teaspoon dried thyme, crushed

⅛　teaspoon black pepper

　Lemon wedges

Sauteed Shrimp and Scallops

START TO FINISH: 30 minutes

NUTRITION FACTS per serving:

CALORIES 265
TOTAL FAT 7 g (1 g sat. fat)
CHOLESTEROL 124 mg
PROTEIN 32 g
CARBOHYDRATE 14 g
FIBER 3 g
SODIUM 669 mg

EXCHANGES 0.5 Starch, 4 Very Lean Meat, 1 Vegetable, 0.5 Fat

1 Thaw scallops and shrimp, if frozen. Peel and devein shrimp. Rinse scallops and shrimp; pat dry with paper towels. In a very large nonstick skillet heat 2 teaspoons oil over medium-high heat. Add scallops and shrimp; cook for 2 to 4 minutes or until shrimp and scallops are opaque. Remove from skillet and set aside.

2 Add remaining 2 teaspoons oil to skillet; add zucchini, carrot, and leek to skillet. Cook and stir for 3 to 5 minutes or until vegetables are crisp-tender. Reduce heat to medium-low. Add mustard, wine, thyme, and black pepper. Stir to coat vegetables.

3 Spoon vegetable mixture onto a serving platter. Top with shrimp and scallops. Serve with lemon wedges. Makes 4 servings.

COOK'S TIP

To store fresh uncooked shrimp, rinse and drain them thoroughly, then tightly cover and refrigerate for no more than two days.

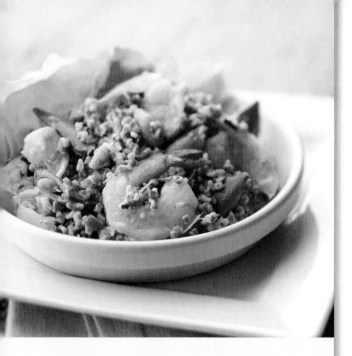

8 ounces fresh or frozen peeled and deveined cooked shrimp with tails, halved lengthwise

1⅓ cups water

⅔ cup bulgur

1 cup fresh pea pods, halved crosswise

½ cup chopped radishes or daikon

½ cup snipped fresh cilantro

¼ cup bias-sliced green onion

½ cup bottled fat-free ranch salad dressing

½ teaspoon finely shredded lime peel

2 tablespoons lime juice

¼ teaspoon crushed red pepper

Lettuce leaves (optional)

Spicy Shrimp Tabbouleh

PREP: 25 minutes

COOK: 15 minutes

NUTRITION FACTS per serving:

CALORIES 201

TOTAL FAT 1 g (0 g sat. fat)

CHOLESTEROL 111 mg

PROTEIN 16 g

CARBOHYDRATE 32 g

FIBER 6 g

SODIUM 495 mg

EXCHANGES 2 Starch, 1.5 Very Lean Meat, 0.5 Vegetable

1 Thaw shrimp, if frozen; set aside. In a medium saucepan combine water and bulgur. Bring to boiling; reduce heat. Cover and simmer about 15 minutes or until most of the water is absorbed and bulgur is tender. Stir in pea pods. Transfer to a large bowl. Stir in radishes or daikon, cilantro, and green onion.

2 In a small bowl combine salad dressing, lime peel, lime juice, and crushed red pepper; stir into bulgur mixture. Stir in shrimp. Serve immediately or cover and chill for up to 8 hours.

3 To serve, if desired, line serving bowl with lettuce leaves; spoon in tabbouleh. Makes 4 servings.

COOK'S TIP

Reduce the pungency of radishes by salting and washing them to remove some of the peppery flavor. To increase crispness of radishes, soak them in ice water for several hours before serving.

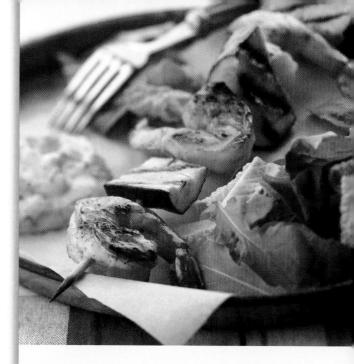

1	8-ounce carton fat-free or light dairy sour cream
½	cup snipped fresh basil
3	tablespoons snipped fresh chives
½	teaspoon salt
⅛	teaspoon black pepper
1¼	pounds fresh or frozen large shrimp
2	medium zucchini, halved lengthwise and cut into 1-inch-thick slices (about 1 pound total)
2	tablespoons olive oil
½	teaspoon finely shredded orange peel or lime peel
1	tablespoon orange juice or lime juice
¼	teaspoon cayenne pepper
5	cups torn fresh spinach, arugula, and/or romaine

1 For sauce, in a food processor or blender combine sour cream, basil, chives, ¼ teaspoon salt, and black pepper. Cover and process or blend until nearly smooth. Cover and chill until ready to serve.

2 Thaw shrimp, if frozen. Peel and devein shrimp, leaving tails intact if desired. Rinse shrimp; pat dry with paper towels. On long skewers,* alternately thread shrimp and zucchini, leaving a ¼-inch space between pieces. In a small bowl combine oil, orange or lime peel, orange or lime juice, cayenne pepper, and remaining ¼ teaspoon salt; brush evenly on shrimp and zucchini. Discard any remaining oil-juice mixture.

3 For a charcoal grill, place kabobs on the greased rack of an uncovered grill directly over medium coals. Grill about 10 minutes or until shrimp are opaque, turning once halfway through grilling. (For a gas grill, preheat grill. Reduce heat to medium. Place kabobs on greased grill rack over heat. Cover and grill as above.)

4 Serve kabobs with greens and sauce. Makes 6 servings.

*If using wooden skewers, soak in enough water to cover for 30 minutes; drain before using.

Shrimp-Zucchini Kabobs with Basil Cream Sauce

PREP: 40 minutes

GRILL: 10 minutes

NUTRITION FACTS per serving:

CALORIES 171
TOTAL FAT 6 g (1 g sat. fat)
CHOLESTEROL 108 mg
PROTEIN 19 g
CARBOHYDRATE 10 g
FIBER 2 g
SODIUM 447 mg

EXCHANGES 2 Very Lean Meat, 2 Vegetable, 1 Fat

Cajun Shrimp with Mango-Edamame Salsa

START TO FINISH: 30 minutes

NUTRITION FACTS per serving:

- -

CALORIES 317
TOTAL FAT 12 g (2 g sat. fat)
CHOLESTEROL 129 mg
PROTEIN 27 g
CARBOHYDRATE 29 g
FIBER 6 g
SODIUM 287 mg

EXCHANGES 1 Starch, 0.5 Fruit, 3.5 Very Lean Meat, 0.5 Vegetable, 1.5 Fat

1   pound fresh or frozen large shrimp
2   teaspoons purchased salt-free Cajun seasoning or Homemade Cajun Seasoning
1   tablespoon canola oil
1   recipe Mango-Edamame Salsa
    Belgian endive leaves (optional)

1 Thaw shrimp, if frozen. Peel and devein shrimp, leaving tails intact if desired. Rinse shrimp; pat dry with paper towels. Set aside.

2 In a large bowl toss shrimp with Cajun seasoning. In a heavy large skillet heat oil over medium-high heat. Add shrimp; cook and stir about 5 minutes or until shrimp are opaque.

3 Serve shrimp with Mango-Edamame Salsa and, if desired, Belgian endive leaves. Makes 4 servings.

Homemade Cajun Seasoning: In a small bowl stir together ½ teaspoon onion powder, ½ teaspoon paprika, ¼ teaspoon white pepper, ¼ teaspoon garlic powder, ¼ teaspoon cayenne pepper, and ¼ teaspoon black pepper.

Mango-Edamame Salsa: In a medium bowl combine 2 seeded, peeled, and chopped mangoes; 1 cup fresh or frozen shelled sweet soybeans (edamame), cooked and cooled; 1 red sweet pepper, seeded and chopped; ½ cup finely chopped green onion; ¼ cup snipped fresh cilantro; 2 tablespoons lime juice; 2 teaspoons canola oil; and ¼ teaspoon salt. Toss gently to mix. Cover and chill until serving time or for up to 2 hours. Makes 3 cups.

On the opener: Artichoke-Basil Lasagna (*see recipe, page 179*)

9   dried whole grain lasagna noodles
    Nonstick cooking spray
1   medium onion, chopped
4   cloves garlic, minced
1   cup vegetable broth
1   tablespoon snipped fresh
    rosemary or 1 teaspoon dried
    rosemary, crushed
1   14-ounce package frozen
    broccoli florets
2   10-ounce packages frozen
    chopped spinach, thawed
    and well drained
1   26- to 28-ounce jar meatless
    tomato pasta sauce
2   cups shredded part-skim
    mozzarella cheese (8 ounces)
    Fresh rosemary sprigs (optional)

1 Preheat oven to 375°F. Cook lasagna noodles according to package directions. Drain noodles; rinse with cold water and drain well. Set aside.

2 Meanwhile, lightly coat an unheated large skillet with nonstick cooking spray. Add onion and garlic; cook over medium heat for 3 minutes, stirring occasionally. Stir in vegetable broth and snipped or dried rosemary; bring to boiling. Stir in broccoli. Return to boiling; reduce heat. Cover and simmer for 1 minute. Uncover and stir in spinach; remove from heat.

3 Lightly coat a 3-quart rectangular baking dish with nonstick cooking spray. Spread ½ cup pasta sauce evenly in bottom of dish. Arrange 3 lasagna noodles on the sauce. Layer with half of the spinach mixture; sprinkle with ½ cup mozzarella cheese. Spoon ¾ cup pasta sauce on the cheese. Top with 3 more noodles, the remaining spinach mixture, ½ cup mozzarella cheese, and ¾ cup pasta sauce. Top with remaining 3 noodles. Spoon remaining pasta sauce on the noodles. Sprinkle with remaining 1 cup mozzarella cheese.

4 Cover and bake for 40 minutes. Uncover and bake about 15 minutes more or until hot in the center. Let stand for 10 minutes before serving. If desired, garnish with rosemary sprigs. Makes 8 servings.

Broccoli-Spinach Lasagna

PREP: 35 minutes   **BAKE:** 55 minutes
STAND: 10 minutes   **OVEN:** 375°F

NUTRITION FACTS per serving:

CALORIES 249
TOTAL FAT 6 g (3 g sat. fat)
CHOLESTEROL 18 mg
PROTEIN 16 g
CARBOHYDRATE 33 g
FIBER 9 g
SODIUM 696 mg

EXCHANGES 1.5 Starch, 1 Lean Meat,
2 Vegetable

Make-Ahead Directions: Prepare lasagna as at left through step 3. Cover with plastic wrap, then foil and refrigerate for up to 24 hours.
To serve, preheat oven to 375°F. Remove plastic wrap. Bake, covered with foil, for 50 minutes. Uncover and bake about 15 minutes more or until hot in the center. Let stand for 10 minutes before serving.

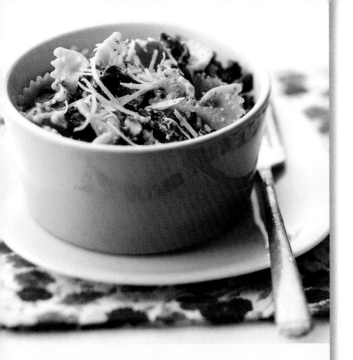

4 ounces dried whole grain bow tie
or mostaccioli pasta

6 ounces fresh Swiss chard
or spinach

1½ teaspoons olive oil

2 cloves garlic, minced

⅓ cup light ricotta cheese

2 tablespoons fat-free milk

2 tablespoons snipped fresh basil or
1 teaspoon dried basil, crushed

⅛ teaspoon salt

⅛ teaspoon black pepper

Dash ground nutmeg

1 medium tomato, seeded
and chopped

2 tablespoons shredded
Parmesan cheese

Pasta with Swiss Chard

START TO FINISH: 35 minutes

NUTRITION FACTS per serving:

CALORIES 307
TOTAL FAT 8 g (2 g sat. fat)
CHOLESTEROL 14 mg
PROTEIN 14 g
CARBOHYDRATE 51 g
FIBER 8 g
SODIUM 435 mg

EXCHANGES 3 Starch, 0.5 Lean Meat,
1 Vegetable, 1 Fat

1 Cook pasta according to package directions, except omit any oil or salt. Drain well. Return pasta to hot saucepan. Cover and keep warm.

2 Meanwhile, cut out and discard center ribs from Swiss chard or remove stems from spinach. Coarsely chop greens; set aside. In a large nonstick skillet heat oil over medium heat. Add garlic; cook for 15 seconds. Add Swiss chard or spinach. Cook over medium-low heat about 3 minutes or until greens are wilted and tender, stirring frequently. Stir in ricotta cheese, milk, basil, salt, pepper, and nutmeg. Cook and stir for 3 to 5 minutes more or until heated through.

3 Add ricotta mixture and tomato to cooked pasta; toss gently to combine. Sprinkle individual servings with Parmesan cheese. Makes 2 servings.

9   dried whole grain lasagna noodles

1   tablespoon olive oil

2   8- or 9-ounce packages frozen artichoke hearts, thawed and well drained

¼   cup pine nuts

4   cloves garlic, minced

1   15-ounce carton light ricotta cheese

1½ cups reduced-fat shredded Italian-blend cheese or part-skim mozzarella cheese (6 ounces)

1   cup snipped fresh basil or 4 teaspoons dried basil, crushed

1   egg

¼   teaspoon salt

1   cup reduced-sodium chicken broth

¼   cup all-purpose flour

2   cups fat-free milk

Chopped fresh tomato (optional)

Snipped fresh parsley (optional)

1 Preheat oven to 350°F. Cook lasagna noodles according to package directions. Drain noodles; rinse with cold water and drain well. Set aside.

2 In a large skillet heat oil over medium heat. Add artichokes, pine nuts, and garlic; cook about 5 minutes or until artichokes, nuts, and garlic start to brown, stirring frequently. Transfer to a large bowl. Stir in ricotta cheese, ½ cup Italian-blend cheese, ½ cup fresh basil or 1 tablespoon dried basil, egg, and salt.

3 For sauce, in a medium saucepan whisk together chicken broth and flour until smooth. Stir in milk. Cook and stir over medium heat until sauce is slightly thickened and bubbly. Remove from heat. Stir in remaining ½ cup fresh basil or 1 teaspoon dried basil.

4 Pour 1 cup sauce into a 3-quart rectangular baking dish. Top with 3 cooked lasagna noodles. Dollop with one-third of the ricotta mixture (about 1⅓ cups); carefully spread evenly over noodles. Top with one-third of the remaining sauce (about ⅔ cup). Sprinkle with ⅓ cup of the remaining Italian-blend cheese. Repeat layers twice more, beginning with lasagna noodles and ending with the Italian-blend cheese.

Artichoke-Basil Lasagna

PREP: 45 minutes   **BAKE:** 40 minutes
STAND: 15 minutes   **OVEN:** 350°F

NUTRITION FACTS per serving:

CALORIES 330
TOTAL FAT 12 g (5 g sat. fat)
CHOLESTEROL 52 mg
PROTEIN 21 g
CARBOHYDRATE 35 g
FIBER 8 g
SODIUM 431 mg

EXCHANGES 2 Starch, 2 Lean Meat, 1 Vegetable, 1 Fat

5 Bake, uncovered, about 40 minutes or until heated through and top is lightly browned. Let stand for 15 minutes before serving. If desired, top with tomato and parsley. Makes 8 servings.

1   9-ounce package refrigerated whole wheat linguine

1   pound fresh asparagus, trimmed and cut into 2-inch-long pieces

1   cup evaporated fat-free milk

2   ounces reduced-fat cream cheese (Neufchâtel), cubed

2   ounces Gorgonzola or other blue cheese, crumbled (½ cup)

¼   teaspoon salt

2   tablespoons chopped walnuts, toasted

1 Cook pasta and asparagus according to package directions for the pasta; drain well. Return pasta and asparagus to pan. Cover and keep warm.

2 Meanwhile, for sauce, in a medium saucepan combine milk, cream cheese, half of the Gorgonzola cheese, and salt. Bring to boiling over medium heat, whisking constantly; reduce heat. Simmer, uncovered, for 2 minutes, stirring frequently (sauce may appear slightly curdled).

3 Pour sauce over pasta mixture; toss gently to coat. Transfer to four shallow bowls. Sprinkle individual servings with remaining Gorgonzola cheese and walnuts. Serve immediately (sauce will thicken upon standing). Makes 4 servings.

Linguine with Gorgonzola Sauce

START TO FINISH: 25 minutes

NUTRITION FACTS per serving:

- -

CALORIES 361
TOTAL FAT 13 g (6 g sat. fat)
CHOLESTEROL 42 mg
PROTEIN 19 g
CARBOHYDRATE 44 g
FIBER 7 g
SODIUM 476 mg

EXCHANGES 2 Starch, 0.5 Milk, 1 High-Fat Meat, 1 Vegetable, 0.5 Fat

NUTRITION NOTE

Whole wheat pasta requires slightly longer cooking time than traditional pasta, but the added fiber and protein make whole wheat worth the wait.

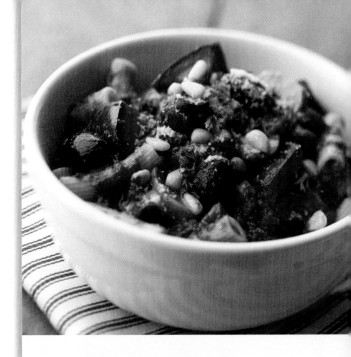

1 medium eggplant, cut into 1-inch cubes

1 28-ounce can Italian-style whole peeled tomatoes in puree, undrained, cut up

1 6-ounce can no-salt-added tomato paste

1 4-ounce can or jar (drained weight) sliced mushrooms, drained

½ cup chopped onion

¼ cup dry red wine or water

¼ cup water

1½ teaspoons dried oregano, crushed

2 cloves garlic, minced

½ cup pitted kalamata olives or pitted ripe olives

Salt

Black pepper

8 ounces dried multigrain or whole grain rotini or penne pasta, cooked according to package directions

⅓ cup grated reduced-fat Parmesan cheese

2 tablespoons snipped fresh parsley

2 tablespoons pine nuts, toasted (optional)

Pasta with Eggplant Sauce

PREP: 25 minutes

COOK: 7 to 8 hours (low) or 3½ to 4 hours (high)

NUTRITION FACTS per serving:

CALORIES 265
TOTAL FAT 5 g (1 g sat. fat)
CHOLESTEROL 4 mg
PROTEIN 13 g
CARBOHYDRATE 43 g
FIBER 10 g
SODIUM 634 mg

EXCHANGES 1.5 Starch, 1 Other Carbohydrates, 1 Lean Meat, 1 Vegetable

1 In a 4- to 5-quart slow cooker combine eggplant, undrained tomatoes, tomato paste, mushrooms, onion, dry red wine, water, oregano, and garlic.

2 Cover and cook on low-heat setting for 7 to 8 hours or on high-heat setting for 3½ to 4 hours.

3 Stir in olives. Season to taste with salt and pepper. Serve over hot cooked pasta. Top with Parmesan cheese, parsley, and, if desired, toasted pine nuts. Makes 6 servings.

Range-Top Directions: In a 4-quart Dutch oven combine eggplant, undrained tomatoes, tomato paste, mushrooms, onion, dry red wine, water, oregano, and garlic. Bring to boiling; reduce heat. Cover and simmer 15 minutes or until eggplant and onion are tender. Simmer, uncovered, about 10 minutes more or until sauce is desired consistency. Stir in olives. Season to taste with salt and pepper. Serve as above.

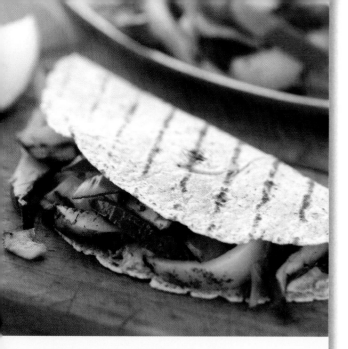

Mushroom-Vegetable Fajitas

PREP: 25 minutes

GRILL: 15 minutes

NUTRITION FACTS per serving:

CALORIES 233
TOTAL FAT 10 g (2 g sat. fat)
CHOLESTEROL 0 mg
PROTEIN 11 g
CARBOHYDRATE 26 g
FIBER 15 g
SODIUM 475 mg

EXCHANGES 1.5 Starch, 1.5 Vegetable, 1.5 Fat

1   small avocado, halved, seeded, and peeled

1   tablespoon lime juice

1   clove garlic, minced

½   teaspoon ground cumin

½   teaspoon dried oregano, crushed

¼   teaspoon salt

⅛   teaspoon black pepper

3   small fresh portobello mushrooms, stems and gills removed

2   medium red, yellow and/or green sweet peppers, halved, stemmed, and seeded

½   of a medium red onion, cut into ½-inch-thick slices

    Nonstick cooking spray

4   7- to 8-inch whole wheat flour tortillas

    Lime wedges (optional)

1 Place avocado halves in a small bowl. With a potato masher or fork, mash avocado until nearly smooth. Stir in lime juice and garlic. Cover the surface of the avocado mixture with plastic wrap and chill until ready to serve.

2 In a small bowl combine cumin, oregano, salt, and black pepper. Coat mushrooms, sweet pepper halves, and red onion slices with nonstick cooking spray. Sprinkle cumin mixture on vegetables.

3 For a charcoal grill, place mushrooms, sweet pepper halves, and onion slices on rack of an uncovered grill directly over medium coals. Grill until vegetables are crisp-tender, turning once halfway through grilling and removing vegetables when they are done. Allow 8 to 10 minutes for the sweet peppers, 10 to 15 minutes for the mushrooms, and 15 to 20 minutes for the onion slices. (For a gas grill, preheat grill. Reduce heat to medium. Place vegetables on grill rack directly over heat. Cover and grill as above.)

4 Place tortillas on grill rack directly over medium coals. Grill for 20 to 30 seconds or until warm, turning once. Remove from grill and cover to keep warm. Thinly slice mushrooms and sweet peppers. Coarsely chop onion slices.

5 Spread avocado mixture on warm tortillas. Divide vegetables among tortillas. Fold over. If desired, serve with lime wedges. Makes 4 servings.

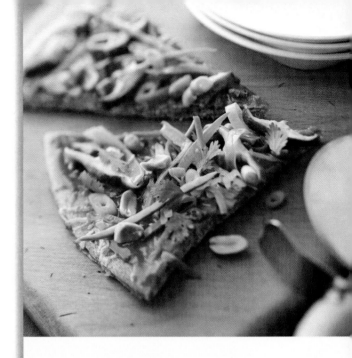

1   12-inch (10-ounce) whole wheat Italian bread shell (such as Boboli brand)

     Nonstick cooking spray

1   cup sliced fresh shiitake or button mushrooms

⅔   cup fresh pea pods cut into thin strips

¼   cup coarsely shredded carrot

¼   cup sliced green onion

¼   to ⅓ cup bottled peanut sauce

2   tablespoons chopped peanuts

2   tablespoons fresh cilantro leaves

1 Preheat oven to 450°F. Place bread shell on an ungreased baking sheet. Bake for 6 to 8 minutes or until lightly browned and crisp.

2 Meanwhile, lightly coat an unheated large nonstick skillet with nonstick cooking spray. Preheat over medium heat. Add mushrooms, pea pods, and carrot to hot skillet; cook about 2 minutes or just until tender. Stir in green onion. Remove from heat.

3 Carefully spread hot bread shell with peanut sauce. Top with hot vegetable mixture; sprinkle with peanuts and cilantro leaves. Makes 4 servings.

COOK'S TIP

Check for freshness in pea pods such as sugar snap or snow peas by snapping one in half. If it sounds crisp when snapped, it's fresh and ready to eat.

Thai-Style Veggie Pizza

PREP: 20 minutes   **BAKE:** 6 minutes

COOK: 2 minutes   **OVEN:** 450°F

NUTRITION FACTS per serving:

CALORIES 286
TOTAL FAT 8 g (2 g sat. fat)
CHOLESTEROL 0 mg
PROTEIN 12 g
CARBOHYDRATE 46 g
FIBER 8 g
SODIUM 598 mg

EXCHANGES 3 Starch, 0.5 Vegetable, 1 Fat

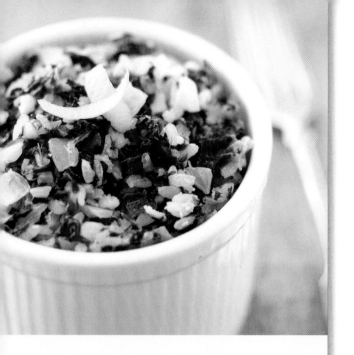

1 tablespoon olive oil

1 medium onion, chopped

4 eggs

½ cup low-fat cottage cheese

3 ounces reduced-fat feta cheese, crumbled

1 tablespoon snipped fresh dill or ½ teaspoon dried dill

½ teaspoon salt

2 10-ounce packages frozen chopped spinach, thawed and well drained

2 cups cooked brown rice

1 tablespoon lemon juice

Fresh lemon peel strips (optional)

Brown Rice-Spinach Custards

PREP: 25 minutes **BAKE:** 25 minutes
OVEN: 350°F

NUTRITION FACTS per serving:

- -

CALORIES 213
TOTAL FAT 8 g (3 g sat. fat)
CHOLESTEROL 146 mg
PROTEIN 14 g
CARBOHYDRATE 20 g
FIBER 4 g
SODIUM 648 mg

EXCHANGES 1 Starch, 1.5 Lean Meat, 1 Vegetable, 0.5 Fat

1 Preheat oven to 350°F. In a small skillet heat oil over medium heat. Add onion; cook until tender, stirring occasionally. Cool slightly.

2 In a large bowl beat eggs with a fork. Stir in cottage cheese, feta cheese, dill, salt, and cooked onion. Add spinach, cooked brown rice, and lemon juice, stirring until well mixed. Place six 8- to 10-ounce ramekins or custard cups in a 15×10×1-inch baking pan. Divide rice mixture among the dishes. Bake for 25 to 30 minutes or until a knife inserted near the center of each custard comes out clean. If desired, garnish with lemon peel. Makes 6 servings.

COOK'S TIP

Cottage cheese is more perishable than other cheeses. A good sign that it's past its prime is when the cheese mixture separates and becomes watery. Store cottage cheese in the coldest part of the refrigerator for up to 10 days beyond the date stamped on the container.

- 4 medium green, red, and/or yellow sweet peppers
- 1 cup cooked brown rice
- 1 15-ounce can spicy chili beans or mild chili beans
- 1 cup shredded reduced-fat Monterey Jack cheese (4 ounces)
- 1 4½-ounce can stewed tomatoes, undrained, cut up

1 Remove tops from sweet peppers; set tops aside. Remove membranes and seeds from sweet peppers. In a medium bowl stir together cooked brown rice, undrained beans, and cheese; spoon into sweet peppers. Pour stewed tomatoes into the bottom of a 5- to 6-quart slow cooker. Place sweet peppers, filled sides up, in cooker on tomatoes. Replace sweet pepper tops.

2 Cover and cook on low-heat setting for 6 to 6½ hours or on high-heat setting for 3 to 3½ hours. Makes 4 servings.

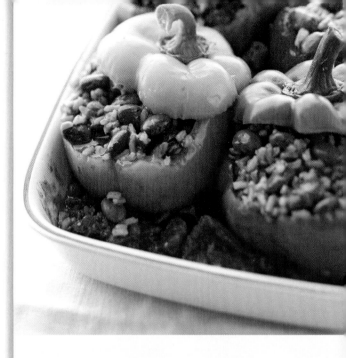

Spicy Bean- and Rice-Stuffed Peppers

PREP: 15 minutes

COOK: 6 to 6½ hours (low) or 3 to 3½ hours (high)

NUTRITION FACTS per serving:

CALORIES 290
TOTAL FAT 8 g (4 g sat. fat)
CHOLESTEROL 20 mg
PROTEIN 15 g
CARBOHYDRATE 42 g
FIBER 9 g
SODIUM 848 mg

EXCHANGES 2 Starch, 1 Lean Meat, 2 Vegetable, 0.5 Fat

Triple-Pepper Nachos

PREP: 25 minutes   **BAKE:** 13 minutes
OVEN: 425°F

NUTRITION FACTS per serving:

CALORIES 201
TOTAL FAT 7 g (3 g sat. fat)
CHOLESTEROL 13 mg
PROTEIN 15 g
CARBOHYDRATE 24 g
FIBER 11 g
SODIUM 838 mg

EXCHANGES 1.5 Starch, 1.5 Lean Meat, 0.5 Vegetable

5   7- to 8-inch whole wheat flour tortillas or 4 ounces baked tortilla chips (about 5 cups)
    Nonstick cooking spray (optional)

1   15-ounce can black beans, rinsed and drained

¾   cup purchased chunky salsa

1   cup shredded reduced-fat Colby and Monterey Jack cheese (4 ounces)

¾   cup bottled roasted red sweet peppers, drained and cut into strips

1   bottled pepperoncini salad pepper, seeded and cut into strips

2   to 4 tablespoons bottled sliced pickled jalapeño chile peppers, chopped*
    Thinly sliced green onion
    Light dairy sour cream (optional)
    Purchased chunky salsa (optional)

1 Preheat oven to 425°F. If using whole wheat flour tortillas, lightly coat both sides of each tortilla with nonstick cooking spray. Cut each tortilla into six wedges. Place wedges in a single layer on a very large ungreased baking sheet. Bake for 8 to 10 minutes or until lightly browned and crisp, turning once halfway through baking. Tortilla wedges will continue to crisp as they cool.

2 Meanwhile, in a medium saucepan combine black beans and ¾ cup salsa; cook and stir over medium heat just until heated through.

3 On a very large ovenproof platter arrange tortilla chips one to two layers deep, overlapping slightly. Spoon bean mixture on chips. Sprinkle cheese, roasted red peppers, pepperoncini pepper, and jalapeño peppers over bean mixture on chips.

4 Bake about 5 minutes or until cheese is melted. Sprinkle with green onion. If desired, serve with sour cream and additional salsa. Makes 6 servings.

*See chile pepper handling note, page 188.

½ cup whole wheat couscous

2 tablespoons whole wheat flour

¼ teaspoon baking soda

⅛ teaspoon salt

1 egg

¾ cup buttermilk or sour fat-free milk*

1 tablespoon canola oil

1 recipe Black Bean Salsa
  Nonstick cooking spray

1 In a medium bowl combine uncooked couscous, whole wheat flour, baking soda, and salt. In a small bowl beat egg with a fork. Stir in buttermilk and oil. Stir buttermilk mixture into couscous mixture. Let stand for 20 minutes (batter will thicken as it stands).

2 Meanwhile, prepare Black Bean Salsa; set aside. Preheat oven to 200°F.

3 Lightly coat an unheated griddle or large nonstick skillet with nonstick cooking spray. Preheat over medium heat. For each cake, spoon 2 slightly rounded tablespoons of the batter onto the hot griddle or skillet; quickly spread to 3½-inch rounds. Cook about 2 minutes per side or until browned, turning when bottoms are lightly browned and edges are slightly dry. Keep warm in oven while cooking remaining cakes.

4 To serve, spoon Black Bean Salsa over cakes. Makes 4 servings.

Black Bean Salsa: In a medium bowl stir together ¾ cup loose-pack frozen whole kernel corn, thawed; ½ of a 15-ounce can black beans (¾ cup), rinsed and drained; ¾ cup purchased fresh salsa;** ½ cup chopped, peeled jicama; 1 tablespoon snipped fresh cilantro; 1 tablespoon lime juice; and ½ teaspoon ground cumin. Makes 2 cups.

*To make ¾ cup sour fat-free milk, place 2 teaspoons lemon juice or vinegar in a glass measuring cup. Add enough fat-free milk to make ¾ cup total liquid; stir. Let stand for 5 minutes before using.

**Look for fresh salsa in the deli or produce section of your supermarket.

Couscous Cakes with Salsa

PREP: 20 minutes   **STAND:** 20 minutes

COOK: 4 minutes per batch   **OVEN:** 200°F

NUTRITION FACTS per serving:

CALORIES 270
TOTAL FAT 6 g (1 g sat. fat)
CHOLESTEROL 55 mg
PROTEIN 13 g
CARBOHYDRATE 46 g
FIBER 8 g
SODIUM 639 mg

EXCHANGES 3 Starch, 0.5 Very Lean Meat, 0.5 Fat

COOK'S TIP

Couscous is widely available in grocery stores, but the whole wheat variety may be hard to find. If you do not see it with rice or pasta, try a health food store or specialty market.

Southwest Quinoa Pilaf

START TO FINISH: 40 minutes

NUTRITION FACTS per serving:

- -

CALORIES 261
TOTAL FAT 5 g (1 g sat. fat)
CHOLESTEROL 0 mg
PROTEIN 12 g
CARBOHYDRATE 48 g
FIBER 7 g
SODIUM 443 mg

EXCHANGES 3 Starch, 0.5 Vegetable, 0.5 Fat

COOK'S TIP

When you've cut into a jicama and find more than you need for one recipe, wrap the excess tightly and store it in the refrigerator for up to one week. Look for tasty ways to add it to recipes—salads, stir-fries, dippers, and crudités.

1 tablespoon olive oil

1½ cups chopped onion

6 cloves garlic, minced

1¼ cups quinoa*

½ teaspoon ground cumin

1 14-ounce can reduced-sodium chicken broth or vegetable broth

1¼ cups water

1 recipe Black Bean, Corn, and Jicama Salsa

2 tablespoons snipped fresh cilantro
Fresh cilantro sprigs (optional)

1 In a 4-quart Dutch oven heat oil over medium heat. Add onion and garlic; cook about 5 minutes or until onion is tender, stirring occasionally. Rinse and drain quinoa. Add quinoa and cumin to onion and garlic in Dutch oven; cook and stir about 3 minutes or until quinoa is lightly browned.

2 Add chicken broth and water to quinoa mixture. Bring to boiling; reduce heat. Cover and simmer for 15 to 20 minutes or until all of the liquid is absorbed and quinoa is tender. Divide quinoa mixture among six serving plates. Top quinoa with Black Bean, Corn, and Jicama Salsa. Sprinkle with snipped cilantro. If desired, garnish with cilantro sprigs. Makes 6 servings.

Black Bean, Corn, and Jicama Salsa: In a large bowl toss together one 15-ounce can black beans, rinsed and drained; 1 cup loose-pack frozen whole kernel corn, thawed; 1 large tomato, chopped; ½ cup peeled, chopped jicama; 2 green onions, thinly sliced; 1 fresh jalapeño chile pepper, halved, seeded, and finely chopped;** 2 tablespoons lime juice; and ¼ teaspoon salt. Makes 4 cups.

*Look for quinoa (pronounced KEEN-wa) at health food stores or in the grains section of large supermarkets.

**Because chile peppers contain volatile oils that can burn your skin and eyes, avoid direct contact with them as much as possible. When working with chile peppers, wear plastic or rubber gloves. If your bare hands do touch the peppers, wash your hands and nails well with soap and warm water.

- 1   18.8- to 19-ounce can ready-to-serve lentil soup
- 1   15-ounce can black beans, rinsed and drained
- 1   cup small fresh mushrooms, sliced
- 1   cup sliced carrot
- 1   cup loose-pack frozen whole kernel corn
- ½   cup regular barley
- ⅓   cup bulgur
- ¼   cup chopped onion
- ½   teaspoon black pepper
- ¼   teaspoon salt
- ¾   cup water
- ½   cup shredded reduced-fat cheddar cheese (2 ounces)

1 Preheat oven to 350°F. In an ungreased 2-quart casserole combine lentil soup, black beans, mushrooms, carrot, corn, uncooked barley, uncooked bulgur, onion, pepper, and salt; stir in the water.

2 Cover and bake about 1¼ hours or until barley and bulgur are tender, stirring twice. Stir again; sprinkle with cheese. Cover; let stand about 5 minutes or until cheese is melted. Makes 5 servings.

Vegetable Two-Grain Casserole

PREP: 20 minutes   **BAKE:** 1¼ hours
STAND: 5 minutes   **OVEN:** 350°F

NUTRITION FACTS per serving:

- -

CALORIES 292
TOTAL FAT 4 g (2 g sat. fat)
CHOLESTEROL 10 mg
PROTEIN 17 g
CARBOHYDRATE 55 g
FIBER 13 g
SODIUM 828 mg

EXCHANGES 3.5 Starch, 1 Very Lean Meat, 0.5 Vegetable

Tofu and Eggplant

START TO FINISH: 30 minutes

NUTRITION FACTS per serving:

- -

CALORIES 272
TOTAL FAT 8 g (1 g sat. fat)
CHOLESTEROL 0 mg
PROTEIN 11 g
CARBOHYDRATE 38 g
FIBER 7 g
SODIUM 334 mg

EXCHANGES 2 Starch, 0.5 Very Lean Meat,
1 Vegetable, 1 Fat

¾   cup cold water

3   tablespoons dry sherry or water

2   tablespoons reduced-sodium soy sauce

2   teaspoons cornstarch

1   to 2 teaspoons Asian chili sauce

1   teaspoon sugar

1   tablespoon cooking oil

2   Japanese eggplants, halved lengthwise and cut into ¼-inch-thick slices

2   medium red sweet peppers, seeded and cut into strips

1   tablespoon grated fresh ginger

2   to 3 cloves garlic, minced

12   to 16 ounces firm tofu (fresh bean curd), cut into ½-inch cubes

2   cups hot cooked brown rice

    Fresh cilantro or basil leaves (optional)

1 For sauce, in a small bowl stir together water, dry sherry, soy sauce, cornstarch, chili sauce, and sugar; set aside.

2 In a large nonstick skillet or wok heat oil over medium-high heat. Add eggplant slices and sweet pepper. Cook for 3 to 4 minutes or just until eggplant is tender, stirring often. Remove eggplant mixture from skillet. Add ginger and garlic to skillet; cook for 1 minute. Stir sauce and add to skillet. Cook and stir until thickened and bubbly. Cook and stir for 1 minute more. Add eggplant mixture and tofu to skillet; gently stir to combine. Heat through. Serve over hot cooked rice. If desired, garnish with cilantro or basil leaves. Makes 4 servings.

- 2½ cups water
- 1¼ cups bulgur
- ¼ cup lemon juice
- 3 tablespoons purchased basil pesto
- 2 cups fresh or thawed frozen shelled sweet soybeans (edamame)
- 2 cups cherry tomatoes, cut up
- ⅓ cup crumbled, reduced-fat feta cheese
- ⅓ cup thinly sliced green onion
- 2 tablespoons snipped fresh parsley
- ¼ teaspoon black pepper
  Fresh parsley sprigs (optional)

1 In a medium saucepan bring water to boiling; add uncooked bulgur. Return to boiling; reduce heat. Cover and simmer about 15 minutes or until most of the liquid is absorbed. Transfer to a large bowl.

2 In a small bowl whisk together lemon juice and pesto. Add lemon juice mixture to cooked bulgur along with soybeans, cherry tomatoes, feta cheese, green onion, snipped parsley, and pepper. Toss gently to combine. If desired, garnish with parsley sprigs. Makes 6 servings.

Make-Ahead Directions: Prepare as above. Cover and chill for up to 4 hours.

Tabbouleh with Edamame and Feta

PREP: 25 minutes
COOK: 15 minutes

NUTRITION FACTS per serving:

CALORIES 313
TOTAL FAT 12 g total fat (1 g sat. fat)
CHOLESTEROL 3 mg
PROTEIN 18 g
CARBOHYDRATE 37 g
FIBER 10 g
SODIUM 187 mg

EXCHANGES 2 Starch, 1.5 Very Lean Meat, 0.5 Vegetable, 2 Fat

NUTRITION NOTE

Soybeans are great for health. Feel confident including more soybeans in your diet to provide protein, iron, calcium, and vitamin C. Add them to soups, salads, and pasta dishes.

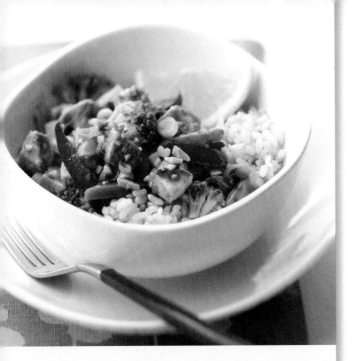

¼ cup finely chopped peanuts

1 tablespoon sesame seeds

1 teaspoon grated fresh ginger or ½ teaspoon ground ginger

⅛ teaspoon crushed red pepper

1 12-ounce package firm or extra-firm tub-style tofu (fresh bean curd), drained and cut into ½-inch cubes

1 tablespoon olive oil

3 cups loose-pack frozen stir-fry vegetables (any combination), thawed

½ cup bottled stir-fry sauce

2 cups hot cooked brown rice

2 green onions, thinly sliced

1 medium orange, cut into 8 wedges

Sesame-Orange Tofu

START TO FINISH: 30 minutes

NUTRITION FACTS per serving:

CALORIES 330
TOTAL FAT 12 g (2 g sat. fat)
CHOLESTEROL 1 mg
PROTEIN 16 g
CARBOHYDRATE 41 g
FIBER 6 g
SODIUM 854 mg

EXCHANGES 2.5 Starch, 1 Very Lean Meat, 1 Vegetable, 2 Fat

1 In a large bowl combine 1 tablespoon peanuts, sesame seeds, ginger, and crushed red pepper. Add tofu; gently toss to coat.

2 In a large skillet heat oil over medium heat. (If necessary, add more oil during cooking.) Add tofu mixture to skillet. Cook, stirring gently, until sesame seeds are toasted and tofu begins to brown.

3 Push tofu mixture to side of skillet. Add vegetables; cook and stir until heated through. Add stir-fry sauce; cook and stir gently until mixture is bubbly. Serve over hot cooked brown rice. Sprinkle individual servings with remaining 3 tablespoons peanuts and green onion. Serve with orange wedges. Makes 4 servings.

NUTRITION NOTE

Soy protein products such as tofu can be substituted for animal protein. Soy protein is a complete protein that has all the essential amino acids and often contains less fat, especially saturated fat, than animal proteins.

On the opener: Roasted Potatoes and Tomatoes (*see recipe, page 204*)

- 4 cups fresh baby spinach
- 1 medium green-skinned apple (such as Granny Smith), cored and sliced
- ¼ cup thin wedges red onion
- 2 tablespoons snipped dried tart red cherries
- ¼ cup Thyme-Dijon Vinaigrette
- ½ cup crumbled reduced-fat feta cheese or crumbled blue cheese (2 ounces) (optional)

1 In a large bowl toss together spinach, apple, red onion, and dried cherries. Drizzle with Thyme-Dijon Vinaigrette. Toss gently to coat. If desired, top individual servings with cheese. Makes 4 (about 1-cup) servings.

Thyme-Dijon Vinaigrette: In a screw-top jar combine ¼ cup olive oil; ¼ cup white balsamic vinegar or regular balsamic vinegar; 2 teaspoons snipped fresh thyme or ½ teaspoon dried thyme, crushed; 1 teaspoon Dijon-style mustard; and ¼ teaspoon salt. Cover; shake well to mix. Chill for up to 1 week. Shake before serving. Makes ⅔ cup.

Apple-Spinach Salad with Thyme-Dijon Vinaigrette

START TO FINISH: 25 minutes

NUTRITION FACTS per serving:

CALORIES 91
TOTAL FAT 5 g (1 g sat. fat)
CHOLESTEROL 0 mg
PROTEIN 1 g
CARBOHYDRATE 11 g
FIBER 2 g
SODIUM 91 mg

EXCHANGES 0.5 Fruit, 1 Vegetable, 1 Fat

Cranberry-Cucumber Salad

START TO FINISH: 25 minutes

NUTRITION FACTS per serving:

CALORIES 89
TOTAL FAT 8 g (1 g sat. fat)
CHOLESTEROL 0 mg
PROTEIN 1 g
CARBOHYDRATE 6 g
FIBER 1 g
SODIUM 85 mg

EXCHANGES 1 Vegetable, 1.5 Fat

3 cups torn mixed salad greens
1 cup fresh spinach
1 medium cucumber, seeded and chopped
1 cup cherry tomatoes, halved
¼ cup sliced pitted ripe olives
2 tablespoons dried cranberries
3 tablespoons olive oil
2 tablespoons lemon juice
2 tablespoons water
1¼ teaspoons Homemade Spice Mix
Cracked black pepper (optional)

1 In a large bowl combine mixed greens, spinach, cucumber, cherry tomatoes, olives, and dried cranberries. Set aside.

2 For dressing, in a small screw-top jar combine oil, lemon juice, water, and Homemade Spice Mix; shake well. Pour over greens mixture; toss to coat. If desired, sprinkle with black pepper. Makes 6 (about 1-cup) servings.

Homemade Spice Mix: In a small bowl combine ½ teaspoon paprika, ½ teaspoon ground coriander, ½ teaspoon ground cumin, ¼ teaspoon garlic powder, ¼ teaspoon ground turmeric, ⅛ teaspoon salt, and ⅛ teaspoon cayenne pepper. Store any leftover mix in an airtight container at room temperature for up to 6 months. Makes about 2¼ teaspoons.

8 cups mixed baby salad greens

½ cup bottled reduced-fat or fat-free
   balsamic vinaigrette
   salad dressing

4 small cooked beets or two
   8¼-ounce cans whole beets,
   chilled

2 tablespoons snipped fresh basil or
   flat-leaf parsley

¼ teaspoon black pepper

¼ cup coarsely chopped walnuts,
   toasted

2 ounces semisoft goat cheese
   (chèvre), crumbled

1 In a bowl drizzle salad greens with ¼ cup salad dressing. Set aside.

2 If using canned beets, drain beets. Cut beets into bite-size pieces. In a medium bowl combine beets, basil or parsley, and pepper. Drizzle with remaining ¼ cup salad dressing; toss to coat. Toss beet mixture with salad greens. Transfer to a serving platter. Sprinkle with walnuts and goat cheese. Makes 4 servings.

Beet Salad with Goat Cheese and Walnuts

START TO FINISH: 15 minutes

NUTRITION FACTS per serving:

CALORIES 147
TOTAL FAT 10 g (3 g sat. fat)
CHOLESTEROL 7 mg
PROTEIN 6 g
CARBOHYDRATE 11 g
FIBER 3 g
SODIUM 571 mg

EXCHANGES 0.5 Medium-Fat Meat,
2.5 Vegetable, 1.5 Fat

NUTRITION NOTE

Read labels when buying bottled salad dressings. Even those low in calories and fat may have a high amount of sodium or sugar.

Marinated Vegetable Salad

PREP: 25 minutes

STAND: 30 to 60 minutes

NUTRITION FACTS per serving:

CALORIES 64
TOTAL FAT 5 g (1 g sat. fat)
CHOLESTEROL 0 mg
PROTEIN 1 g
CARBOHYDRATE 5 g
FIBER 1 g
SODIUM 7 mg

EXCHANGES 1 Vegetable, 1 Fat

2 medium red and/or yellow tomatoes or 4 plum tomatoes, cut into wedges

1 medium green sweet pepper, seeded and chopped

1 small zucchini or yellow summer squash, thinly sliced (about 1 cup)

½ of a small red onion, thinly sliced

2 tablespoons snipped fresh parsley

2 tablespoons olive oil

2 tablespoons balsamic vinegar or wine vinegar

2 tablespoons water

1 tablespoon snipped fresh thyme or basil or 1 teaspoon dried thyme or basil, crushed

1 clove garlic, minced

Toasted pine nuts (optional)

1 In a medium bowl combine tomato wedges, sweet pepper, zucchini, red onion, and parsley; set aside.

2 For dressing, in a screw-top jar combine oil, vinegar, water, thyme, and garlic. Cover; shake well. Pour over vegetable mixture. Toss lightly to coat.

3 Let salad stand at room temperature for 30 to 60 minutes, stirring occasionally. If desired, garnish with pine nuts. Serve with a slotted spoon. Makes 6 (⅔-cup) servings.

Make-Ahead Directions: Prepare as above through step 2. Cover and chill for 4 to 24 hours, stirring once or twice. Let stand at room temperature about 30 minutes before serving. If desired, garnish with pine nuts. Serve with a slotted spoon.

COOK'S TIP

To peel garlic cloves easily, set a clove on a cutting board. Holding a knife with a broad blade (such as a chef's knife) horizontally above the clove, press down firmly or gently strike with the knife to separate the clove from its skin. When using several cloves, strike the cloves with the bottom of a skillet.

3　large yellow sweet peppers,
　　seeded and thinly sliced into
　　rings (about 3 cups)

4　cups fresh watercress or
　　baby spinach

3　or 4 medium tomatoes (about
　　1 pound), cut into wedges

1　recipe Herb-Dijon Vinaigrette

¼　cup crumbled Gorgonzola or
　　blue cheese (1 ounce)

1 In a covered Dutch oven cook sweet pepper rings in a large amount of boiling water for 1 to 2 minutes or just until crisp-tender. Drain and rinse with cold water to cool. Drain well.

2 Arrange watercress on a platter. Top with sweet pepper rings and tomato wedges. Shake dressing; drizzle over salad. Sprinkle with cheese. Makes 8 servings.

Herb-Dijon Vinaigrette: In a screw-top jar combine 2 tablespoons olive oil, 2 tablespoons white wine vinegar or balsamic vinegar, 1 tablespoon snipped fresh chives, 2 teaspoons snipped fresh basil, ½ teaspoon sugar, ½ teaspoon Dijon-style mustard, and ⅛ teaspoon black pepper. Cover and shake well to combine; use immediately or cover and chill for up to 3 days. Shake before serving. Makes ¼ cup.

Tomato and Sweet Pepper Salad

START TO FINISH: 25 minutes

NUTRITION FACTS per serving:

CALORIES 85
TOTAL FAT 5 g (1 g sat. fat)
CHOLESTEROL 3 mg
PROTEIN 3 g
CARBOHYDRATE 9 g
FIBER 2 g
SODIUM 78 mg

EXCHANGES 1.5 Vegetable, 1 Fat

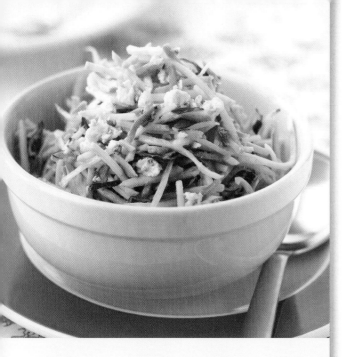

¼ cup cider vinegar or rice vinegar

2 tablespoons canola oil

1 teaspoon sugar

½ teaspoon dry mustard

¼ teaspoon onion powder

⅛ teaspoon salt

⅛ teaspoon white pepper or
   black pepper

2½ cups packaged shredded broccoli
   (broccoli slaw mix)

2 tablespoons crumbled blue cheese

1 For dressing, in a screw-top jar combine vinegar, oil, sugar, dry mustard, onion powder, salt, and pepper. Cover and shake well. Chill until serving time.

2 To serve, in a large bowl combine broccoli and blue cheese. Shake dressing; drizzle over cabbage mixture, gently tossing to coat. Makes 4 (about ½-cup) servings.

Make-Ahead Hints: The dressing may be chilled for up to 1 week. The dressed salad may be covered and chilled for up to 24 hours before serving.

Blue Cheese Coleslaw

START TO FINISH: 15 minutes

NUTRITION FACTS per serving:

CALORIES 100
TOTAL FAT 8 g (1 g sat. fat)
CHOLESTEROL 3 mg
PROTEIN 2 g
CARBOHYDRATE 5 g
FIBER 1 g
SODIUM 148 mg

EXCHANGES 0.5 Vegetable, 1.5 Fat

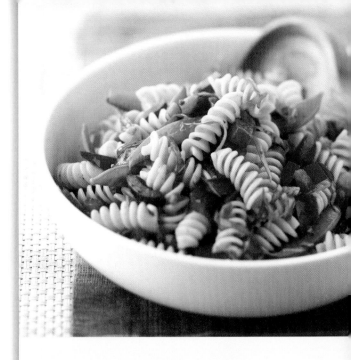

4 ounces dried whole wheat rotini, penne, or bow tie pasta (about 1½ cups)

1 cup fresh sugar snap peas (4 ounces), trimmed

½ cup chopped red sweet pepper

¼ cup shredded fresh basil*

2 tablespoons pitted kalamata or niçoise olives, quartered

2 tablespoons red wine vinegar

2 tablespoons olive oil

1 clove garlic, minced

⅛ teaspoon salt

Dash black pepper

1 Cook pasta according to package directions, adding sugar snap peas for the last 1 minute of cooking. Drain well. Rinse with cold water; drain again. In a large bowl combine pasta mixture, sweet pepper, basil, and olives. Set aside.

2 For dressing, in a screw-top jar combine red wine vinegar, oil, garlic, salt, and black pepper. Cover and shake well. Pour dressing over pasta and vegetables; toss gently to coat. Makes 6 (½-cup) servings.

*To shred (chiffonade) fresh basil, stack several leaves and roll up the leaves. Starting at one end, use a sharp knife to cut crosswise into thin slices.

Italian Pasta Salad

START TO FINISH: 25 minutes

NUTRITION FACTS per serving:

CALORIES 123
TOTAL FAT 5 g (1 g sat. fat)
CHOLESTEROL 0 mg
PROTEIN 3 g
CARBOHYDRATE 16 g
FIBER 2 g
SODIUM 81 mg

EXCHANGES 1 Starch, 1 Fat

2 cups water
½ cup wild rice, rinsed and drained
¼ cup barley
1 cup fresh pea pods, cut into thirds
⅓ cup golden raisins
3 green onions, sliced
1 teaspoon finely shredded
   orange peel
⅓ cup orange juice
1 tablespoon olive oil
¼ teaspoon salt
⅛ teaspoon black pepper
2 tablespoons snipped fresh mint
Shredded orange peel (optional)

Minted Wild Rice and Barley Salad

PREP: 30 minutes   **CHILL:** 4 to 6 hours
COOK: 40 minutes

NUTRITION FACTS per serving:

CALORIES 136
TOTAL FAT 3 g (0 g sat. fat)
CHOLESTEROL 0 mg
PROTEIN 4 g
CARBOHYDRATE 26 g
FIBER 3 g
SODIUM 103 mg

EXCHANGES 1 Starch, 0.5 Fruit, 0.5 Fat

1 In a medium saucepan bring water to boiling; stir in uncooked wild rice and barley. Return to boiling; reduce heat. Cover and simmer about 40 minutes or until wild rice and barley are tender. Drain off liquid. Transfer wild rice and barley to a large bowl.

2 Stir in pea pods, golden raisins, green onion, orange peel, orange juice, oil, salt, and pepper. Cover and chill for 4 to 6 hours.

3 Stir in mint. If desired, garnish with additional orange peel. Makes 6 (about ⅔-cup) servings.

- 1 tablespoon olive oil
- 1 cup quartered fresh mushrooms
- 1½ cups water
- ¾ cup quinoa*
- 1 cup canned red beans, rinsed and drained
- 1 cup chopped zucchini
- 1 cup cherry tomatoes, halved if desired
- 1 tablespoon snipped fresh basil or 1 teaspoon dried basil, crushed
- 1 tablespoon red wine vinegar
- 6 cloves garlic, minced
- ¼ teaspoon salt
- ¼ teaspoon black pepper
- Snipped fresh basil (optional)

1 In a very large skillet heat olive oil over medium heat. Add mushrooms; cook about 5 minutes or until golden brown, stirring occasionally. Add water; bring to boiling. Add quinoa. Return to boiling; reduce heat. Cover and simmer about 15 minutes or until liquid is nearly absorbed.

2 Stir beans, zucchini, cherry tomatoes, the 1 tablespoon snipped basil, the vinegar, garlic, salt, and pepper into quinoa mixture. Heat through. Remove from heat; let stand, covered, for 5 minutes before serving. If desired, sprinkle with additional snipped basil. Makes 6 (1-cup) servings.

*Look for quinoa at a health food store or in the grains section of a large supermarket.

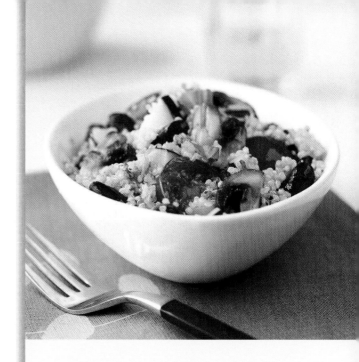

Hearty Grain Medley

PREP: 20 minutes   **COOK:** 15 minutes
STAND: 5 minutes

NUTRITION FACTS per serving:

CALORIES 149
TOTAL FAT 4 g (0 g sat. fat)
CHOLESTEROL 0 mg
PROTEIN 6 g
CARBOHYDRATE 24 g
FIBER 4 g
SODIUM 264 mg

EXCHANGES 1.5 Starch, 0.5 Vegetable, 0.5 Fat

NUTRITION NOTE

Quinoa is not only high in protein, but it is also a complete protein, which means that it includes all the essential amino acids.

1 pound tiny new potatoes (10 to 12), scrubbed and quartered

2 tablespoons olive oil

2 teaspoons snipped fresh oregano or ½ teaspoon dried oregano, crushed

¼ teaspoon salt

¼ teaspoon black pepper

4 plum tomatoes, quartered lengthwise

½ cup pitted kalamata olives

3 cloves garlic, minced

¼ cup grated Parmesan cheese

Roasted Potatoes and Tomatoes

PREP: 15 minutes   **BAKE:** 25 minutes

OVEN: 450°F

NUTRITION FACTS per serving:

CALORIES 102
TOTAL FAT 5 g (1 g sat. fat)
CHOLESTEROL 2 mg
PROTEIN 3 g
CARBOHYDRATE 11 g
FIBER 2 g
SODIUM 208 mg

EXCHANGES 1 Starch, 1 Fat

1 Preheat oven to 450°F. Lightly grease a 15×10×1-inch baking pan; place potatoes in pan. In a small bowl combine oil, oregano, salt, and pepper; drizzle over potatoes, tossing to coat.

2 Bake for 20 minutes, stirring once. Add tomatoes, olives, and garlic; toss to combine. Bake for 5 to 10 minutes more or until potatoes are tender and brown on the edges and tomatoes are soft. Transfer to a serving dish. Sprinkle with Parmesan cheese. Makes 8 (½-cup) servings.

1 pound round red, Yukon gold, or round white potatoes, scrubbed and quartered

1 teaspoon bottled minced roasted garlic

¼ cup light dairy sour cream

2 to 4 tablespoons fat-free milk

1 teaspoon snipped fresh thyme or ½ teaspoon dried thyme, crushed

¼ teaspoon salt

⅛ teaspoon black pepper

Snipped fresh thyme (optional)

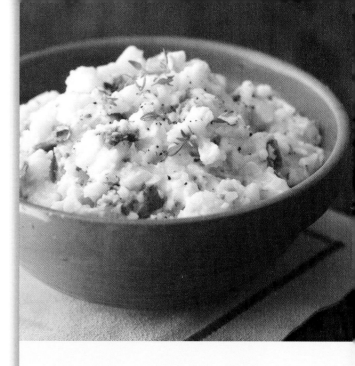

1 In a covered large saucepan cook potatoes in enough boiling water to cover for 20 to 25 minutes or until tender. Drain well and return to saucepan.

2 Add garlic to potatoes. Mash with a potato masher or an electric mixer on low speed. Add sour cream, 2 tablespoons milk, snipped thyme, salt, and pepper. Beat until light and fluffy, adding remaining 2 tablespoons milk if necessary. If desired, sprinkle with additional snipped thyme. Makes 4 (about ⅔-cup) servings.

COOK'S TIP

If you prefer roasting the garlic yourself, it's supereasy. Scatter unpeeled garlic cloves on a baking sheet, drizzle with olive oil, and bake at 375°F for 30 minutes. Squeeze the garlic out of the skins to use it for any roasted garlic called for in recipes.

Roasted Garlic Mashed Potatoes

PREP: 15 minutes
COOK: 20 minutes

NUTRITION FACTS per serving:

CALORIES 106
TOTAL FAT 1 g (1 g sat. fat)
CHOLESTEROL 5 mg
PROTEIN 4 g
CARBOHYDRATE 19 g
FIBER 2 g
SODIUM 162 mg

EXCHANGES 1.5 Starch

3 cups fresh green beans (about 10 ounces), trimmed if desired

¼ cup sliced almonds, toasted

1 tablespoon olive oil

½ teaspoon Homemade Spice Mix

1 In a covered large saucepan cook beans in a small amount of boiling water for 8 to 10 minutes or until crisp-tender. Drain well. Return to hot pan. Stir in almonds, oil, and Homemade Spice Mix. Heat through. Makes 6 (about ½-cup) servings.

Homemade Spice Mix: In a small bowl combine ½ teaspoon paprika, ½ teaspoon ground coriander, ½ teaspoon ground cumin, ¼ teaspoon garlic powder, ¼ teaspoon ground turmeric, ⅛ teaspoon salt, and ⅛ teaspoon cayenne pepper. Store any leftover mix in an airtight container at room temperature for up to 6 months. Makes about 2¼ teaspoons.

Green Beans with Toasted Almonds

START TO FINISH: 20 minutes

NUTRITION FACTS per serving:

- -

CALORIES 59
TOTAL FAT 4 g (0 g sat. fat)
CHOLESTEROL 0 mg
PROTEIN 2 g
CARBOHYDRATE 5 g
FIBER 2 g
SODIUM 14 mg

EXCHANGES 1 Vegetable, 0.5 Fat

1½ pounds broccoli rabe or 3½ cups broccoli florets

1 tablespoon olive oil

3 cloves garlic, minced

2 tablespoons reduced-sodium chicken broth

¼ teaspoon black pepper

⅛ teaspoon salt

1 If using broccoli rabe, remove large leaves and, if necessary, cut stems to 6- to 8-inch-long pieces. In a 4-quart Dutch oven cook broccoli rabe or broccoli, half at a time if necessary, in a large amount of boiling water for 3 minutes if using broccoli rabe or 6 minutes if using broccoli florets. Drain well; gently squeeze vegetable if necessary to get it really dry.

2 In the same Dutch oven heat oil over medium heat. Add garlic; cook and stir for 30 seconds. Carefully add drained broccoli rabe or broccoli florets (oil will spatter if the vegetable is not drained well); cook and stir for 1 minute. Add chicken broth. Cook, uncovered, until all of the broth has evaporated, stirring frequently. Stir in pepper and salt. Serve immediately. Makes 6 (½-cup) servings.

COOK'S TIP

Americans rarely eat the greens of broccoli rabe because of their bitter taste, yet they are packed with the same nutrients in cabbage and turnips. Italian cuisine often combines garlic with broccoli rabe, cutting the bitterness with garlic's mellow taste.

Broccoli Rabe with Garlic

START TO FINISH: 20 minutes

NUTRITION FACTS per serving:

CALORIES 48
TOTAL FAT 3 g (0 g sat. fat)
CHOLESTEROL 0 mg
PROTEIN 4 g
CARBOHYDRATE 4 g
FIBER 3 g
SODIUM 98 mg

EXCHANGES 1 Vegetable, 0.5 Fat

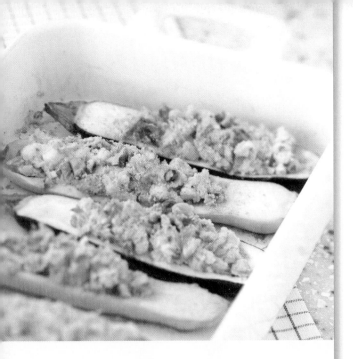

4 medium yellow summer squash or zucchini

½ of an 8-ounce package reduced-fat cream cheese (Neufchâtel), softened

½ cup shredded carrot

⅓ cup crumbled blue cheese

⅓ cup thinly sliced green onion

⅓ cup fine dry bread crumbs

¼ cup fat-free or light dairy sour cream

⅛ teaspoon black pepper

2 tablespoons chopped walnuts

Snipped fresh parsley (optional)

Blue Cheese-Stuffed Summer Squash

PREP: 25 minutes **BAKE:** 20 minutes
OVEN: 400°F

NUTRITION FACTS per serving:

CALORIES 107
TOTAL FAT 6 g (3 g sat. fat)
CHOLESTEROL 15 mg
PROTEIN 5 g
CARBOHYDRATE 8 g
FIBER 1 g
SODIUM 179 mg

EXCHANGES 0.5 Medium-Fat Meat, 1 Vegetable, 1 Fat

1 Preheat oven to 400°F. Grease a 3-quart rectangular baking dish; set aside.

2 Halve the squash lengthwise. Remove seeds from each squash half with a spoon, leaving a shell about ¼ inch thick. Place squash halves, cut sides down, in prepared baking dish. Bake, uncovered, for 10 minutes. Turn squash halves cut sides up.

3 Meanwhile, in a medium bowl stir together cream cheese, shredded carrot, blue cheese, green onion, ¼ cup bread crumbs, sour cream, and pepper. (Mixture will be stiff.)

4 Spoon cream cheese mixture evenly into squash halves. Sprinkle with walnuts and remaining bread crumbs. Bake, uncovered, about 10 minutes or until squash is tender and filling is heated through. If desired, sprinkle with parsley. Makes 8 servings.

> ### COOK'S TIP
> Summer squash is perishable and should be refrigerated tightly covered in a bag for no more than four days.

On the opener: Guacamole-Stuffed Tomatoes (*see recipe, page 216*)

- 2 tablespoons tub-style light cream cheese spread with garden vegetables
- 2 tablespoons light mayonnaise or salad dressing
- 1 teaspoon apple cider vinegar
- ¼ teaspoon black pepper
- 1 9-ounce package refrigerated cooked chicken breast strips, cut into bite-size pieces
- ½ cup chopped celery
- ¼ cup dried cranberries
- 3 medium apples, cored and thinly sliced

1 For chicken salad, in a medium bowl combine cream cheese, mayonnaise, vinegar, and pepper. Stir in chicken breast, celery, and dried cranberries. Serve with apple slices. Makes 6 servings.

Make-Ahead Directions: Prepare as above in step 1. Cover and chill for up to 24 hours. Serve as above.

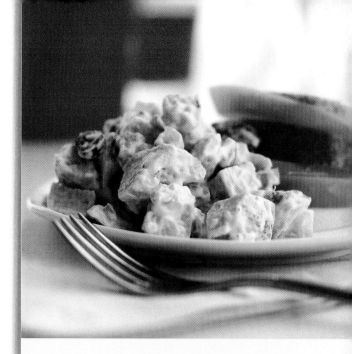

Chicken Salad with Apple Slices

START TO FINISH: 15 minutes

NUTRITION FACTS per serving:

CALORIES 125
TOTAL FAT 3 g (1 g sat. fat)
CHOLESTEROL 27 mg
PROTEIN 12 g
CARBOHYDRATE 15 g
FIBER 2 g
SODIUM 201 mg

EXCHANGES 1 Fruit, 1.5 Very Lean Meat, 0.5 Fat

1 3-ounce can chunk white tuna (water pack), drained and broken into chunks
½ cup seedless red grapes, halved
¼ cup finely chopped red onion
2 tablespoons light mayonnaise or salad dressing
2 cloves garlic, minced
¼ teaspoon black pepper
⅛ teaspoon salt
3 large celery stalks, ends trimmed

1 In a medium bowl combine tuna, grapes, red onion, mayonnaise, garlic, pepper, and salt.

2 To serve, cut each celery stalk crosswise into four pieces. Serve tuna mixture with celery pieces. Makes 4 servings.

Make-Ahead Directions: Prepare as above in step 1. Cover and chill for up to 24 hours. Serve as above.

COOK'S TIP

For the equivalent of two cloves of fresh garlic minced, use a teaspoon of prepared minced garlic.

Inside-Out Tuna Salad Snack

START TO FINISH: 15 minutes

NUTRITION FACTS per serving:
- -

CALORIES 76
TOTAL FAT 3 g (1 g sat. fat)
CHOLESTEROL 12 mg
PROTEIN 6 g
CARBOHYDRATE 6 g
FIBER 1 g
SODIUM 237 mg

EXCHANGES 0.5 Very Lean Meat, 0.5 Vegetable, 0.5 Fat

- 4 slices reduced-sodium bacon
- ¼ cup light dairy sour cream
- 2 tablespoons light mayonnaise or salad dressing
- 1½ teaspoons white vinegar
- 1 teaspoon sugar
- ⅛ teaspoon salt
- ⅛ teaspoon black pepper
- 1 medium tomato, seeded and chopped
- 8 leaves butterhead (Boston or Bibb) lettuce (about 1 small head)

1 Line a microwave-safe plate with a microwave-safe paper towel. Arrange bacon on the paper towel. Cover bacon with another microwave-safe paper towel. Microwave on 100% power (high) for 3 to 4 minutes or until bacon is crisp. Cool bacon; crumble and set aside.

2 In a small bowl combine sour cream, mayonnaise, vinegar, sugar, salt, and pepper. Gently stir in tomato and crumbled bacon.

3 To serve, spoon a scant 2 tablespoons bacon mixture on each lettuce leaf; roll up. Makes 4 (2-wrap) servings.

Make-Ahead Directions: Prepare as above through step 2. Cover and chill for up to 6 hours. Serve as above.

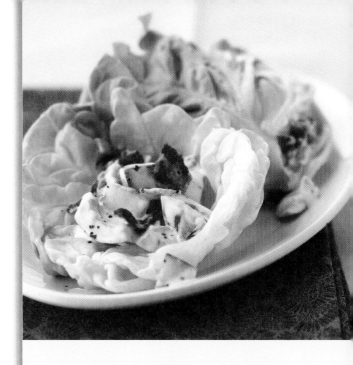

Bacon-Tomato Lettuce Wraps

START TO FINISH: 15 minutes

NUTRITION FACTS per serving:

- -

CALORIES 88
TOTAL FAT 7 g (2 g sat. fat)
CHOLESTEROL 12 mg
PROTEIN 4 g
CARBOHYDRATE 4 g
FIBER 1 g
SODIUM 228 mg

EXCHANGES 1 Vegetable, 1.5 Fat

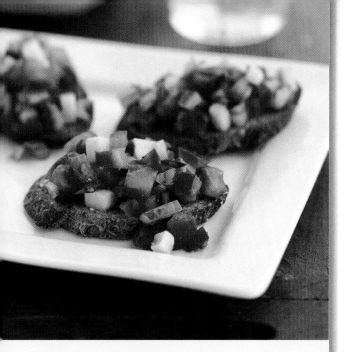

2	medium tomatoes, seeded and chopped
⅓	cup reduced-fat mozzarella cheese cut into small cubes
¼	cup finely chopped red onion
2	tablespoons shredded fresh basil
2	teaspoons olive oil
1	teaspoon balsamic vinegar
¼	teaspoon salt
¼	teaspoon black pepper
12	slices whole grain baguette, toasted

1 In a medium bowl combine chopped tomatoes, mozzarella cheese, red onion, basil, oil, balsamic vinegar, salt, and pepper. Serve immediately or cover and chill for up to 24 hours. Serve on toasted baguette slices. Makes 4 servings.

Caprese Bruschetta

START TO FINISH: 20 minutes

NUTRITION FACTS per serving:

- -

CALORIES 163
TOTAL FAT 5 g (1 g sat. fat)
CHOLESTEROL 5 mg
PROTEIN 10 g
CARBOHYDRATE 22 g
FIBER 6 g
SODIUM 334 mg

EXCHANGES 1.5 Starch, 0.5 Medium-Fat Meat, 0.5 Vegetable

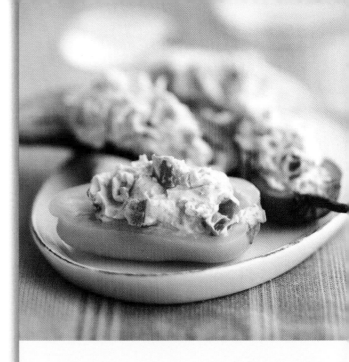

12 fresh jalapeño chile peppers* and/
    or miniature sweet peppers

1   8-ounce package reduced-fat
    cream cheese (Neufchâtel),
    softened

2   green onions, thinly sliced

½   to 1 canned chipotle chile pepper
    in adobo sauce, finely chopped*

⅛   teaspoon salt

⅛   teaspoon black pepper

1   small tomato, seeded and chopped

1 Cut the jalapeño chile peppers or miniature sweet peppers in half lengthwise. Remove pepper seeds and ribs. Set aside.

2 In a medium bowl stir together cream cheese, green onion, chipotle pepper, salt, and black pepper. Gently stir in tomato.

3 To serve, spoon cream cheese mixture into pepper halves. Makes 6 servings (4 pepper halves per serving).

*Because chile peppers contain volatile oils that can burn your skin and eyes, avoid direct contact with them as much as possible. When working with chile peppers, wear plastic or rubber gloves. If your bare hands do touch the peppers, wash your hands and nails well with soap and warm water.

Make-Ahead Directions: Prepare as above through step 2. Cover and chill for up to 24 hours. Serve as above.

Creamy Stuffed Peppers

START TO FINISH: 20 minutes

NUTRITION FACTS per serving:

CALORIES 111
TOTAL FAT 9 g (6 g sat. fat)
CHOLESTEROL 29 mg
PROTEIN 5 g
CARBOHYDRATE 4 g
FIBER 1 g
SODIUM 205 mg

EXCHANGES 1 Medium-Fat Meat, 0.5 Vegetable, 1 Fat

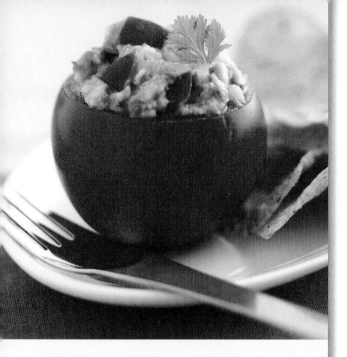

Guacamole-Stuffed Tomatoes

START TO FINISH: 20 minutes

NUTRITION FACTS per serving:

- -

CALORIES 164
TOTAL FAT 10 g (1 g sat. fat)
CHOLESTEROL 0 mg
PROTEIN 7 g
CARBOHYDRATE 19 g
FIBER 5 g
SODIUM 152 mg

EXCHANGES 1 Starch, 1 Vegetable, 2 Fat

4 medium tomatoes
(about 6 ounces each)
1 ripe avocado, halved, seeded,
peeled, and chopped
1 tablespoon finely chopped onion
2 teaspoons snipped fresh cilantro
2 teaspoons lemon juice
1 clove garlic, minced
⅛ teaspoon salt
Fresh cilantro leaves (optional)
2 ounces multigrain tortilla chips

1 Cut a ¼-inch-thick slice from the stem end of each tomato. Using a spoon, carefully scoop out the tomato pulp, leaving a ¼- to ½-inch-thick shell. Discard seeds. Set tomatoes, cut sides down, on paper towels until ready to stuff. Chop enough tomato pulp to measure ⅓ cup; discard remaining pulp.

2 In a medium bowl mash avocado slightly; stir in chopped tomato pulp, onion, snipped cilantro, lemon juice, garlic, and salt. Stuff avocado mixture evenly into tomato shells. If desired, garnish with fresh cilantro leaves. Serve with tortilla chips. Makes 4 servings.

COOK'S TIP

To get juice flowing from a lemon, press on the fruit and roll it a few times on a hard surface. Getting the juice you need should be simple. If the lemon is still stubborn, warm it in the microwave for 15 seconds.

2	cloves garlic
2	tablespoons fresh parsley leaves
4	teaspoons fresh oregano leaves or ½ teaspoon dried oregano, crushed
1	15-ounce can garbanzo beans (chickpeas) or cannellini beans (white kidney beans), rinsed and drained
2	tablespoons light dairy sour cream
1	tablespoon lemon juice
¼	teaspoon ground black pepper
¼	teaspoon bottled hot pepper sauce
18	slices whole wheat baguette, toasted

1 In a food processor combine garlic, parsley, and oregano; cover and process with several on/off turns until finely chopped. Add garbanzo beans, sour cream, lemon juice, black pepper, and hot pepper sauce. Cover and process until blended. Transfer to serving bowl.

2 Serve with toasted baguette slices. Makes 6 servings (about 3 tablespoons spread and 3 baguette slices per serving).

Make-Ahead Directions: Prepare as above in step 1. Cover and chill for up to 24 hours. Serve as above.

Herby Garbanzo Bean Spread on Toast

START TO FINISH: 15 minutes

NUTRITION FACTS per serving:

- -

CALORIES 187
TOTAL FAT 3 g (1 g sat. fat)
CHOLESTEROL 1 mg
PROTEIN 9 g
CARBOHYDRATE 33 g
FIBER 6 g
SODIUM 394 mg

EXCHANGES 2 Starch, 0.5 Fat

1 ripe avocado, halved, seeded, and peeled

1 tablespoon lemon juice or lime juice

½ cup light dairy sour cream

1 clove garlic, minced

⅛ teaspoon salt

4 medium sweet peppers, seeded and cut into strips

1 In a medium bowl use a fork to mash avocado with lemon juice. Stir in sour cream, garlic, and salt. Serve with sweet pepper strips. Makes 8 servings (2 tablespoons dip and half a sweet pepper per serving).

Make-Ahead Directions: Prepare as above in step 1. Cover the surface of the dip with plastic wrap and chill for up to 4 hours. Serve as above.

Lemony Avocado Dip

START TO FINISH: 15 minutes

NUTRITION FACTS per serving:

CALORIES 61
TOTAL FAT 4 g (1 g sat. fat)
CHOLESTEROL 4 mg
PROTEIN 1 g
CARBOHYDRATE 6 g
FIBER 2 g
SODIUM 49 mg

EXCHANGES 1 Vegetable, 1 Fat

NUTRITION NOTE

An avocado spread makes a great substitute for mayo-based spreads on sandwiches and wraps. The avocado spread adds moistness, flavor, and heart-healthy monounsaturated fat.

1 cup round toasted oat cereal with nuts and honey

¾ cup bite-size whole grain fish-shape cheddar cheese crackers

½ cup honey wheat braided pretzel twists, broken into bite-size pieces

½ cup semisweet or dark chocolate pieces

1 In a large bowl combine cereal, crackers, pretzels, and chocolate pieces. Makes 6 (½-cup) servings.

Sweet 'n' Salty Snack Mix

START TO FINISH: 5 minutes

NUTRITION FACTS per serving:
- -

CALORIES 129
TOTAL FAT 6 g (3 g sat. fat)
CHOLESTEROL 2 mg
PROTEIN 2 g
CARBOHYDRATE 20 g
FIBER 1 g
SODIUM 146 mg

EXCHANGES 1 Starch, 1 Fat

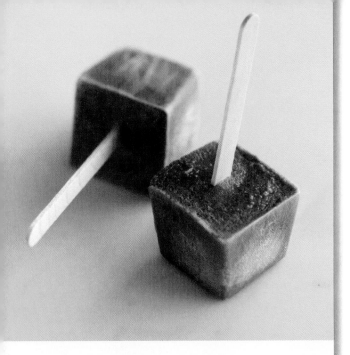

Mocha Frappuccino Pops

PREP: 10 minutes

FREEZE: 4 hours

NUTRITION FACTS per pop:

CALORIES 21
TOTAL FAT 0 g (0 g sat. fat)
CHOLESTEROL 1 mg
PROTEIN 0 g
CARBOHYDRATE 4 g
FIBER 0 g
SODIUM 28 mg

EXCHANGES Free

3   cups brewed coffee, chilled
¾   cup fat-free half-and-half
½   cup reduced-calorie or sugar-free
      chocolate-flavored syrup
15   3-ounce frozen pop molds or
      3-ounce plastic cups
15   wooden craft sticks or
      plastic spoons (optional)

1 In a medium bowl combine coffee and half-and-half. Whisk in chocolate syrup until well mixed.

2 Pour coffee mixture into frozen pop molds; cover. (Or pour into plastic cups. Cover cups with foil. With a sharp knife make a slit in each of the foil tops. Insert sticks or spoons into the slits for handles.) Freeze about 4 hours or until firm. Makes 15 pops.

- 1 cup frozen unsweetened whole strawberries
- 1 cup cut-up cantaloupe
- ⅓ cup orange juice
- ¼ cup fat-free milk
- 1 tablespoon honey
- 1 cup calorie-free citrus-flavored sparkling water
- 12 3-ounce frozen pop molds or 3-ounce plastic cups
- 12 wooden craft sticks or plastic spoons (optional)

1 In a blender combine strawberries, cantaloupe, orange juice, milk, and honey. Cover and blend until smooth. Stir in sparkling water.

2 Pour melon mixture into frozen pop molds; cover. (Or pour into plastic cups. Cover cups with foil. With a sharp knife make a slit in each of the foil tops. Insert sticks or spoons into the slits for handles.) Freeze about 4 hours or until firm. Makes 12 pops.

COOK'S TIP

For a fun summer treat pour the melon mixture into ice cube trays. Once frozen, put a generous amount of melon-berry cubes in a glass; top with sparkling water or orange juice for a healthful cool refresher.

Melon-Berry Smoothie Pops

PREP: 20 minutes

FREEZE: 4 hours

NUTRITION FACTS per pop:
- -

CALORIES 18 cal
TOTAL FAT 0 g (0 g sat. fat)
CHOLESTEROL 0 mg
PROTEIN 0 g
CARBOHYDRATE 4 g
FIBER 0 g
SODIUM 5 mg

EXCHANGES Free

2 cups fat-free milk

1 medium banana, sliced and frozen*

3 tablespoons unsweetened cocoa powder

2 tablespoons honey

1 teaspoon vanilla

1 In a blender combine milk, frozen banana, cocoa powder, honey, and vanilla. Cover and blend until smooth and frothy. Makes 4 (about 8-ounce) servings.

*Peel and slice banana. Place banana slices in a single layer on a baking sheet lined with plastic wrap. Freeze about 1 hour or until firm.

Chocolate-Banana Sipper

START TO FINISH: 5 minutes

NUTRITION FACTS per serving:

CALORIES 120
TOTAL FAT 1 g (0 g sat. fat)
CHOLESTEROL 2 mg
PROTEIN 5 g
CARBOHYDRATE 23 g
FIBER 1 g
SODIUM 52 mg

EXCHANGES 0.5 Other Carbohydrates, 0.5 Fruit, 0.5 Milk

- 1 2-quart-size envelope low-calorie lemonade-flavor soft drink mix
- 5 cups water
- 8 medium fresh strawberries, hulled and quartered
- 1 2-quart-size envelope low-calorie cherry- or raspberry-flavor soft drink mix
- 1 1-liter bottle club soda, chilled
  Ice cubes

1 In a 2-quart pitcher stir together lemonade drink mix and water. Place one strawberry quarter in each of 32 compartments of ice cube trays; fill trays with 3 cups of lemonade mixture. Freeze about 4 hours or until solid.

2 Stir cherry or raspberry drink mix into remaining lemonade mixture in pitcher. Cover and chill until serving time.

3 To serve, slowly pour club soda into lemonade mixture in pitcher. Put four ice cubes in each of eight glasses. Pour lemonade mixture into glasses. Makes 8 (6-ounce) servings.

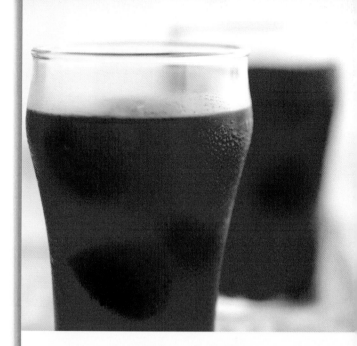

Sparkling Berry Lemonade

PREP: 15 minutes

FREEZE: 4 hours

NUTRITION FACTS per serving:

CALORIES 4
TOTAL FAT 0 g (0 g sat. fat)
CHOLESTEROL 0 mg
PROTEIN 0 g
CARBOHYDRATE 1 g
FIBER 0 g
SODIUM 31 mg

EXCHANGES Free

1   2-quart-size envelope low-calorie cherry- or punch-flavored soft drink mix

1   cup orange juice

1   2-liter bottle carbonated water, chilled

    Ice cubes

1 In a large pitcher combine drink mix and orange juice. Add carbonated water. Stir to dissolve drink mix. Serve immediately over ice cubes. Makes 10 to 12 (about 6-ounce) servings.

To make 1 serving: Stir together drink mix and orange juice and keep in a covered container in the refrigerator for up to 1 week. Add 4 to 5 teaspoons orange juice mixture to ¾ to 1 cup carbonated water; stir to combine. Serve over ice cubes.

Cherry-Citrus Cooler

START TO FINISH: 10 minutes

NUTRITION FACTS per serving:

CALORIES 11
TOTAL FAT 0 g (0 g sat. fat)
CHOLESTEROL 0 mg
PROTEIN 0 g
CARBOHYDRATE 3 g
FIBER 0 g
SODIUM 43 mg

EXCHANGES Free

Chapter 14

Desserts

On the opener: Piled-High Shortcake (*see recipe, page 236*)

- 1¼ cups rolled oats
- 1 cup all-purpose flour
- ½ teaspoon baking powder
- ½ teaspoon baking soda
- 4 ounces soft silken-style tofu (fresh bean curd)
- 2 tablespoons butter, softened
- ½ cup granulated sugar
- ½ cup packed brown sugar
- ¼ cup canola oil
- ½ teaspoon vanilla
- 4 ounces dark chocolate chunks or bittersweet chocolate pieces

1 Preheat oven to 375°F. Place oats in a food processor or blender. Cover and process or blend until oats resemble coarse flour. In a medium bowl stir together oats, flour, baking powder, and baking soda. Set aside. Place tofu in food processor or blender. Cover and process or blend until smooth. Set aside.

2 In a large bowl beat butter with an electric mixer on medium to high speed for 30 seconds. Add tofu; beat until combined, scraping side of bowl occasionally. Add granulated sugar and brown sugar; beat until combined. Beat in oil and vanilla. Beat in as much of the flour mixture as you can with the mixer. Using a wooden spoon, stir in any remaining flour mixture. Stir in chocolate.

3 Drop dough by rounded teaspoons 2 inches apart onto an ungreased cookie sheet. Bake for 8 to 10 minutes or until edges are golden brown. Transfer cookies to a wire rack; cool. Makes about 24 cookies.

Chocolate Chunk Cookies

PREP: 30 minutes

BAKE: 8 minutes per batch

OVEN: 375°F

NUTRITION FACTS per cookie:

CALORIES 125
TOTAL FAT 5 g (1 g sat. fat)
CHOLESTEROL 3 mg
PROTEIN 1 g
CARBOHYDRATE 18 g
FIBER 1 g
SODIUM 40 mg

EXCHANGES 1 Other Carbohydrates, 1 Fat

COOK'S TIP

Adding tofu to cookies may seem odd. With its bland flavor, versatile tofu takes on the flavors of the other ingredients in a recipe. It can add nutrition to beverages, baked goods, dressings, soups, spreads, and casseroles.

½ cup butter, softened

¼ cup packed brown sugar

1 teaspoon baking powder

¼ teaspoon baking soda

¼ teaspoon salt

¼ teaspoon ground cinnamon

2 eggs, lightly beaten

¼ cup honey

½ teaspoon vanilla

1¼ cups all-purpose flour

1 cup white whole wheat flour or whole wheat flour

½ cup miniature semisweet chocolate pieces

3 ounces bittersweet chocolate or ½ cup miniature semisweet chocolate pieces

½ teaspoon shortening

Chocolate-Drizzled Graham Cookies

PREP: 30 minutes   **BAKE:** 8 minutes per batch
STAND: 30 minutes   **OVEN:** 375°F

NUTRITION FACTS per cookie:

- -

CALORIES 68
TOTAL FAT 3 g (2 g sat. fat)
CHOLESTEROL 14 mg
PROTEIN 1 g
CARBOHYDRATE 9 g
FIBER 1 g
SODIUM 41 mg

EXCHANGES 0.5 Other Carbohydrates, 0.5 Fat

1 Preheat oven to 375°F. In a large bowl beat butter with an electric mixer on medium to high speed for 30 seconds. Add brown sugar, baking powder, baking soda, salt, and cinnamon. Beat until light and fluffy, scraping side of bowl occasionally.

2 Beat in eggs, honey, and vanilla until combined. Beat in as much of the all-purpose flour and the whole wheat flour as you can with the mixer. Using a wooden spoon, stir in any remaining flour. Stir in ½ cup semisweet chocolate pieces.

3 Shape dough into 1-inch balls. Place balls 1 inch apart on an ungreased cookie sheet. Flatten slightly. Bake for 8 to 9 minutes or until bottoms are lightly browned. Transfer cookies to a wire rack; cool.

4 In a small saucepan combine bittersweet chocolate and shortening; heat over low heat until melted and smooth, stirring often. Cool slightly. Transfer melted chocolate mixture to a small resealable plastic bag; seal bag. Snip a small hole in one corner of the bag; pipe chocolate on tops of cookies. Let stand about 30 minutes or until set. Makes about 48 cookies.

Chocolate-Chocolate-Drizzled Graham Cookies: Prepare as above, except add ¼ cup unsweetened cocoa powder with the all-purpose flour.

Nutrition Facts per cookie: 70 cal., 3 g total fat (2 g sat. fat), 14 mg chol., 41 mg sodium, 9 g carbo., 1 g fiber, 1 g pro.
Exchanges: 0.5 Other Carbohydrates, 0.5 Fat

COOK'S TIP

Honey will crystallize and harden when refrigerated and when exposed to air. Store it, tightly sealed, in a cool, dry area. If honey crystallizes, place it in warm water or microwave it for only a few seconds until it turns to liquid.

- ¼ cup butter, softened
- ½ cup packed brown sugar
- ½ teaspoon baking powder
- ¼ teaspoon ground cinnamon or ground cardamom
- ⅛ teaspoon baking soda
- 2 egg whites
- ½ teaspoon vanilla
- ½ cup all-purpose flour
- ¼ cup white whole wheat flour or whole wheat flour
- 1 cup quick-cooking rolled oats
- 1 egg white
- ¾ cup finely chopped walnuts and/or pecans
- ¼ cup low-sugar strawberry, apricot, and/or red raspberry preserves

Walnut-Crusted Oatmeal-Raspberry Thumbprints

1 In a large bowl beat butter with an electric mixer on medium to high speed for 30 seconds. Add brown sugar, baking powder, cinnamon, and baking soda. Beat until combined, scraping side of bowl occasionally. Beat in 2 egg whites and vanilla until combined. Beat in as much of the all-purpose flour and whole wheat flour as you can with the mixer. Using a wooden spoon, stir in any remaining flour and oats. Cover and chill dough about 2 hours or until easy to handle.

2 Preheat oven to 375°F. Lightly grease two large cookie sheets or line with parchment paper. Shape dough into ¾-inch balls. In a small bowl lightly beat 1 egg white; roll dough balls in egg white. Roll in nuts to coat. Place on prepared cookie sheets. Using your thumb, make an indentation in the center of each cookie.

3 Bake for 7 to 8 minutes or until edges are golden brown. If indentations puff during baking, gently press the back of a measuring teaspoon into indentations when cookies are removed from oven. Cool cookies on cookie sheet for 1 minute. Transfer to a wire rack; cool.

4 Just before serving, spoon preserves into indentations in cookies. Makes about 36 cookies.

PREP: 30 minutes   **CHILL:** 2 hours
BAKE: 7 minutes per batch   **COOL:** 1 minute
OVEN: 375°F

NUTRITION FACTS per cookie:

CALORIES 61
TOTAL FAT 3 g (1 g sat. fat)
CHOLESTEROL 3 mg
PROTEIN 1 g
CARBOHYDRATE 8 g
FIBER 1 g
SODIUM 23 mg

EXCHANGES 0.5 Other Carbohydrates, 0.5 Fat

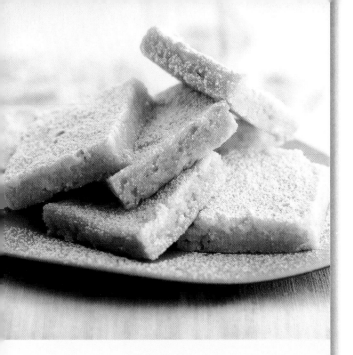

Nonstick cooking spray

¾ cup all-purpose flour

¼ cup granulated sugar

Dash salt

¼ cup butter

2 eggs, beaten

¾ cup granulated sugar

2 tablespoons all-purpose flour

1 teaspoon finely shredded lemon peel

⅓ cup lemon juice

⅓ cup fat-free half-and-half

Powdered sugar (optional)

Lemon Bars

PREP: 30 minutes **BAKE:** 40 minutes

OVEN: 350°F

NUTRITION FACTS per bar:

- -

CALORIES 113

TOTAL FAT 4 g (2 g sat. fat)

CHOLESTEROL 34 mg

PROTEIN 1 g

CARBOHYDRATE 19 g

FIBER 0 g

SODIUM 44 mg

EXCHANGES 1 Other Carbohydrates, 1 Fat

1 Preheat oven to 350°F. Coat an 8×8×2-inch baking pan with nonstick cooking spray; set aside. In a small bowl combine ¾ cup flour, ¼ cup granulated sugar, and salt. Using a pastry blender, cut in butter until crumbly. Using the back of a large spoon, pat mixture into prepared baking pan. Bake for 15 minutes.

2 Meanwhile, for filling, in a medium bowl stir together eggs, ¾ cup granulated sugar, and 2 tablespoons flour. Stir in lemon peel, lemon juice, and half-and-half. Pour filling over hot crust. Bake about 25 minutes more or until surface is set. Cool in pan on a wire rack.

3 If desired, sift powdered sugar over cooled recipe. Cut into bars. Cover and store in the refrigerator. Makes 16 bars.

Nonstick cooking spray

¾ cup all-purpose flour

¼ cup whole wheat flour

½ cup sugar or sugar substitute*
  equivalent to ½ cup sugar

1½ teaspoons pumpkin pie spice

1 teaspoon baking powder

⅛ teaspoon salt

1 cup finely shredded carrot

¾ cup chopped walnuts or pecans,
  toasted

1 egg, lightly beaten

¼ cup cooking oil

¼ cup fat-free milk

1 recipe Fluffy
  Cream Cheese Frosting

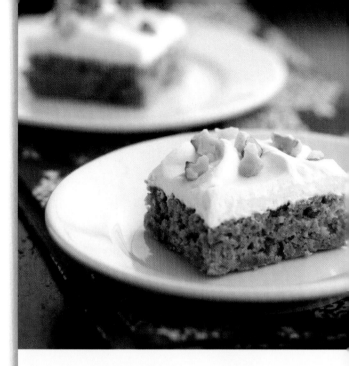

1 Preheat oven to 350°F. Line a 9×9×2-inch baking pan with foil, extending foil over the edges of the pan. Lightly coat foil with nonstick cooking spray. Set aside.

2 In a medium bowl combine all-purpose flour, whole wheat flour, sugar, pumpkin pie spice, baking powder, and salt. Add carrot, ½ cup nuts, egg, oil, and milk. Stir just until combined. Spread mixture evenly in the prepared pan.

3 Bake for 15 to 18 minutes or until a toothpick inserted near center comes out clean. Cool bars in pan on a wire rack.

4 Using the edges of the foil, lift uncut bars out of the pan. Spread top evenly with Fluffy Cream Cheese Frosting. Sprinkle with remaining ¼ cup nuts. Cut into 20 bars. Store, covered, in refrigerator. Makes 20 bars.

*Sugar Substitute: Choose Sweet'N Low bulk or packets. Follow package directions to use product amount equivalent to ½ cup sugar.

Per serving with substitute: same as above, except 102 cal., 7 g carbo.
Exchanges: 0.5 Other Carbohydrates

Nutty Carrot Cake Cheesecake Bars

PREP: 25 minutes   **BAKE:** 15 minutes
OVEN: 350°F

NUTRITION FACTS per bar:

- -

CALORIES 123
TOTAL FAT 8 g (2 g sat. fat)
CHOLESTEROL 15 mg
PROTEIN 3 g
CARBOHYDRATE 12 g
FIBER 1 g
SODIUM 60 mg

EXCHANGES 1 Other Carbohydrates, 1 Fat

Fluffy Cream Cheese Frosting: Thaw ½ cup frozen light whipped topping. In a medium bowl beat half of an 8-ounce package reduced-fat cream cheese (Neufchâtel), softened, with an electric mixer on medium speed until smooth. Beat in ¼ cup vanilla low-fat yogurt until smooth. Fold whipped topping into cream cheese mixture.

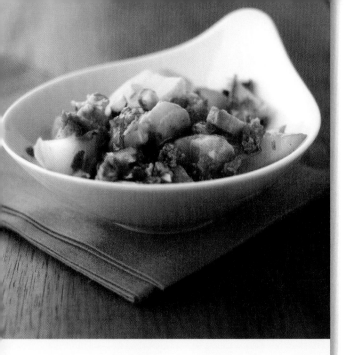

Pear-Rhubarb Crisp

PREP: 25 minutes   **BAKE:** 40 minutes
COOL: 30 minutes   **OVEN:** 375°F

NUTRITION FACTS per serving:

CALORIES 169
TOTAL FAT 5 g (2 g sat. fat)
CHOLESTEROL 7 mg
PROTEIN 2 g
CARBOHYDRATE 32 g
FIBER 4 g
SODIUM 55 mg

EXCHANGES 0.5 Starch, 0.5 Other
Carbohydrates, 1 Fruit, 1 Fat

4	medium Bartlett pears or cooking apples (such as Rome, Braeburn, or Jonathan), cored and thinly sliced
2	cups sliced fresh rhubarb or frozen unsweetened sliced rhubarb*
¼	cup all-purpose flour
½	teaspoon ground nutmeg
¼	cup honey
2	tablespoons apple juice or apple cider
1	cup oat square cereal, crushed
¼	cup whole bran cereal, crushed
¼	cup chopped almonds or pecans
2	tablespoons butter, melted
1	tablespoon honey
	Honey (optional)

1 Preheat oven to 375°F. In a large bowl combine pear or apple slices, rhubarb, flour, and nutmeg. Add ¼ cup honey and apple juice; toss gently to coat. Transfer fruit mixture to a 2-quart square baking dish. Cover and bake for 30 to 40 minutes or just until pear or apple slices are tender.

2 Meanwhile, for topping, in a medium bowl combine crushed cereals and nuts. Add butter and 1 tablespoon honey; toss to coat. Sprinkle over partially baked fruit mixture. Bake, uncovered, about 10 minutes more or until fruit is very tender and topping is lightly browned.

3 Cool on a wire rack for 30 minutes. Serve warm. If desired, drizzle with additional honey. Makes 9 servings.

*If using frozen rhubarb, measure while still frozen. Allow rhubarb to thaw in a large bowl 1 hour or until the fruit is partially thawed but still icy; do not drain rhubarb. Continue as above.

- ⅓ cup sugar or sugar substitute* equivalent to ⅓ cup sugar
- 2 tablespoons cornstarch
- ½ teaspoon ground cinnamon
- 10 cups sliced, pitted, peeled fresh peaches (3½ to 4 pounds) or 10 cups frozen unsweetened peach slices, thawed
- ½ cup water
- 1¼ cups whole wheat flour
- 2 tablespoons sugar or sugar substitute* equivalent to 2 tablespoons sugar
- ¾ teaspoon baking powder
- ¼ teaspoon baking soda
- ¼ teaspoon salt
- ¼ cup butter
- ½ cup buttermilk
- 4 cups vanilla frozen yogurt (optional)

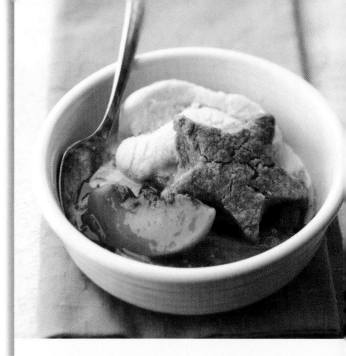

Old-Fashioned Peach Cobbler

PREP: 30 minutes **BAKE:** 25 minutes
COOL: 30 minutes **OVEN:** 400°F

NUTRITION FACTS per serving:

CALORIES 175
TOTAL FAT 4 g (3 g sat. fat)
CHOLESTEROL 11 mg
PROTEIN 3 g
CARBOHYDRATE 34 g
FIBER 4 g
SODIUM 129 mg

EXCHANGES 1 Other Carbohydrates, 1 Fruit, 1 Fat

1 Preheat oven to 400°F. For filling, in a very large bowl stir together ⅓ cup sugar, cornstarch, and cinnamon; add peaches and toss gently to mix. Gently stir in water. Spread fruit mixture evenly in a 3-quart rectangular baking dish. Set aside.

2 For topping, in a medium bowl stir together whole wheat flour, 2 tablespoons sugar, baking powder, baking soda, and salt. Using a pastry blender, cut in butter until mixture resembles coarse crumbs. Make a well in the center of the flour mixture. Add buttermilk all at once. Using a fork, stir just until moistened. Knead mixture gently to shape into a ball.

3 On a lightly floured surface, roll dough to ½-inch thickness. Using a 2- to 2½-inch star cookie cutter, cut out 12 stars, rerolling dough as needed. Arrange stars on fruit mixture.

4 Bake for 25 to 30 minutes or until stars are lightly browned and fruit mixture is bubbly in the center. Cool on a wire rack for 30 minutes. Serve warm. If desired, serve with frozen yogurt. Makes 12 servings.

***Sugar Substitutes:** Choose from Splenda granular or Sweet'N Low bulk or packets. Follow package directions to use product amounts equivalent to ⅓ cup and 2 tablespoons sugar.

Per serving with substitute: same as above, except 147 cal., 28 carbo.
Exchanges: 0.5 Other Carbohydrates

COOK'S TIP

An easy way to peel a peach is to blanch it in boiling water for 30 seconds, then plunge it into ice water. Drain off the water, then pull off the skins using a paring knife if necessary.

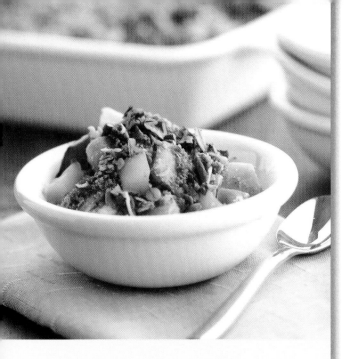

Nonstick cooking spray
- ¾ cup all-purpose flour
- ¾ cup rolled oats
- ½ cup toasted wheat germ
- ½ cup packed brown sugar or brown sugar substitute*
- 1½ teaspoons ground cinnamon
- ¼ cup canola oil
- 4 Granny Smith apples
- 2 red sweet apples (such as Gala, Fuji, or Rome Beauty)
- 3 tablespoons lime juice
- 2 medium mangoes, seeded, peeled, and chopped
- ⅓ cup chopped pecans

Frozen light whipped dessert topping, thawed, or low-fat vanilla frozen yogurt (optional)

Apple-Mango Crisp

PREP: 25 minutes   **BAKE:** 40 minutes
OVEN: 375°F

NUTRITION FACTS per serving:

CALORIES 169
TOTAL FAT 6 g (1 g sat. fat)
CHOLESTEROL 0 mg
PROTEIN 4 g
CARBOHYDRATE 28 g
FIBER 3 g
SODIUM 4 mg

EXCHANGES 1 Other Carbohydrates, 1 Fruit, 1 Fat

NUTRITION NOTE

Apples contain pectin, a soluble fiber that slows the digestion of complex carbohydrates. It helps you feel full longer.

1 Preheat oven to 375°F. Coat two 1½- or 2-quart baking dishes or a 3-quart rectangular baking dish with nonstick cooking spray.

2 In a medium bowl stir together ½ cup flour, oats, wheat germ, brown sugar, and cinnamon. Stir in oil; set aside.

3 Core apples; chop apples and place in a very large bowl. Sprinkle chopped apples with lime juice; stir. Stir in remaining ¼ cup flour. Fold in chopped mangoes.

4 Place apple-mango mixture in the prepared baking dish(es). Evenly sprinkle flour-oat mixture over fruit. Bake, uncovered, for 30 minutes. Sprinkle with pecans; bake for 10 to 15 minutes more or until apples are tender. Cool slightly. Serve warm. If desired, top individual servings with whipped topping.
Makes 16 servings.

*****Sugar Substitutes:** Choose from Sweet'N Low Brown or Sugar Twin Granulated Brown. Follow package directions to use product amount equivalent to ½ cup brown sugar.

Per serving with substitute: same as above, except 158 cal., 25 g carbo., 2 mg sodium
Exchanges: 0.5 Other Carbohydrates

Nonstick cooking spray

- 1 cup all-purpose flour
- 2 tablespoons packed brown sugar or brown sugar substitute* equivalent to 2 tablespoons brown sugar
- 1½ teaspoons finely snipped crystallized ginger or ½ teaspoon ground ginger
- 1 teaspoon baking powder
- ⅛ teaspoon baking soda
- 2 tablespoons butter
- ½ cup buttermilk or sour fat-free milk**
- ¾ cup frozen fat-free whipped dessert topping, thawed
- ¼ cup fat-free dairy sour cream
- ¼ teaspoon ground ginger
- 1 cup chopped fresh strawberries and/or small fresh blueberries

Finely snipped crystallized ginger (optional)

1 Preheat oven to 450°F. Lightly coat a baking sheet with nonstick cooking spray; set aside. In a medium bowl combine flour, brown sugar, 1½ teaspoons crystallized ginger or ½ teaspoon ground ginger, baking powder, and baking soda. Using a pastry blender, cut in butter until mixture resembles coarse crumbs. Make a well in the center of flour mixture. Add buttermilk all at once. Using a fork, stir just until moistened.

2 Drop dough by slightly rounded tablespoons into 12 mounds on the prepared baking sheet. Bake for 8 to 10 minutes or until lightly golden and a toothpick inserted into centers comes out clean. Cool on a wire rack.

3 In a medium bowl combine whipped topping, sour cream, and ¼ teaspoon ground ginger. Set aside ⅓ cup of the topping mixture. Fold the berries into remaining topping mixture.

4 Split shortcakes in half horizontally. Spoon berry mixture onto bottom halves of shortcakes. Add tops; dollop with reserved topping mixture. If desired, garnish with additional snipped crystallized ginger. Makes 12 bites.

*Sugar Substitutes: Choose from Sweet'N Low Brown or Sugar Twin Granulated Brown. Follow package directions to use product amount equivalent to 2 tablespoons brown sugar.

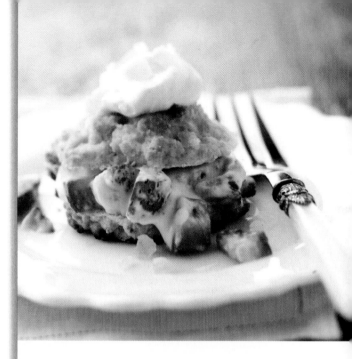

Gingered Shortcake Bites

PREP: 25 minutes   **BAKE:** 8 minutes
OVEN: 450°F

NUTRITION FACTS per bite:

CALORIES 83
TOTAL FAT 2 g (1 g sat. fat)
CHOLESTEROL 6 mg
PROTEIN 2 g
CARBOHYDRATE 14 g
FIBER 1 g
SODIUM 65 mg

EXCHANGES 0.5 Starch, 0.5 Other Carbohydrates, 0.5 Fat

Per serving with substitute: same as above, except 75 cal., 11 g carbo., 64 mg sodium

**To make ½ cup sour fat-free milk, place 1½ teaspoons lemon juice or vinegar in a glass measuring cup. Add enough fat-free milk to make ½ cup total liquid; stir. Let stand for 5 minutes before using.

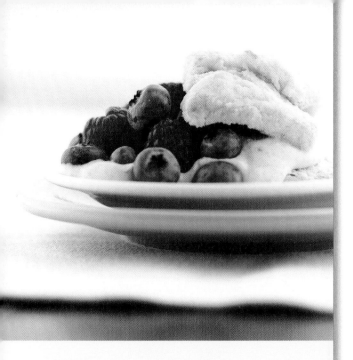

Piled-High Shortcake

PREP: 25 minutes   **BAKE:** 7 minutes
OVEN: 425°F

NUTRITION FACTS per serving:

CALORIES 212
TOTAL FAT 10 g (6 g sat. fat)
CHOLESTEROL 62 mg
PROTEIN 6 g
CARBOHYDRATE 25 g
FIBER 1 g
SODIUM 232 mg

EXCHANGES 1.5 Other Carbohydrates,
2 Fat

NUTRITION NOTE

The deep color of blackberries is telling
of the antioxidant content. Generally the
darker the fruits or veggies, the more
antioxidants. Color isn't the only way to
measure antioxidant content, but it is a
simple guide.

¾ cup all-purpose flour
2 teaspoons sugar
1 teaspoon baking powder
⅛ teaspoon baking soda
  Dash salt
2 tablespoons butter
¼ cup buttermilk
1 egg yolk, lightly beaten
  Nonstick cooking spray
½ of an 8-ounce package reduced-
   fat cream cheese (Neufchâtel),
   softened
1 cup plain low-fat yogurt
3 tablespoons low-sugar
   strawberry preserves
1½ cups fresh raspberries, blueberries,
   blackberries, cut-up nectarine,
   and/or peeled and
   cut-up kiwifruit

1 Preheat oven to 425°F. For shortcakes, in
a medium bowl stir together flour, sugar,
baking powder, baking soda, and salt. Using
a pastry blender, cut in butter until mixture
resembles coarse crumbs. Make a well in center
of flour mixture. In a small bowl combine
buttermilk and egg yolk. Add to flour mixture
all at once, stirring just until moistened.

2 Lightly coat a baking sheet with nonstick
cooking spray; set aside. On a lightly floured
surface, pat or roll dough to ½-inch thickness.
Using a floured 1½- to 2-inch cookie cutter, cut
dough into desired shapes, rerolling scraps as
necessary. Place on prepared baking sheet. Bake
for 7 to 8 minutes or until golden. Cool on a
wire rack.

3 In a medium bowl beat cream cheese with
an electric mixer on medium speed for
30 seconds. Gradually beat in yogurt and
preserves until smooth.

4 Split shortcakes in half horizontally. Divide
shortcake bottoms among six dessert plates;
top each with some of the fresh fruit and yogurt
mixture. Add shortcake tops. Serve immediately.
Makes 6 servings.

Nonstick cooking spray

- ½ cup yellow cornmeal
- ⅓ cup whole wheat flour
- 2 tablespoons sugar or sugar substitute* equivalent to 2 tablespoons sugar
- 1½ teaspoons finely shredded lemon peel
- 1 teaspoon baking powder
- ⅛ teaspoon baking soda
- ⅛ teaspoon salt
- ⅔ cup buttermilk
- ⅔ cup shredded, cored red cooking apple (such as Gala or Jonathan)
- 2 egg whites, lightly beaten
- 3 tablespoons finely chopped dried figs (about 5 figs)
- 1 small red cooking apple (such as Gala or Jonathan)
- ½ cup apple juice or apple cider
- ½ teaspoon cornstarch

1 Preheat oven to 400°F. Lightly coat six 3¼- to 3½-inch muffin cups with nonstick cooking spray. Set aside.

2 In a large bowl combine cornmeal, whole wheat flour, sugar, lemon peel, baking powder, baking soda, and salt; set aside. In a medium bowl combine buttermilk, shredded apple, egg whites, and figs. Add apple mixture to cornmeal mixture. Stir just until moistened.

3 Core whole apple. Cut whole apple horizontally into six rings, each about ¼ inch thick. Place one ring in each muffin cup, cutting slices to fit if necessary. Spoon cornmeal batter evenly into muffin cups on top of apple slices, filling each about half full.

4 Bake for 15 to 20 minutes or until tops are golden brown and a toothpick inserted into cakes comes out clean.

5 Meanwhile, in a small saucepan whisk together apple juice and cornstarch. Cook and stir until slightly thickened and bubbly; cook and stir 2 minutes more.

6 Let cakes cool in muffin cups on a wire rack for 10 minutes. Run a thin metal spatula around edges of cakes to loosen from sides of muffin cups. Invert pan onto a baking sheet;

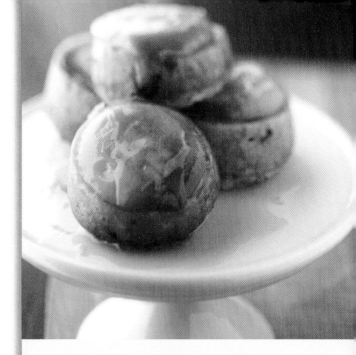

Upside-Down Apple-Corn Cakes

PREP: 25 minutes **BAKE:** 15 minutes
COOL: 10 minutes **OVEN:** 400°F

NUTRITION FACTS per serving:

CALORIES 133
TOTAL FAT 1 g (0 g sat. fat)
CHOLESTEROL 1 mg
PROTEIN 5 g
CARBOHYDRATE 29 g
FIBER 3 g
SODIUM 167 mg

EXCHANGES 1 Starch, 1 Fruit

remove pan. Transfer cakes to a serving platter. While hot, slowly drizzle cakes with hot apple juice mixture. Serve warm. Makes 6 servings.

*Sugar Substitutes: Choose from Splenda granular, Equal Spoonful or packets, or Sweet'N Low bulk or packets. Follow package directions to use product amount equivalent to 2 tablespoons sugar.

Per serving with substitute: same as above, except 119 cal., 25 g carbo. Exchanges: 0.5 Starch

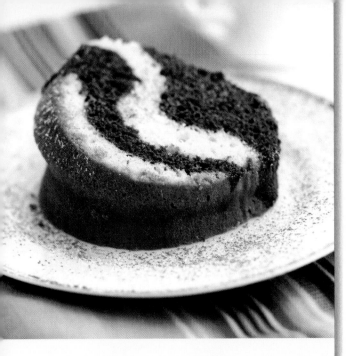

Coffee-Chocolate Marble Cake

PREP: 25 minutes **BAKE:** 30 minutes
COOL: 15 minutes **OVEN:** 350°F

NUTRITION FACTS per serving:

CALORIES 231
TOTAL FAT 8 g (1 g sat. fat)
CHOLESTEROL 27 mg
PROTEIN 4 g
CARBOHYDRATE 36 g
FIBER 0 g
SODIUM 128 mg

EXCHANGES 2.5 Other Carbohydrates, 1.5 Fat

***Sugar Substitutes:** Choose from Equal Sugar Lite or Splenda Sugar Blend for Baking. Follow package directions to use product amount equivalent to 1¼ cups for cake and 1 tablespoon for Coffee Drizzle.
Per serving with substitute: same as above, except 198 cal., 27 carbo. Exchanges: 2 Other Carbohydrates

Coffee Drizzle: In a small bowl combine ½ cup boiling water, 1 tablespoon sugar or sugar substitute blend* equivalent to 1 tablespoon sugar, and 2 teaspoons instant espresso coffee powder or instant coffee crystals. Stir until sugar and espresso powder are dissolved.

2½	cups sifted cake flour or 2¼ cups all-purpose flour
1½	teaspoons baking powder
½	teaspoon baking soda
¼	teaspoon salt
1¼	cups buttermilk
1¼	cups granulated sugar or sugar substitute blend* equivalent to 1¼ cups sugar
½	cup canola oil or cooking oil
2	eggs
2	teaspoons vanilla
⅓	cup unsweetened cocoa powder
2	tablespoons instant espresso coffee powder or instant coffee crystals
1	recipe Coffee Drizzle
2	teaspoons powdered sugar and/or unsweetened cocoa powder

1 Preheat oven to 350°F. Grease and lightly flour a 10-inch fluted tube pan; set aside. Set aside ½ cup flour. In a large bowl combine remaining 2 cups cake flour or 1¾ cups all-purpose flour, baking powder, baking soda, and salt.

2 In another large bowl whisk together buttermilk, granulated sugar, oil, eggs, and vanilla. Add buttermilk mixture to flour mixture. Whisk just until combined. In a medium bowl combine cocoa powder and espresso powder. Add half of the buttermilk-flour mixture (about 1¾ cups) to cocoa mixture, stirring until smooth. Add reserved ½ cup flour to remaining buttermilk-flour mixture, whisking just until combined.

3 Evenly spoon half of the white batter into prepared pan. Carefully spoon half of the cocoa batter onto the white batter in pan in an even layer. Repeat layers.

4 Bake for 30 minutes or until a toothpick inserted near center of cake comes out clean. Cool in pan on a wire rack for 15 minutes. Remove cake from pan. Place cake on a wire rack set over a sheet of waxed paper. Using a long wooden skewer, poke cake all the way through to bottom of cake in several places. Slowly pour Coffee Drizzle evenly over cake. Cool completely. Sprinkle with powdered sugar and/or additional cocoa powder. Makes 16 servings.

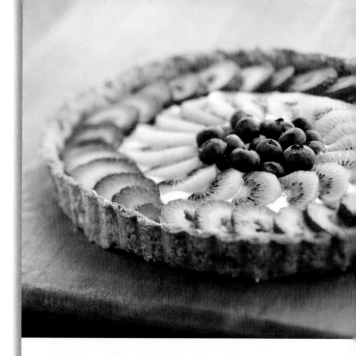

- ⅔ cup quick-cooking rolled oats
- ½ cup white whole wheat flour or whole wheat flour
- ¼ cup pecans, toasted and ground
- 1 8-ounce package reduced-fat cream cheese (Neufchâtel), softened
- 2 tablespoons butter, softened
- 2 tablespoons packed brown sugar
- ¼ teaspoon baking soda
- ⅛ teaspoon salt
  Nonstick cooking spray
- ⅓ cup fat-free vanilla yogurt
- 1 tablespoon honey
- 2½ cups assorted fresh fruit (such as blueberries, sliced strawberries, sliced kiwifruit, raspberries, and/or sliced, pitted, peeled peaches)

1 For tart dough, in a small bowl combine oats, whole wheat flour, and ground pecans; set aside. In a large bowl combine half of the cream cheese and butter; beat with an electric mixer on medium to high speed for 30 seconds. Add brown sugar, baking soda, and salt; beat until well mixed. Beat in as much of the oat mixture as you can with the mixer. Using a wooden spoon, stir in any remaining oat mixture. If necessary, cover and chill for 30 to 60 minutes or until easy to handle.

2 Preheat oven to 400°F. Pat dough evenly on the bottom and up the side of a lightly greased 9-inch tart pan with a removable bottom. Coat a double thickness of foil with nonstick cooking spray. Line the pastry with foil, coated side down. Bake for 6 minutes. Remove foil. Bake for 7 to 8 minutes more or until crust is golden brown. Cool completely on a wire rack.

3 Meanwhile, in a medium bowl beat remaining cream cheese with an electric mixer on medium speed until smooth. Beat in yogurt and honey; cover and chill for 30 minutes to 4 hours.

4 Spread cream cheese mixture on the crust. Top with fruit. Serve immediately or cover and chill for up to 4 hours. Makes 12 servings.

Fruit Pizza

PREP: 40 minutes

CHILL: 30 minutes to 4 hours

BAKE: 13 minutes   **OVEN:** 400°F

NUTRITION FACTS per serving:

CALORIES 145
TOTAL FAT 8 g (4 g sat. fat)
CHOLESTEROL 20 mg
PROTEIN 4 g
CARBOHYDRATE 15 g
FIBER 2 g
SODIUM 145 mg

EXCHANGES 1 Starch, 1.5 Fat

1   4-serving-size package fat-free, sugar-free instant chocolate pudding mix

1 ¾   cups fat-free milk

1   teaspoon vanilla

½   of an 8-ounce package reduced-fat cream cheese (Neufchâtel), softened

½   of an 8-ounce container frozen light whipped dessert topping, thawed

1   6-ounce chocolate-flavor crumb pie shell

1   cup fresh raspberries

1   tablespoon grated semisweet chocolate

Chocolate Cream Cheese Pie

PREP: 20 minutes

CHILL: 4 hours

NUTRITION FACTS per serving:

CALORIES 180
TOTAL FAT 8 g (4 g sat. fat)
CHOLESTEROL 9 mg
PROTEIN 4 g
CARBOHYDRATE 22 g
FIBER 1 g
SODIUM 285 mg

EXCHANGES 1.5 Other Carbohydrates, 1.5 Fat

1 In a medium bowl prepare pudding mix according to package directions using the 1¾ cups milk. Stir in vanilla; set aside.

2 Place cream cheese in a large microwave-safe bowl. Microwave, uncovered, on 100% power (high) for 15 seconds; stir. Microwave on 100% power (high) for 15 seconds more. Beat cream cheese with an electric mixer on medium speed for 15 seconds. Add half of the pudding mixture; beat until smooth. Add remaining pudding mixture; beat until smooth. Fold in half of the whipped topping. Spread mixture in pie shell. Chill about 4 hours or until set.

3 Top individual servings with remaining whipped topping, raspberries, and grated chocolate. Makes 10 servings.

Make-Ahead Directions: Prepare as above through step 2. Cover and chill for up to 24 hours. Serve as above in step 3.

2   eggs, lightly beaten

2   cups fat-free milk

3   tablespoons packed brown sugar

1   teaspoon vanilla

½   teaspoon pumpkin pie spice or ground cinnamon

5   cups dry oatmeal bread cubes*

2   medium bananas, halved lengthwise and sliced

½   cup chopped walnuts or pecans, toasted (optional)

1 Preheat oven to 350°F. In a medium bowl whisk together eggs, milk, brown sugar, vanilla, and pumpkin pie spice; set aside. In an ungreased 2-quart square baking dish toss together bread cubes, banana slices, and, if desired, nuts. Pour egg mixture evenly over bread mixture. Toss until bread is moistened.

2 Bake for 35 to 40 minutes or until a knife inserted near the center comes out clean. Cool slightly before serving. Makes 9 servings.

*For 5 cups dry bread cubes, preheat oven to 350°F. Spread 8½ cups bread cubes (11 slices) in a shallow baking pan. Bake for 10 to 15 minutes or until bread cubes are dry, stirring twice; cool.

Oatmeal-Banana Bread Pudding

PREP: 25 minutes   **BAKE:** 35 minutes
OVEN: 350°F

NUTRITION FACTS per serving:

CALORIES 167
TOTAL FAT 3 g (1 g sat. fat)
CHOLESTEROL 48 mg
PROTEIN 6 g
CARBOHYDRATE 30 g
FIBER 2 g
SODIUM 239 mg

EXCHANGES 1 Starch, 0.5 Other Carbohydrates, 0.5 Fruit, 0.5 Fat

NUTRITION NOTE

Bananas, a good source of fiber, vitamin C, and potassium, should be stored, uncovered, at room temperature. Hanging them on a banana hanger prevents bruises.

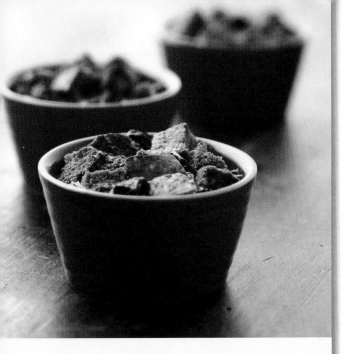

Nonstick cooking spray

2 cups firm-textured whole grain bread cubes (about 3 ounces)

3 tablespoons snipped dried tart red cherries

1 tablespoon toasted wheat germ

⅔ cup fat-free milk

¼ cup semisweet chocolate pieces

1 egg

1 egg white

1 teaspoon finely shredded orange peel

½ teaspoon vanilla

Frozen light whipped dessert topping, thawed (optional)

Unsweetened cocoa powder (optional)

Cherry-Chocolate Bread Puddings

PREP: 20 minutes   **BAKE:** 15 minutes
OVEN: 350°F

NUTRITION FACTS per serving:

CALORIES 168
TOTAL FAT 5 g (2 g sat. fat)
CHOLESTEROL 54 mg
PROTEIN 7 g
CARBOHYDRATE 27 g
FIBER 3 g
SODIUM 148 mg

EXCHANGES 1 Starch, 1 Other Carbohydrates, 0.5 Fat

1 Preheat oven to 350°F. Coat four 6-ounce individual soufflé dishes or custard cups with nonstick cooking spray. Divide bread cubes, dried cherries, and wheat germ among the dishes.

2 In a small saucepan combine milk and chocolate pieces. Cook and stir over low heat until the chocolate melts; remove from heat. If necessary, beat smooth with a wire whisk.

3 In a small bowl beat together egg and egg white with a fork or wire whisk. Gradually stir chocolate mixture into eggs. Stir in orange peel and vanilla. Pour chocolate mixture over bread cubes in dishes. Press lightly with the back of a spoon to thoroughly moisten bread.

4 Bake for 15 to 20 minutes or until pudding tops appear firm and a knife inserted near the centers comes out clean. Serve warm. If desired, serve with whipped topping and sprinkle with cocoa powder. Makes 4 servings.

Make-Ahead Directions: Prepare as above through step 3. Cover and chill for up to 2 hours. Preheat oven to 350°F. Continue with step 4.

4 egg yolks, lightly beaten
1 cup fat-free milk
2 tablespoons sugar
1 teaspoon vanilla
½ cup finely crushed
   graham crackers
¼ cup chopped toasted
   sliced almonds
⅛ teaspoon ground cinnamon
1½ cups fresh raspberries and/or
   sliced strawberries
1½ cups fresh blueberries
   Toasted sliced almonds (optional)

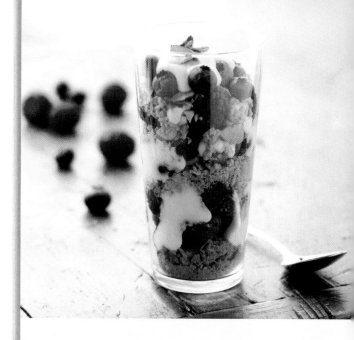

1 For custard, in a heavy small saucepan stir together egg yolks, milk, and sugar. Cook and stir over medium heat until mixture is thickened and coats the back of a metal spoon (do not boil).

2 Remove saucepan from heat. Quickly cool milk mixture by placing saucepan in a large bowl of ice water for 1 to 2 minutes, stirring constantly. Stir in vanilla. Pour mixture into a small bowl. Cover surface with plastic wrap to prevent a skin from forming. Chill for 2 to 24 hours before serving. Do not stir. (Custard will be thickened but will not be set.)

3 In a small bowl combine finely crushed graham crackers, ¼ cup almonds, and cinnamon.

4 Divide one-third of the graham cracker mixture among six tall 8-ounce glasses, small parfait glasses, or small dessert dishes. Divide half of the raspberries and one-third of the chilled custard among the glasses. Layer another one-third of the graham cracker mixture in the glasses. Top with half of the blueberries and another one-third of the custard. Divide remaining raspberries, graham cracker mixture, and blueberries among the glasses. Top each with some of the remaining custard. If desired, garnish with additional almonds. Serve immediately. Makes 6 servings.

Custard Towers

PREP: 25 minutes

CHILL: 2 to 24 hours

NUTRITION FACTS per serving:

CALORIES 157
TOTAL FAT 6 g (1 g sat. fat)
CHOLESTEROL 137 mg
PROTEIN 5 g
CARBOHYDRATE 19 g
FIBER 5 g
SODIUM 62 mg

EXCHANGES 1 Other Carbohydrates, 0.5 Fruit, 0.5 Medium Fat Meat, 0.5 Fat

COOK'S TIP

Toasting nuts intensifies their flavor and adds crunch. To toast nuts, place a single layer of them in a skillet over medium-high heat. Stir or shake the nuts continually until they turn golden.

2 6-ounce cartons peach fat-free yogurt with artificial sweetener

1 8-ounce package fat-free cream cheese, softened

½ of an 8-ounce container frozen light whipped dessert topping, thawed

1 cup chopped, pitted, peeled fresh peach; frozen unsweetened peach slices, thawed, drained, and chopped; or one 8¼-ounce can peach slices (juice pack), drained and chopped

1 cup fresh or frozen unsweetened blueberries, raspberries, and/ or strawberries, thawed and drained if frozen

Fresh mint leaves (optional)

Fresh berries (optional)

Peach-Berry Frozen Dessert

PREP: 20 minutes   **FREEZE:** 8 hours

STAND: 45 minutes

NUTRITION FACTS per serving:

CALORIES 89
TOTAL FAT 2 g (2 g sat. fat)
CHOLESTEROL 3 mg
PROTEIN 6 g
CARBOHYDRATE 12 g
FIBER 1 g
SODIUM 159 mg

EXCHANGES 1 Other Carbohydrates, 1 Very Lean Meat

1 In a medium bowl combine yogurt and cream cheese. Beat with an electric mixer on medium speed until smooth. Fold in whipped topping, peach, and 1 cup berries.

2 Spoon into a 2-quart square baking dish; spread evenly. Cover and freeze about 8 hours or until firm.

3 To serve, let stand at room temperature about 45 minutes to thaw slightly. Cut into squares. If desired, garnish with mint leaves and additional berries. Makes 9 servings.

COOK'S TIP

Fresh peaches are available from May through October. To ripen peaches, place them in a brown paper bag that has been pierced several times and let sit at room temperature for a couple of days.

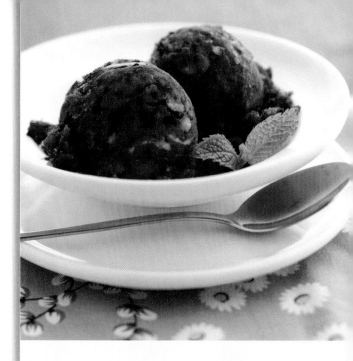

- 2 cups fresh blueberries
- 2 cups fresh raspberries
- ½ cup cold water
- ¼ cup frozen pineapple-orange-banana juice concentrate or citrus beverage concentrate
- Fresh mint sprigs (optional)

1 Place berries in a single layer on a baking sheet lined with waxed paper. Freeze for 1 to 2 hours or until solid.

2 In a large bowl combine frozen berries, water, and frozen concentrate. Place half of the berry mixture in a food processor. Cover and process until almost smooth. Spoon into serving dishes. Repeat with remaining berry mixture. If desired, garnish with fresh mint. Serve immediately. Makes 6 to 8 servings.

Make-Ahead Directions: Prepare as above. Transfer berry mixture to a baking dish. Cover and freeze about 4 hours or until firm. Use within 2 days. If desired, scoop frozen mixture into sugar cones.

Easy-Freezy Sorbet

PREP: 10 minutes

FREEZE: 1 to 2 hours

NUTRITION FACTS per serving:

CALORIES 66
TOTAL FAT 0 g (0 g sat. fat)
CHOLESTEROL 0 mg
PROTEIN 1 g
CARBOHYDRATE 15 g
FIBER 3 g
SODIUM 4 mg

EXCHANGES 1 Fruit

NUTRITION NOTE

Sorbets are a healthy alternative to ice cream because they are lower in calories and usually fat-free. The next time you're standing at an ice cream shop, look for a sorbet. You'll still enjoy a dessert that's sweet and cold without the fat.

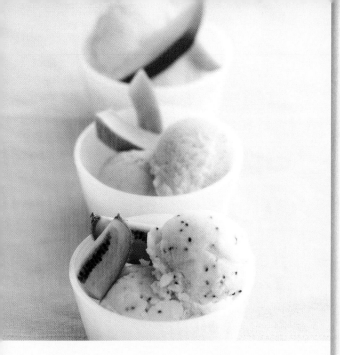

1 cup sugar or sugar substitute* equivalent to 1 cup sugar

1 envelope unflavored gelatin

2 cups unsweetened pineapple juice or orange juice

2 cups chopped, peeled mango, kiwifruit, or strawberry papaya

1 cup buttermilk

1 teaspoon finely shredded lime peel or lemon peel

¼ cup lime juice or lemon juice

3 drops yellow, green, red, or orange food coloring (optional)

Mango, kiwifruit, or strawberry papaya (optional)

Choose-a-Fruit Tropical Sherbet

PREP: 20 minutes   **CHILL:** 4 hours

FREEZE: per manufacturer's directions

RIPEN: 4 hours (optional)

NUTRITION FACTS per serving:

CALORIES 90
TOTAL FAT 0 g (0 g sat. fat)
CHOLESTEROL 1 mg
PROTEIN 2 g
CARBOHYDRATE 21 g
FIBER 0 g
SODIUM 20 mg

EXCHANGES 1 Other Carbohydrates, 0.5 Fruit

1 In a medium saucepan combine sugar and unflavored gelatin. Stir in pineapple juice. Cook and stir until sugar and gelatin dissolve. Remove from heat.

2 Place chopped mango, kiwifruit, or papaya in a blender or food processor; cover and blend or process until pureed.

3 In a large bowl stir together pureed fruit, gelatin mixture, buttermilk, lime peel, and lime juice. If desired, add food coloring to tint desired color (green for kiwifruit, yellow for mango, or pink or orange for papaya). Cover and chill mixture about 4 hours or until completely chilled.

4 Transfer mixture to a 4- to 5-quart ice cream freezer; freeze according to manufacturer's directions. If desired, ripen for 4 hours.** If desired, garnish with additional mango, kiwifruit, or strawberry papaya. Makes 16 (about ½-cup) servings.

***Sugar Substitutes:** Choose from Splenda granular, Equal Spoonful or packets, or Sweet'N Low bulk or packets. Follow package directions to use product amount equivalent to 1 cup sugar.

Per serving with substitute: same as at left, except 44 cal., 10 g carbo. Exchanges: 0.5 Fruit

****Ripening or hardening homemade sherbet isn't essential, but it improves the texture and prevents the sherbet from melting too quickly when served.

To ripen in a traditional-style ice cream freezer, after churning remove the lid and dasher and cover the top of the freezer can with waxed paper or foil. Plug the hole in the lid with a small piece of cloth; replace the lid. Pack the outer freezer bucket with enough ice and rock salt to cover the top of the freezer can (use 1 cup salt for each 4 cups ice). Ripen about 4 hours.

When using an ice cream freezer with an insulated freezer bowl, transfer the ice cream to a covered freezer container and ripen by freezing in your regular freezer about 4 hours (or follow the manufacturer's recommendations).

Freezer Directions: Prepare as above through step 3. Transfer mixture to a 2-quart rectangular baking dish or freezer container. Cover; freeze for 4½ to 5 hours or until almost firm. Break mixture into small chunks; transfer to a large chilled bowl. Beat with an electric mixer on medium speed about 2 minutes or until smooth but not melted. Return to dish or container. Cover and freeze about 4 hours more or until firm.

Chapter 15

Shortcut Meals

On the opener: Chicken Penne Alfredo *(see recipe, page 252)*

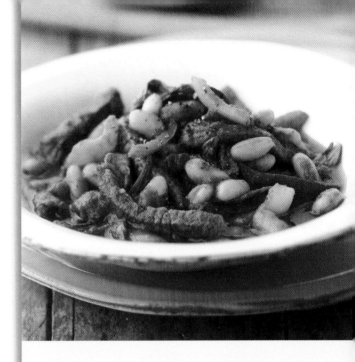

- 2 teaspoons olive oil
- 12 ounces packaged beef stir-fry strips
- 1 16-ounce package frozen (yellow, green, and red) peppers and onion stir-fry vegetables
- 1 15-ounce can cannellini beans (white kidney beans), rinsed and drained
- 1½ cups purchased roasted garlic and herb pasta sauce or your favorite tomato-based pasta sauce
- ½ cup water
- ¼ teaspoon coarsely ground black pepper
- 2 cups packaged fresh baby spinach
  Coarsely ground black pepper (optional)

1 In a large skillet heat oil over medium-high heat. Add beef strips; cook for 3 to 4 minutes or until desired doneness. Stir in stir-fry vegetables, cannellini beans, pasta sauce, water, and black pepper; heat through. Stir in spinach. If desired, garnish individual servings with additional pepper. Makes 4 (about 1½-cup) servings.

Seasoned Steak Ragout

START TO FINISH: 20 minutes

NUTRITION FACTS per serving:

CALORIES 273
TOTAL FAT 7 g (2 g sat. fat)
CHOLESTEROL 52 mg
PROTEIN 27 g
CARBOHYDRATE 30 g
FIBER 7 g
SODIUM 601 mg

EXCHANGES 1 Starch, 2.5 Lean Meat, 3 Vegetable

- 1 12-inch whole wheat thin Italian bread shell (such as Boboli brand)
- 1 9-ounce package frozen chopped cooked chicken, thawed
- ½ cup bottled barbecue sauce
- 2 cups packaged fresh baby spinach
- 1 cup shredded reduced-fat Monterey Jack cheese or part-skim mozzarella cheese (4 ounces)
- 2 tablespoons snipped fresh cilantro

1 Preheat oven to 450°F. Place bread shell on a large baking sheet. In a medium bowl combine chicken and barbecue sauce. Evenly spread chicken mixture on bread shell. Sprinkle with spinach. Top with cheese.

2 Bake for 10 to 12 minutes or until cheese is melted and pizza is heated through. Sprinkle with cilantro. Makes 4 servings.

Spinach Barbecue Chicken Pizza

PREP: 15 minutes   **BAKE:** 10 minutes
OVEN: 450°F

NUTRITION FACTS per serving:

CALORIES 385
TOTAL FAT 13 g (5 g sat. fat)
CHOLESTEROL 65 mg
PROTEIN 33 g
CARBOHYDRATE 40 g
FIBER 6 g
SODIUM 1,258 mg

EXCHANGES 2 Starch, 0.5 Other Carbohydrates, 4 Lean Meat

NUTRITION NOTE

Spinach provides more than 20 percent of the daily recommended value of more than 11 vitamins and minerals, including vitamin K, vitamin A, folate, magnesium, iron, vitamin C, calcium, and potassium.

8 7- or 8-inch whole wheat flour tortillas

Nonstick cooking spray

1 15-ounce can hot or mild chili beans in chili gravy

1 9-ounce package frozen grilled chicken breast strips, thawed

1 cup purchased chunky salsa

1 cup shredded reduced-fat Colby and Monterey Jack cheese (4 ounces)

1 8-ounce can no-salt-added tomato sauce

1 Preheat oven to 350°F. Wrap tortillas tightly in foil. Bake for 10 minutes to soften. Lightly coat a 3-quart rectangular baking dish with nonstick cooking spray; set aside.

2 For filling, in a medium bowl stir together undrained chili beans, chicken breast strips, ½ cup salsa, and ½ cup cheese. Divide chicken mixture evenly among warm tortillas; roll up tortillas. Arrange filled tortillas, seam sides down, in prepared baking dish.

3 In a small bowl stir together remaining ½ cup salsa and tomato sauce. Spoon sauce down center of filled tortillas.

4 Bake, covered, about 30 minutes or until heated through. Top with remaining ½ cup cheese. Bake, uncovered, about 5 minutes more or until cheese is melted. Makes 8 servings.

Saucy Chicken Enchiladas

PREP: 15 minutes   **BAKE:** 35 minutes
OVEN: 350°F

NUTRITION FACTS per serving:

CALORIES 282
TOTAL FAT 8 g (3 g sat. fat)
CHOLESTEROL 33 mg
PROTEIN 23 g
CARBOHYDRATE 28 g
FIBER 14 g
SODIUM 889 mg

EXCHANGES 2 Starch, 2.5 Very Lean Meat, 0.5 Fat

6 ounces dried multigrain or whole wheat penne pasta

2 cups packaged peeled baby carrots

3 cups broccoli florets

1 9-ounce package frozen grilled chicken breast strips, thawed

½ of an 8-ounce tub light cream cheese spread with garden vegetables

½ to 1 cup fat-free milk

½ teaspoon cracked black pepper

Cracked black pepper (optional)

Chicken Penne Alfredo

START TO FINISH: 25 minutes

NUTRITION FACTS per serving:

CALORIES 354
TOTAL FAT 8 g (4 g sat. fat)
CHOLESTEROL 59 mg
PROTEIN 30 g
CARBOHYDRATE 43 g
FIBER 7 g
SODIUM 627 mg

EXCHANGES 2.5 Starch, 3 Very Lean Meat, 1 Vegetable, 0.5 Fat

1 In a 4-quart Dutch oven cook pasta and carrots according to pasta package directions; add broccoli for the last 6 minutes of cooking time. Drain pasta and vegetables; return to Dutch oven.

2 Stir chicken strips, cream cheese spread, ½ cup milk, and pepper into pasta mixture. Cook and stir over low heat until cream cheese is melted. If necessary, stir in enough of the remaining ½ cup milk to make sauce desired consistency. If desired, sprinkle individual servings with additional pepper. Makes 4 (2-cup) servings.

- 1 7-ounce container hummus
- 1 cup bottled roasted red sweet peppers, drained
- ½ teaspoon ground cumin
- 1 tablespoon olive oil or canola oil
- 1 medium zucchini, sliced
- 1 medium yellow summer squash, sliced
- 1 9-ounce package refrigerated or frozen Southwestern-style cooked chicken breast strips, thawed if frozen

   Toasted pita wedges*

1 In a blender or food processor combine hummus, roasted red peppers, and cumin. Cover and blend or process until smooth; set aside.

2 In a large skillet heat oil over medium-high heat. Add zucchini and yellow squash; cook for 3 to 4 minutes or until tender, stirring occasionally. Add chicken; heat through. Divide mixture among four serving plates. Serve with hummus mixture and toasted pita wedges. Makes 4 servings.

*To toast pita wedges, preheat oven to 375°F. Split two whole wheat pita bread rounds in half horizontally. Cut each half into eight wedges. Arrange wedges in a single layer on a baking sheet. Bake for 8 to 10 minutes or until toasted. Makes 32 wedges.

Chicken and Vegetables with Red Pepper Hummus

START TO FINISH: 30 minutes
OVEN: 375°F

NUTRITION FACTS per serving:

CALORIES 309
TOTAL FAT 11 g (2 g sat. fat)
CHOLESTEROL 41 mg
PROTEIN 21 g
CARBOHYDRATE 34 g
FIBER 6 g
SODIUM 875 mg

EXCHANGES 1.5 Starch, 2 Very Lean Meat, 2 Vegetable, 1.5 Fat

NUTRITION NOTE

Tahini, or sesame seed paste, is an important ingredient in hummus—it provides essential fatty acids.

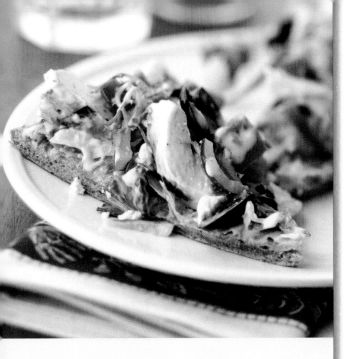

1 12-inch whole wheat Italian bread shell (such as Boboli brand)

½ cup shredded reduced-fat mozzarella cheese (2 ounces)

2 cups packaged European mixed salad greens

2 cups thin-cut grilled chicken breast strips

2 medium plum tomatoes, chopped

¼ cup thinly sliced quartered red onion

2 tablespoons halved pitted kalamata olives

3 tablespoons bottled light Caesar salad dressing

2 tablespoons crumbled reduced-fat feta cheese

Chicken Caesar Salad Pizza

START TO FINISH: 20 minutes

OVEN: 450°F

NUTRITION FACTS per serving:

- -

CALORIES 388
TOTAL FAT 11 g (3 g sat. fat)
CHOLESTEROL 70 mg
PROTEIN 35 g
CARBOHYDRATE 39 g
FIBER 6 g
SODIUM 830 mg

EXCHANGES 2 Starch, 4 Very Lean Meat, 1 Vegetable, 1.5 Fat

1 Preheat oven to 450°F. Sprinkle bread shell with mozzarella cheese. Place shell directly on middle oven rack. Bake about 5 minutes or until cheese is melted.

2 Meanwhile, in a large bowl toss together salad greens, chicken, tomato, onion, and olives. Add salad dressing; toss to coat. Remove bread shell from oven; immediately top with salad greens mixture. Sprinkle with feta cheese. Cut into wedges. Serve immediately. Makes 4 servings.

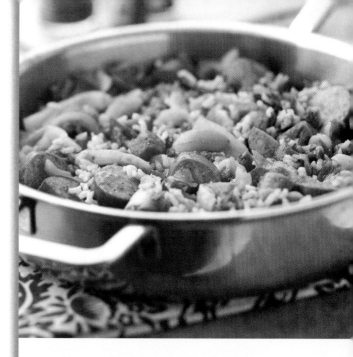

1 16-ounce package frozen (yellow, green, and red) peppers and onion stir-fry vegetables

1 14½-ounce can diced tomatoes, undrained

12 ounces smoked turkey sausage, sliced

1 teaspoon Cajun seasoning

1 8.8-ounce pouch cooked brown rice

1 In a large skillet combine stir-fry vegetables, undrained tomatoes, sausage, and Cajun seasoning. Bring to boiling; reduce heat. Cover and simmer about 5 minutes or just until vegetables are tender. Stir in cooked rice; heat through. Makes 6 (1-cup) servings.

COOK'S TIP

Chicken and turkey sausages are becoming more readily available in supermarkets. They are often located near meat alternatives such as tofu and organic poultry.

Jambalaya-Style Sausage and Rice

START TO FINISH: 20 minutes

NUTRITION FACTS per serving:

CALORIES 189
TOTAL FAT 6 g (1 g sat. fat)
CHOLESTEROL 38 mg
PROTEIN 12 g
CARBOHYDRATE 22 g
FIBER 2 g
SODIUM 671 mg

EXCHANGES 1 Starch, 1 Medium-Fat Meat, 2 Vegetable

1/3 cup bottled light Catalina
    salad dressing

2 tablespoons crunchy
    peanut butter

1 tablespoon reduced-sodium soy
    sauce

1 tablespoon canola oil

1 16-ounce package frozen broccoli
    stir-fry vegetable blend

16 ounces fresh or frozen peeled and
    deveined cooked shrimp*
    (tails intact if desired)

3 cups hot cooked brown rice

1/4 cup chopped peanuts

1 In a small bowl whisk together salad dressing, peanut butter, and soy sauce; set aside.

2 In a wok or very large skillet heat oil over medium-high heat. Add frozen vegetables; cook and stir for 5 to 7 minutes or until vegetables are crisp-tender. Stir in salad dressing mixture and shrimp; heat through.

3 Serve over hot cooked brown rice. Sprinkle individual servings with peanuts. Makes 6 servings (¾ cup shrimp mixture and ½ cup rice per serving).

*Thaw and drain shrimp, if frozen.

Shrimp and Peanut Stir-Fry

START TO FINISH: 20 minutes

NUTRITION FACTS per serving:

- - - - - - - - - - - - - - - - - - - -

CALORIES 323
TOTAL FAT 10 g (1 g sat. fat)
CHOLESTEROL 147 mg
PROTEIN 23 g
CARBOHYDRATE 34 g
FIBER 4 g
SODIUM 546 mg

EXCHANGES 2 Starch, 2 Very Lean Meat,
1 Vegetable, 1.5 Fat

NUTRITION NOTE

Asian dishes are often high in sodium. To cut it down, use reduced-sodium soy sauce. One tablespoon of reduced-sodium soy sauce has less than half the sodium of the full-sodium version.

1   14½-ounce can diced tomatoes
    and green chile peppers,
    undrained

1   medium red sweet pepper, seeded
    and cut into bite-size strips

¼   teaspoon salt

¼   teaspoon ground saffron
    or turmeric

¼   teaspoon bottled
    hot pepper sauce

12 ounces peeled and deveined
    cooked shrimp* (tails intact
    if desired)

1   8.8-ounce pouch cooked
    whole grain brown rice

1   cup loose-pack frozen peas

    Snipped fresh parsley (optional)

1 In a large saucepan combine undrained
tomatoes, sweet pepper, salt, saffron, and
hot pepper sauce. Bring to boiling; reduce heat.
Simmer, uncovered, for 5 minutes. Stir in shrimp,
cooked rice, and peas. Cook for 1 to 2 minutes
or until heated through, stirring occasionally. If
desired, sprinkle individual servings with parsley.
Makes 4 (1¼-cup) servings.

*Thaw and drain shrimp, if frozen.

COOK'S TIP

By weight, saffron threads are the most
expensive spice in the world, selling for
about $40 an ounce. Most supermarkets
carry powdered saffron in tiny packets in
the spice aisle. Although still expensive, it is
a perfect substitute for threads.

Shrimp Paella

START TO FINISH: 20 minutes

NUTRITION FACTS per serving:

CALORIES 241
TOTAL FAT 3 g (0 g sat. fat)
CHOLESTEROL 166 mg
PROTEIN 23 g
CARBOHYDRATE 30 g
FIBER 3 g
SODIUM 827 mg

EXCHANGES 1.5 Starch, 2.5 Very Lean
Meat, 1 Vegetable

4   4-ounce fresh or frozen catfish
     fillets, ½ to ¾ inch thick
     Nonstick cooking spray
½   of a 20-ounce package
     refrigerated red potato wedges
     (about 30 wedges)
2   teaspoons olive oil
¼   teaspoon garlic powder
¾   cup herb-seasoned stuffing mix
1   tablespoon olive oil
     Fresh parsley sprigs (optional)

1 Thaw fish, if frozen. Rinse fish; pat dry with paper towels. Set aside.

2 Preheat oven to 450°F. Line a 15×10×1-inch baking pan with foil. Coat foil with nonstick cooking spray. Arrange potato wedges in a single layer in half of the baking pan. Brush potatoes with 2 teaspoons oil; sprinkle with garlic powder. Set aside.

3 In a small bowl stir together stuffing mix and the 1 tablespoon oil. Place fish in baking pan next to potatoes. Sprinkle stuffing mixture on fish, pressing lightly. Bake for 9 to 12 minutes or until fish flakes easily when tested with a fork and potatoes are hot and beginning to brown. If desired, garnish individual servings with parsley. Makes 4 servings (1 piece of fish and 7 or 8 potato wedges per serving).

Seasoned Fish with Potato Wedges

PREP: 15 minutes   **BAKE:** 9 minutes
OVEN: 450°F

NUTRITION FACTS per serving:

CALORIES 290
TOTAL FAT 15 g (3 g sat. fat)
CHOLESTEROL 53 mg
PROTEIN 21 g
CARBOHYDRATE 17 g
FIBER 3 g
SODIUM 285 mg

EXCHANGES 1 Starch, 3 Very Lean Meat, 2 Fat

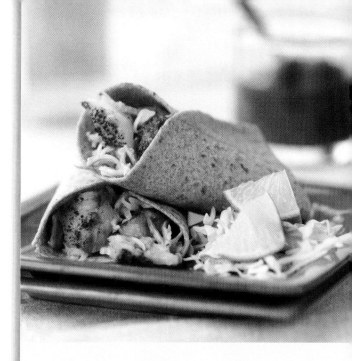

- 1 pound fresh or frozen skinless halibut fillets, ½ to ¾ inch thick

  Olive oil nonstick cooking spray

- 1 teaspoon ancho chili powder or chili powder
- ¼ cup light dairy sour cream
- ¼ cup desired flavor purchased fruit salsa (such as pineapple, peach, or mango-peach)
- 2 cups packaged shredded cabbage with carrot (coleslaw mix)
- 4 8-inch whole grain flour tortillas

  Packaged shredded cabbage with carrot (coleslaw mix) (optional)

  Lime wedges (optional)

  Desired flavor purchased fruit salsa (optional)

1 Thaw fish, if frozen. Preheat broiler. Rinse fish; pat dry with paper towels. Lightly coat the unheated rack of a broiler pan with nonstick cooking spray. Place fish on rack. Sprinkle with chili powder. Broil 4 to 5 inches from heat for 4 to 6 minutes per ½-inch thickness or until fish flakes easily when tested with a fork. Cool fish slightly. Using a fork, flake fish into bite-size chunks.

2 Meanwhile, in a medium bowl stir together sour cream and salsa. Add cabbage; toss to coat. Divide cabbage mixture among tortillas. Top with fish. Roll up tortillas. If desired, serve with additional cabbage and lime wedges. If desired, pass additional salsa. Makes 4 servings.

Fish Taco Wraps

START TO FINISH: 20 minutes

NUTRITION FACTS per serving:

CALORIES 294
TOTAL FAT 7 g (2 g sat. fat)
CHOLESTEROL 40 mg
PROTEIN 32 g
CARBOHYDRATE 21 g
FIBER 11 g
SODIUM 450 mg

EXCHANGES 1 Starch, 0.5 Other Carbohydrates, 4 Very Lean Meat, 0.5 Fat

NUTRITION NOTE

Halibut, a low-fat fish, has primarily monounsaturated and polyunsaturated fat. Halibut also contains plenty of protein, magnesium, potassium, phosphorous, and several B vitamins.

4   8-inch whole wheat flour tortillas

     Olive oil nonstick cooking spray

1½   cups canned fat-free spicy refried beans, warmed

1½   cups shredded leaf lettuce

¾   cup purchased fresh deli salsa

½   cup shredded reduced-fat Mexican-blend cheese (2 ounces)

1 Preheat oven to 425°F. Lightly coat both sides of each tortilla with nonstick cooking spray. Place tortillas on a very large baking sheet. Bake for 10 to 12 minutes or until lightly browned and crisp, turning once. Cool tortillas on a wire rack.

2 Evenly spread warm refried beans on tortillas. Top with lettuce, salsa, and cheese. Makes 4 servings.

Spicy Bean Tostadas

PREP: 15 minutes   **BAKE:** 10 minutes

OVEN: 425°F

NUTRITION FACTS per serving:

- -

CALORIES 255
TOTAL FAT 6 g (3 g sat. fat)
CHOLESTEROL 5 mg
PROTEIN 17 g
CARBOHYDRATE 32 g
FIBER 15 g
SODIUM 1,252 mg

EXCHANGES 2 Starch, 2 Lean Meat

- 1 14½-ounce can Italian-style stewed tomatoes, undrained
- ½ cup water
- 2 medium zucchini and/or yellow summer squash, halved lengthwise and cut into ½-inch-thick slices
- 1 9-ounce package refrigerated whole wheat four-cheese ravioli
- 1 15- or 16-ounce can cannellini beans (white kidney beans) or navy beans, rinsed and drained
- 2 tablespoons snipped fresh basil or parsley
- 2 tablespoons finely shredded or grated Parmesan cheese

1 In a very large skillet combine undrained tomatoes and water; bring to boiling. Add zucchini and/or yellow summer squash and ravioli. Return to boiling; reduce heat. Cover and boil gently for 6 to 7 minutes or until ravioli is tender, stirring gently once or twice.

2 Stir beans into ravioli mixture; heat through. Sprinkle individual servings with basil and Parmesan cheese.
Makes 4 (1⅔-cup) servings.

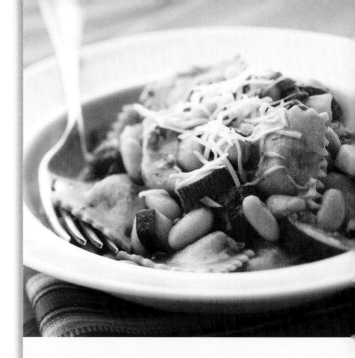

Ravioli Skillet

START TO FINISH: 20 minutes

NUTRITION FACTS per serving:

CALORIES 305
TOTAL FAT 8 g (4 g sat. fat)
CHOLESTEROL 44 mg
PROTEIN 18 g
CARBOHYDRATE 49 g
FIBER 11 g
SODIUM 986 mg

EXCHANGES 2.5 Starch, 1 Lean Meat, 1.5 Vegetable

1 9-ounce package refrigerated whole wheat four-cheese ravioli

1 16-ounce package frozen broccoli stir-fry vegetable blend

¾ cup bottled roasted red sweet peppers, drained

⅓ cup bottled light ranch salad dressing

¼ cup packed fresh basil leaves

1 In a 4-quart Dutch oven cook ravioli according to package directions; add stir-fry vegetables for the last 5 minutes of cooking time. Drain ravioli and vegetables; return to Dutch oven.

2 Meanwhile, for sauce, in a blender or food processor combine roasted red peppers, salad dressing, and basil. Cover and blend or process until smooth. Serve with hot pasta mixture. Makes 4 (1-cup) servings.

Hot Tossed Vegetable Ravioli

START TO FINISH: 20 minutes

NUTRITION FACTS per serving:

CALORIES 278
TOTAL FAT 11 g (4 g sat. fat)
CHOLESTEROL 49 mg
PROTEIN 12 g
CARBOHYDRATE 34 g
FIBER 6 g
SODIUM 673 mg

EXCHANGES 1.5 Starch, 0.5 Medium-Fat Meat, 2 Vegetable, 1.5 Fat

On the opener: Spicy Stir-Fried Chicken with Cashews (*see recipe, page 280*)

- 2 teaspoons olive oil
- 1 large sweet onion (such as Vidalia, Maui, or Walla Walla), halved and thinly sliced
- 1 pound extra-lean ground beef or uncooked ground turkey breast
- 2 teaspoons snipped fresh thyme or ½ teaspoon dried thyme, crushed
- ¼ teaspoon salt
- ¼ teaspoon black pepper
- 1 cup torn arugula
- 4 whole wheat hamburger buns, split and toasted
- ½ cup bottled roasted red sweet peppers, drained and cut into strips
- ¼ cup crumbled blue cheese (1 ounce)

1 In a large skillet heat oil over medium heat. Add onion; cover and cook for 15 minutes, stirring occasionally. Uncover and cook for 5 to 10 minutes more or until onion is very tender and golden brown, stirring frequently.

2 Meanwhile, in a large bowl combine ground beef, thyme, salt, and black pepper; mix well. Form into four ¾-inch-thick patties.

3 For a charcoal grill, place patties on the rack of an uncovered grill directly over medium coals. Grill for 14 to 18 minutes or until done (160°F for beef or 165°F for turkey),* turning once halfway through grilling. (For a gas grill, preheat grill. Reduce heat to medium. Place patties on grill rack over heat. Cover and grill as above.)

4 To serve, place arugula and patties on bun bottoms. Top patties with onion, roasted red peppers, blue cheese, and bun tops. Makes 4 servings.

COOK'S TIP

Can't decide which sweet onion variety to choose? The Maui variety is easy to find because it's available year-round. Vidalia and Walla Walla are widely available in the summer months.

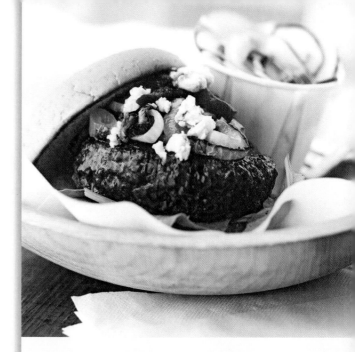

Blue Cheese-Topped Burgers with Caramelized Onions

PREP: 15 minutes   **COOK:** 20 minutes
GRILL: 14 minutes

NUTRITION FACTS per serving:

CALORIES 397
TOTAL FAT 17 g (6 g sat. fat)
CHOLESTEROL 79 mg
PROTEIN 29 g
CARBOHYDRATE 31 g
FIBER 4 g
SODIUM 540 mg

EXCHANGES 2 Starch, 3 Medium-Fat Meat, 0.5 Vegetable

*The internal color of a burger is not a reliable doneness indicator. A beef patty cooked to 160°F or a turkey patty cooked to 165°F is safe, regardless of color. To measure the doneness of a patty, insert an instant-read thermometer through the side of the patty to a depth of 2 to 3 inches.

Buffalo Chicken Tenders

PREP: 30 minutes   **BAKE:** 10 minutes
OVEN: 425°F

NUTRITION FACTS per serving:

CALORIES 265
TOTAL FAT 10 g (2 g sat. fat)
CHOLESTEROL 145 mg
PROTEIN 31 g
CARBOHYDRATE 12 g
FIBER 1 g
SODIUM 444 mg

EXCHANGES 1 Starch, 4 Very Lean Meat, 1 Fat

Nonstick cooking spray
1¼ ounces reduced-fat shredded wheat crackers, broken (½ cup)
1 ounce honey wheat pretzel rods, broken (½ cup)
¼ teaspoon cayenne pepper
2 eggs
¼ cup fat-free milk
1½ pounds chicken breast tenderloins
⅓ cup light mayonnaise or salad dressing
¼ cup crumbled blue cheese (1 ounce)
1 clove garlic, minced
½ cup Buffalo Sauce

1 Preheat oven to 425°F. Line a 15×10×1-inch baking pan with foil; coat with nonstick cooking spray. Set pan aside. Place crackers in a food processor; cover and process until coarsely ground. Add pretzels to food processor; cover and process until pretzels are coarsely ground. Transfer cracker mixture to a shallow dish; stir in cayenne pepper. In another shallow dish whisk together eggs and 2 tablespoons milk.

2 Dip chicken tenderloins into egg mixture, allowing excess to drip off. Dip tenderloins into crumb mixture, turning to coat. Arrange tenderloins in prepared pan. Lightly coat breaded tenderloins with nonstick cooking spray. Bake chicken for 10 to 15 minutes or until no longer pink (170°F).

3 Meanwhile, for blue cheese dip, in a small bowl stir together mayonnaise, blue cheese, remaining 2 tablespoons milk, and garlic. Serve chicken tenderloins with blue cheese dip and Buffalo Sauce. Makes 6 servings.

Buffalo Sauce: In a small saucepan stir together one 8-ounce can tomato sauce, ¼ cup cider vinegar, 2 tablespoons water, 2 teaspoons packed brown sugar, 1½ teaspoons bottled hot pepper sauce, ½ teaspoon dry mustard, ¼ teaspoon celery seeds, and ⅛ teaspoon salt. Bring to boiling; reduce heat. Simmer, uncovered, for 8 to 10 minutes or until mixture is reduced to 1 cup, stirring occasionally. Use immediately or cool, cover, and store in the refrigerator for up to 1 week. Makes 1 cup.

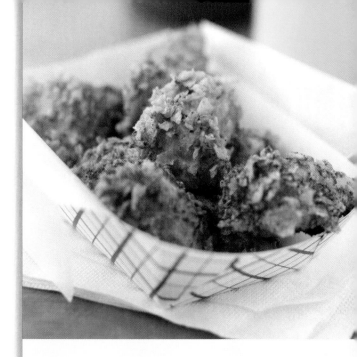

- ⅔ cup crushed cornflakes
- 1 teaspoon paprika
- ½ teaspoon garlic powder
- ½ teaspoon dried oregano, crushed
- ⅛ teaspoon cayenne pepper (optional)
- 1 egg white
- 1 pound skinless, boneless chicken breast, cut into 1-inch pieces

1 Preheat oven to 450°F. In a plastic bag combine crushed cornflakes, paprika, garlic powder, oregano, and, if desired, cayenne pepper. In a small bowl beat egg white with a fork.

2 Dip chicken pieces into egg white, allowing excess to drain off. Add chicken pieces, a few at a time, to cornflake mixture; shake to coat well.

3 Place chicken pieces in a single layer in an ungreased shallow baking pan. Bake for 7 to 9 minutes or until chicken is no longer pink. Makes 4 servings.

Chicken Nuggets

PREP: 20 minutes   **BAKE:** 7 minutes
OVEN: 450°F

NUTRITION FACTS per serving:

CALORIES 191
TOTAL FAT 2 g (0 g sat. fat)
CHOLESTEROL 66 mg
PROTEIN 29 g
CARBOHYDRATE 13 g
FIBER 0 g
SODIUM 228 mg

EXCHANGES 1 Starch, 3.5 Very Lean Meat

NUTRITION NOTE

Breading chicken in cornflakes and baking it is a healthful equivalent to battering in bread crumbs, which contain fat on their own, and frying it, which is how they are commonly prepared at restaurants.

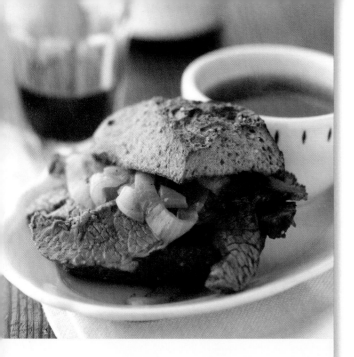

Classic French Dips

PREP: 20 minutes

COOK: 9 to 10 hours (low) or 4½ to 5 hours (high)

NUTRITION FACTS per serving:

CALORIES 339
TOTAL FAT 7 g (2 g sat. fat)
CHOLESTEROL 45 mg
PROTEIN 33 g
CARBOHYDRATE 39 g
FIBER 9 g
SODIUM 453 mg

EXCHANGES 2.5 Starch, 3.5 Lean Meat

NUTRITION NOTE

When you have a choice between a flat cut and point cut of beef brisket, select the flat cut, which is lower in fat. Always cook brisket using a long, slow method.

1 large sweet onion (such as Vidalia, Maui, or Walla Walla), cut into ½-inch-thick slices and separated into rings (1 cup)

1 2- to 2½-pound fresh beef brisket or boneless beef bottom round roast

2 cloves garlic, minced

1 teaspoon dried thyme, marjoram, or oregano, crushed

½ teaspoon black pepper

1 14-ounce can lower-sodium beef broth

2 tablespoons Worcestershire sauce

1 16-ounce loaf whole grain baguette-style bread, cut crosswise into 6 pieces and halved lengthwise, or 6 whole grain hoagie buns, split and if desired, toasted

1 Place onion in a 3½- to 5-quart slow cooker. Trim separable fat from beef. If necessary, cut beef to fit cooker. Place beef on top of onion. Sprinkle with garlic, thyme, and pepper. Pour beef broth and Worcestershire sauce over all.

2 Cover and cook on low-heat setting for 9 to 10 hours for brisket or 8 to 9 hours for bottom round, or on high-heat setting for 4½ to 5 hours for brisket or 4 to 4½ hours for bottom round.

3 Transfer meat to a cutting board; thinly slice across the grain, removing any visible fat as you slice. Using a slotted spoon, remove onion from cooker. Divide sliced brisket and onion slices among bread bottoms. Add bread tops. Skim fat from cooking juices in cooker; pass juices for dipping sandwiches. Makes 6 servings.

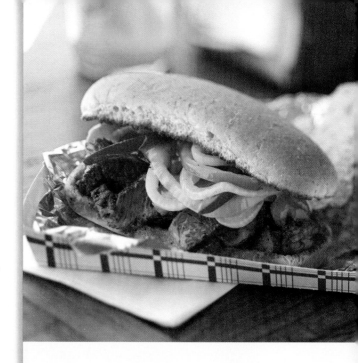

1   12-ounce boneless beef top sirloin steak, cut 1 inch thick

½   teaspoon garlic-pepper seasoning
    Nonstick cooking spray

2   medium red and/or green sweet peppers, seeded and cut into thin strips

1   large onion, thinly sliced and separated into rings

4   whole wheat frankfurter buns, split

½   cup shredded reduced-fat cheddar or reduced-fat Monterey Jack cheese (2 ounces)

1 Preheat broiler. Trim fat from steak. Sprinkle steak with garlic-pepper seasoning. Place seasoned steak on the unheated rack of a broiler pan. Broil 3 to 4 inches from heat until desired doneness. Allow 15 to 17 minutes for medium-rare doneness (145°F) or 20 to 22 minutes for medium doneness (160°F).

2 Meanwhile, coat an unheated very large nonstick skillet* with nonstick cooking spray. Preheat skillet over medium heat. Add sweet pepper and onion. Cover and cook for 5 minutes. Uncover and cook about 5 minutes more or just until tender, stirring occasionally.

3 Place split buns on a large baking sheet. Broil 4 to 5 inches from heat for 1 to 2 minutes or until lightly toasted. Remove bun tops from baking sheet; set aside. Slice steak into bite-size strips. Divide steak strips and sweet pepper mixture among bun bottoms. Sprinkle with cheese. Broil 4 to 5 inches from the heat for 1 to 2 minutes or until cheese is melted. Top with bun tops. Makes 4 servings.

*If you do not have a very large nonstick skillet, use a large nonstick skillet and cook sweet pepper and onion separately.

Philly Steak Sandwiches

PREP: 20 minutes

BROIL: 15 minutes (medium rare) or 20 minutes (medium)

NUTRITION FACTS per serving:

CALORIES 320
TOTAL FAT 12 g (5 g sat. fat)
CHOLESTEROL 52 mg
PROTEIN 25 g
CARBOHYDRATE 29 g
FIBER 4 g
SODIUM 414 mg

EXCHANGES 2 Starch, 2.5 Lean Meat, 0.5 Vegetable, 0.5 Fat

Buffalo Chicken Pizza

PREP: 45 minutes   **RISE:** 30 minutes
BAKE: 20 minutes   **OVEN:** 425°F

NUTRITION FACTS per serving:

CALORIES 431
TOTAL FAT 12 g (5 g sat. fat)
CHOLESTEROL 66 mg
PROTEIN 30 g
CARBOHYDRATE 51 g
FIBER 4 g
SODIUM 656 mg

EXCHANGES 3.5 Starch, 3 Lean Meat

1	recipe Pizza Dough (see recipe below)
½	cup Buffalo Sauce (see page 266)
1½	cups chopped cooked chicken breast (about 8 ounces)
½	cup thinly sliced red onion
¼	cup thinly sliced celery
¾	cup shredded reduced-fat mozzarella cheese (3 ounces)
¼	cup crumbled blue cheese (1 ounce)
2	tablespoons snipped fresh parsley

1 Prepare Pizza Dough. Preheat oven to 425°F. Punch down dough; let rest for 10 minutes. On a lightly floured surface, roll dough to a 12-inch circle. Transfer to a greased 12-inch round pizza pan, building up edge slightly. Using a fork, prick dough all over.

2 Bake crust about 10 minutes or until lightly browned. Spread Buffalo Sauce over partially baked crust. Top with chicken, red onion, and celery. Sprinkle with mozzarella cheese and blue cheese.

3 Bake for 10 to 15 minutes more or until cheese is melted and edge of crust is browned. Sprinkle with parsley. Makes 4 servings.

Pizza Dough: In a small bowl combine 1 package active dry yeast and ⅔ cup warm water (105°F to 115°F). Let stand for 5 minutes. Stir in 1 tablespoon honey and 1 tablespoon olive oil.

In a large bowl combine ¾ cup white whole wheat flour, ¼ cup cornmeal, and ¼ teaspoon salt. Stir in yeast mixture. Stir in as much of ¾ to 1 cup all-purpose flour as you can with a wooden spoon.

Turn dough onto a lightly floured surface. Knead in enough of the remaining all-purpose flour to make a moderately stiff dough that is smooth and elastic (6 to 8 minutes total). Shape dough into a ball. Cover and let rise in a warm place until nearly double in size (30 to 45 minutes). Makes enough for 1 pizza.

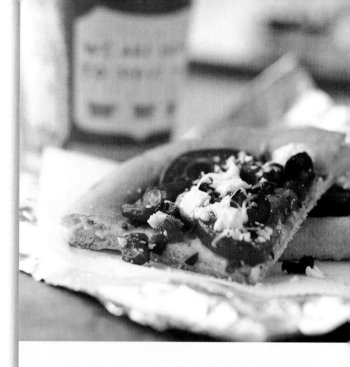

- 1   recipe Pizza Dough (see page 270)
- 1   tablespoon olive oil
- 1   tablespoon snipped fresh oregano or 1 teaspoon dried oregano, crushed
- 2   medium plum tomatoes, thinly sliced
- ¾   cup bottled roasted red sweet peppers, drained and coarsely chopped
- ¼   cup pitted kalamata olives, chopped, or sliced pitted ripe olives
- ¼   cup crumbled, reduced-fat feta cheese (1 ounce)
- ¼   cup finely shredded Parmesan cheese (1 ounce)
-      Snipped fresh oregano (optional)
-      Cracked black pepper (optional)

1 Prepare Pizza Dough. Preheat oven to 425°F. Grease a large baking sheet; set aside. Punch down dough; let rest for 10 minutes. On a lightly floured surface, roll dough to a 14-inch oblong shape. Transfer to prepared baking sheet. Prick dough all over with a fork. Bake for 8 to 10 minutes or until lightly browned.

2 Brush partially baked crust with oil and sprinkle with snipped or dried oregano or 1 teaspoon dried oregano. Top with tomato, roasted red pepper, olives, feta cheese, and Parmesan cheese. Bake for 5 to 10 minutes more or until cheese is melted.

3 To serve, if desired, sprinkle with additional snipped fresh oregano and cracked black pepper. Makes 6 to 8 servings.

Greek-Style Pizza

PREP: 30 minutes   **RISE:** 30 minutes
BAKE: 13 minutes   **OVEN:** 425°F

NUTRITION FACTS per serving:

CALORIES 236
TOTAL FAT 8 g (2 g sat. fat)
CHOLESTEROL 5 mg
PROTEIN 8 g
CARBOHYDRATE 36 g
FIBER 3 g
SODIUM 322 mg

EXCHANGES 2 Starch, 0.5 Vegetable, 1.5 Fat

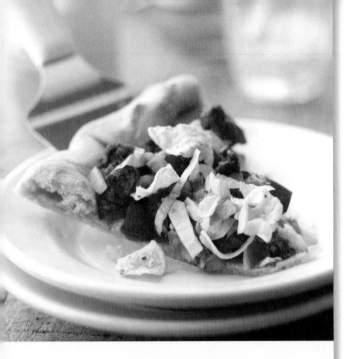

Taco Pizza

PREP: 30 minutes **RISE:** 30 minutes
BAKE: 16 minutes **OVEN:** 425°F

NUTRITION FACTS per serving:

CALORIES 284
TOTAL FAT 10 g (4 g sat. fat)
CHOLESTEROL 38 mg
PROTEIN 17 g
CARBOHYDRATE 33 g
FIBER 3 g
SODIUM 261 mg

EXCHANGES 2 Starch, 1.5 Medium-Fat Meat,
0.5 Vegetable

1 recipe Pizza Dough (see page 270)
1 cup shredded reduced-fat
   cheddar cheese (4 ounces)
12 ounces extra-lean ground beef
1 medium onion, chopped
⅔ cup purchased salsa
1½ cups chopped tomato
½ to 1 cup shredded lettuce and/or
   spinach
1 cup packaged baked tortilla chips,
   coarsely crushed
   Light dairy sour cream (optional)
   Purchased salsa (optional)

1 Prepare Pizza Dough. Preheat oven to
425°F. Grease a 12-inch round pizza pan;
set aside. Punch down dough; let rest for
10 minutes. On a lightly floured surface, roll
dough to a 13-inch circle. Transfer to prepared
pizza pan, allowing excess dough to extend over
edge of pan. Sprinkle half of the cheese in a thin
strip around the edge of the dough. Moisten
edge of dough. Fold edge over cheese and seal
tightly to enclose the cheese. Using a fork, prick
crust inside the cheese edge all over. Bake about
10 minutes or until lightly browned.

2 Meanwhile, in a large skillet cook beef and
onion until beef is brown and onion is
tender. Drain off fat. Stir the ⅔ cup salsa into the
beef mixture. Spoon beef mixture on crust. Bake
for 5 minutes more. Sprinkle with tomatoes and
remaining cheese. Bake for 1 to 2 minutes more
or until cheese melts.

3 To serve, cut pizza into eight wedges. Top
with lettuce and tortilla chips. If desired,
serve with sour cream and additional salsa.
Makes 8 servings.

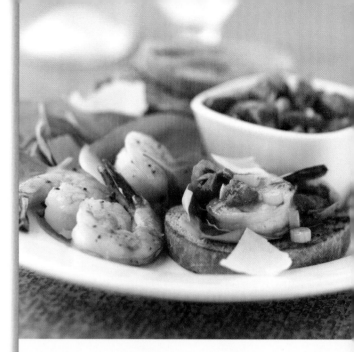

1   pound fresh or frozen peeled, deveined large shrimp with tails

⅛   teaspoon salt

⅛   teaspoon black pepper

3   cups fresh spinach or arugula

1   tablespoon olive oil

6   red and/or yellow plum tomatoes, seeded and coarsely chopped (3 cups)

3   cloves garlic, minced

2   tablespoons white balsamic vinegar or regular balsamic vinegar

1   tablespoon snipped fresh basil

¼   cup thinly sliced green onion

1   ounce Parmesan cheese, shaved

Crusty whole wheat bread slices (optional)

1 Thaw shrimp, if frozen. Rinse shrimp; pat dry with paper towels. Season shrimp with salt and pepper. Chop 1 cup of the spinach; set spinach aside.

2 In a large skillet heat oil over medium-high heat. Add shrimp; cook for 2 to 3 minutes or until opaque, stirring occasionally. Remove shrimp from skillet; keep warm.

3 Add tomato and garlic to hot skillet; cook and stir for 2 minutes. Remove from heat. Stir in 1 cup chopped spinach, balsamic vinegar, and basil.

4 Divide remaining spinach and shrimp among four serving plates. Serve with tomato mixture, green onion, and Parmesan cheese. If desired, serve with bread. Makes 4 servings.

Bruschetta-Style Shrimp

START TO FINISH: 25 minutes

NUTRITION FACTS per serving:

CALORIES 223
TOTAL FAT 8 g (2 g sat. fat)
CHOLESTEROL 177 mg
PROTEIN 28 g
CARBOHYDRATE 10 g
FIBER 2 g
SODIUM 382 mg

EXCHANGES 0.5 Other Carbohydrates, 3.5 Very Lean Meat, 1 Vegetable, 1 Fat

COOK'S TIP

Plum tomatoes are ideal for sauces and drying because of their thick flesh, few seeds, and low acidity. So while other tomato varieties will work, when making sauce, as in this recipe, it's best to use plum tomatoes.

Chicken Parmesan

PREP: 20 minutes **MARINATE:** 2 to 8 hours

BAKE: 20 minutes **OVEN:** 400°F

NUTRITION FACTS per serving:

CALORIES 422
TOTAL FAT 8 g (4 g sat. fat)
CHOLESTEROL 76 mg
PROTEIN 39 g
CARBOHYDRATE 48 g
FIBER 9 g
SODIUM 742 mg

EXCHANGES 3 Starch, 4 Very Lean Meat, 0.5 Vegetable, 0.5 Fat

COOK'S TIP

Always wash fruits and vegetables even when you plan to peel them. Prevent the possibility of peel contamination getting on your hands, cutting board, or knife.

4 skinless, boneless chicken breast halves (1 to 1¼ pounds total)

¾ cup buttermilk

1 cup soft whole wheat bread crumbs

½ cup grated Parmesan cheese

2 teaspoons dried Italian seasoning, crushed

   Olive oil nonstick cooking spray

4 ounces dried multigrain or whole grain spaghetti

1 medium zucchini, halved lengthwise and thinly sliced, or 2 cups (1-inch pieces) peeled eggplant

2 cups purchased tomato-basil pasta sauce

   Grated Parmesan cheese (optional)

1 In a large resealable plastic bag combine chicken and buttermilk. Seal bag; turn to coat chicken. Marinate in the refrigerator for 2 to 8 hours, turning bag occasionally.

2 Preheat oven to 400°F. Place crumbs in a 15×10×1-inch baking pan. Bake for 5 to 7 minutes or until dry and golden brown, stirring once halfway through baking. Cool completely on a wire rack. Transfer crumbs to a shallow dish. Stir in ½ cup Parmesan cheese and Italian seasoning. Line the 15×10×1-inch baking pan with foil; coat foil with nonstick cooking spray.

3 Drain chicken, discarding excess buttermilk. Dip chicken pieces, 1 at a time, in crumb mixture, turning to coat evenly. Place in foil-lined pan. Coat tops of chicken pieces with nonstick cooking spray. Bake for 20 to 25 minutes or until chicken is no longer pink (170°F).

4 Meanwhile, cook spaghetti according to package directions; drain and keep warm. Coat an unheated medium saucepan with nonstick cooking spray. Preheat over medium heat. Add zucchini; cook for 3 to 4 minutes or until tender (5 to 6 minutes for eggplant), stirring occasionally. Add pasta sauce; heat through.

5 Divide spaghetti among four serving plates. Top with chicken and zucchini mixture. If desired, sprinkle with additional Parmesan cheese. Makes 4 servings.

1 tablespoon olive oil

6 small bone-in chicken breast halves, skinned (about 2½ pounds total)

8 ounces fresh mushrooms, sliced (about 3 cups)

1 medium onion, sliced

1 clove garlic, minced

1 14½-ounce can diced tomatoes, undrained

1 6-ounce can tomato paste

½ cup dry white wine or reduced-sodium chicken broth

1 teaspoon dried Italian seasoning, crushed

½ teaspoon salt

⅛ teaspoon black pepper

6 ounces dried multigrain or whole grain fettuccine or linguine, cooked according to package directions

2 tablespoons small fresh basil leaves

Chicken Cacciatore

PREP: 30 minutes

COOK: 30 minutes

NUTRITION FACTS per serving:

CALORIES 311
TOTAL FAT 4 g (1 g sat. fat)
CHOLESTEROL 68 mg
PROTEIN 34 g
CARBOHYDRATE 33 g
FIBER 6 g
SODIUM 427 mg

EXCHANGES 2 Starch, 4 Very Lean Meat, 0.5 Vegetable

1 In a very large skillet heat oil over medium heat. Add chicken; brown chicken on all sides, turning to brown evenly. Remove chicken, reserving drippings in skillet. Set chicken aside.

2 Add mushrooms, onion, and garlic to drippings in skillet. Cook and stir about 5 minutes or just until vegetables are tender. Return chicken to skillet.

3 In a medium bowl combine undrained tomatoes, tomato paste, dry white wine, Italian seasoning, salt, and pepper. Pour over chicken in skillet. Bring to boiling; reduce heat. Cover and simmer for 30 to 35 minutes or until chicken is no longer pink (170°F), turning once during cooking. Serve over hot cooked pasta. Sprinkle with basil. Makes 6 servings.

Chicken and Vegetable Fettuccine

START TO FINISH: 30 minutes

NUTRITION FACTS per serving:

CALORIES 286
TOTAL FAT 7 g (2 g sat. fat)
CHOLESTEROL 40 mg
PROTEIN 25 g
CARBOHYDRATE 35 g
FIBER 2 g
SODIUM 380 mg

EXCHANGES 2 Starch, 2.5 Very Lean Meat, 1 Vegetable, 0.5 Fat

---

8 ounces dried whole wheat or spinach fettuccine

2 cups zucchini and/or yellow summer squash, halved lengthwise and sliced

2 cups broccoli florets

¼ cup snipped dried tomatoes (not oil pack)

2 cups fresh baby spinach

3 tablespoons snipped fresh basil

¼ teaspoon salt

¼ teaspoon freshly cracked black pepper

¾ cup finely shredded Parmesan, Romano, or Asiago cheese (3 ounces)

¼ cup fat-free milk

1 tablespoon olive oil

12 ounces chicken breast tenderloins

2 cloves garlic, minced

   Shredded Parmesan, Romano, or Asiago cheese (optional)

1 In a Dutch oven cook pasta according to package directions, except do not use salt; add zucchini and/or yellow squash, broccoli, and dried tomatoes for the last 3 minutes of cooking; drain. Return pasta mixture to hot Dutch oven. Add spinach, basil, salt, and pepper to pasta; toss gently. Add ¾ cup Parmesan cheese and milk; toss to coat.

2 Meanwhile, in a large skillet heat oil over medium heat. Add chicken and garlic; cook for 3 to 5 minutes or until chicken is no longer pink, stirring occasionally. Add cooked chicken to pasta mixture; toss gently. Divide among six serving plates. If desired, garnish with additional Parmesan cheese. Makes 6 servings.

COOK'S TIP

Look for zucchini and yellow summer squash with skins that are free of soft spots, nicks, and shriveling. Smaller, less mature squash have fewer seeds and a more delicate flavor than the large ones, which can become woody and bitter.

- 8   ounces uncooked bulk turkey sausage or extra-lean ground beef
- ¾   cup chopped onion
- 4   cloves garlic, minced
- 1   15-ounce can tomato sauce
- 1   cup bottled roasted red sweet peppers, drained and chopped
- 2   tablespoons snipped fresh basil or 2 teaspoons dried basil, crushed
- 1   tablespoon snipped fresh oregano or 1 teaspoon dried oregano, crushed
- ¼   teaspoon black pepper
- 6   dried whole grain lasagna noodles
- 1   15-ounce carton light ricotta cheese
- 1   10-ounce package frozen chopped spinach, thawed and well drained
- 1   egg white, lightly beaten
       Nonstick cooking spray
- 1   cup shredded reduced-fat mozzarella cheese (4 ounces)

1 Preheat oven to 375°F. For meat sauce, in a large skillet combine sausage, onion, and garlic; cook over medium heat until meat is brown and vegetables are tender, stirring to break up sausage. Drain off fat, if necessary.

2 Stir tomato sauce, roasted red peppers, dried basil (if using), dried oregano (if using), and black pepper into meat mixture in skillet. Bring to boiling; reduce heat. Cover and simmer for 10 minutes, stirring occasionally. Stir in fresh basil and fresh oregano, if using.

3 Meanwhile, cook lasagna noodles according to package directions, except omit the cooking oil and salt. Drain well. For ricotta mixture, in a medium bowl stir together ricotta cheese, spinach, and egg white.

4 Lightly coat a 2-quart rectangular baking dish with nonstick cooking spray. Place two cooked lasagna noodles in the prepared baking dish. Spread with one-third of the ricotta mixture. Top with one-third of the meat sauce and one-third of the mozzarella cheese. Repeat layers twice, except do not add the last layer of mozzarella cheese.

Sausage and Spinach Lasagna

PREP: 45 minutes   **BAKE:** 30 minutes
STAND: 15 minutes   **OVEN:** 375°F

NUTRITION FACTS per serving:

CALORIES 237
TOTAL FAT 7 g (3 g sat. fat)
CHOLESTEROL 42 mg
PROTEIN 18 g
CARBOHYDRATE 25 g
FIBER 5 g
SODIUM 613 mg

EXCHANGES 1.5 Starch, 2 Lean Meat, 1 Vegetable

5 Bake, covered, for 25 to 30 minutes or until bubbly. Uncover and sprinkle with remaining mozzarella cheese. Bake about 5 minutes more or until cheese is melted. Let stand for 15 minutes before serving. Makes 8 servings.

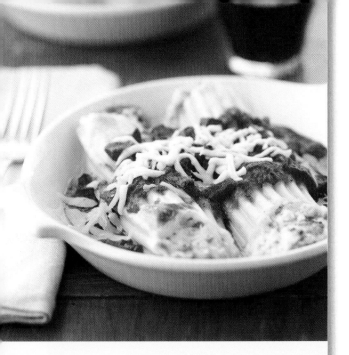

8   dried manicotti shells
    Nonstick cooking spray
1   cup chopped fresh mushrooms
¾   cup shredded carrot
3   or 4 cloves garlic, minced
1   cup light ricotta cheese or low-fat
    cream-style cottage cheese
¾   cup shredded reduced-fat
    mozzarella cheese (3 ounces)
2   eggs, lightly beaten
¼   cup grated Parmesan cheese
2   teaspoons dried Italian seasoning,
    crushed
1   14½-ounce can diced tomatoes
    with basil, garlic, and oregano,
    undrained
1   cup bottled roasted red sweet
    peppers, drained and chopped

Cheese Manicotti with Roasted Pepper Sauce

PREP: 30 minutes   **BAKE:** 25 minutes
STAND: 10 minutes   **OVEN:** 350°F

NUTRITION FACTS per serving:

CALORIES 378
TOTAL FAT 13 g (7 g sat. fat)
CHOLESTEROL 141 mg
PROTEIN 22 g
CARBOHYDRATE 43 g
FIBER 3 g
SODIUM 860 mg

EXCHANGES 2.5 Starch, 2 Lean Meat,
1 Vegetable, 1 Fat

1 Preheat oven to 350°F. Cook manicotti shells according to package directions; drain. Rinse with cold water and drain again. Set aside.

2 Meanwhile, for filling, coat an unheated large nonstick skillet with nonstick cooking spray. Preheat over medium heat. Add mushrooms, carrot, and garlic to hot skillet. Cook for 3 to 5 minutes or just until vegetables are tender, stirring occasionally. Remove from heat; cool slightly. Stir in ricotta cheese, ½ cup mozzarella cheese, eggs, Parmesan cheese, and Italian seasoning. Spoon filling into cooked manicotti shells.

3 For sauce, place undrained tomatoes in a blender or food processor. Cover and blend or process until smooth. Stir in roasted red peppers. Spread about ⅓ cup of the sauce into the bottom of four 12- to 16-ounce ungreased individual baking dishes or a 2-quart rectangular baking dish. Arrange stuffed manicotti shells in the individual baking dishes or on the large baking dish, overlapping shells slightly if necessary. Pour remaining sauce over manicotti.

4 Bake, covered, for 20 to 25 minutes for individual baking dishes, 35 to 40 minutes for large baking dish, or until heated through. Uncover and sprinkle with remaining ¼ cup mozzarella cheese. Bake for 5 minutes more. Let stand for 10 minutes before serving. Makes 4 servings.

COOK'S TIP

Mushrooms can be stored in the refrigerator up to one week. Keep them in the original packaging until ready to use. Once the package is opened, store mushrooms in a porous paper bag or other loosely closed bag. Mushrooms stored in airtight containers spoil quickly.

8 ounces dried multigrain or whole grain penne or mostaccioli

3 cups assorted fresh vegetables (such as red sweet pepper strips, trimmed sugar snap peas, 2-inch-long pieces trimmed asparagus, and/or quartered-lengthwise packaged peeled baby carrots)

1 cup halved cherry tomatoes

½ cup reduced-sodium chicken broth

3 tablespoons all-purpose flour

½ teaspoon salt

1¼ cups low-fat milk

¼ cup dry sherry or reduced-sodium chicken broth

3 ounces Parmesan or Asiago cheese, finely shredded (¾ cup)

½ cup lightly packed fresh basil, coarsely chopped

4 teaspoons snipped fresh thyme or oregano

⅓ cup sliced green onion (optional)

Fresh-Herb Pasta Primavera

START TO FINISH: 35 minutes

NUTRITION FACTS per serving:

CALORIES 253
TOTAL FAT 5 g (3 g sat. fat)
CHOLESTEROL 12 mg
PROTEIN 13 g
CARBOHYDRATE 41 g
FIBER 6 g
SODIUM 496 mg

EXCHANGES 2.5 Starch, 0.5 Medium-Fat Meat, 0.5 Vegetable

1 In a 4-quart Dutch oven cook pasta according to package directions; add 3 cups assorted vegetables for the last 2 minutes of cooking. Drain well. Return to hot Dutch oven. Add cherry tomatoes.

2 In a medium saucepan whisk together chicken broth, flour, and salt until smooth. Stir in milk and sherry. Cook and stir until thickened and bubbly; cook and stir for 2 minutes more. Remove from heat; stir in finely shredded Parmesan cheese, basil, and thyme.

3 Add herb sauce to pasta mixture; toss gently to coat. Divide among six serving plates. If desired, sprinkle with green onion. Makes 6 servings.

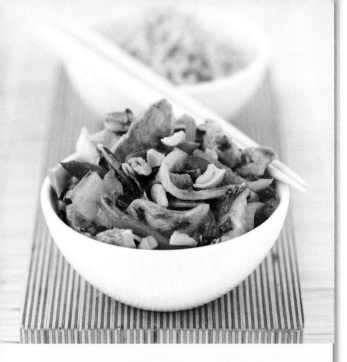

Spicy Stir-Fried Chicken with Cashews

START TO FINISH: 30 minutes

NUTRITION FACTS per serving:

CALORIES 349
TOTAL FAT 10 g (2 g sat. fat)
CHOLESTEROL 49 mg
PROTEIN 26 g
CARBOHYDRATE 41 g
FIBER 4 g
SODIUM 443 mg

EXCHANGES 2.5 Starch, 2.5 Very Lean Meat, 1 Vegetable, 1 Fat

COOK'S TIP

Store bok choy in a perforated plastic bag up to five days in the refrigerator. Before shredding it, pull stalks apart and rinse them in cold water several times to remove any grit.

2 tablespoons bottled oyster sauce
1 tablespoon reduced-sodium soy sauce
1 tablespoon packed brown sugar
2 teaspoons cornstarch
⅓ cup water
1 tablespoon canola oil
2 medium red and/or green sweet peppers, seeded and cut into bite-size strips
1 medium onion, sliced
3 cups coarsely shredded bok choy or napa cabbage
2 to 4 fresh red hot chile peppers, seeded and finely chopped*
1 clove garlic, minced
12 ounces skinless, boneless chicken breast halves, cut into bite-size strips
2 cups hot cooked brown rice
¼ cup lightly salted roasted cashews, coarsely chopped

1 For sauce, in a small bowl stir together oyster sauce, soy sauce, brown sugar, and cornstarch. Stir in water. Set aside.

2 In a large wok or very large nonstick skillet heat oil over medium-high heat. Add sweet pepper and onion; stir-fry for 2 minutes. Add bok choy, chile pepper, and garlic; stir-fry for 1 to 2 minutes more or until peppers and onion are crisp-tender. Remove vegetable mixture from wok and set aside.

3 Add chicken to wok. Stir-fry for 3 to 4 minutes or until no longer pink. Push chicken to the side of wok. Stir sauce; add to wok. Cook and stir until thickened and bubbly. Return vegetable mixture to wok. Cook and stir for 1 minute more or until heated through. Serve over rice and sprinkle with cashews. Makes 4 servings.

*Because chile peppers contain volatile oils that can burn your skin and eyes, avoid direct contact with them as much as possible. When working with chile peppers, wear plastic or rubber gloves. If your bare hands do touch the peppers, wash your hands and nails well with soap and warm water.

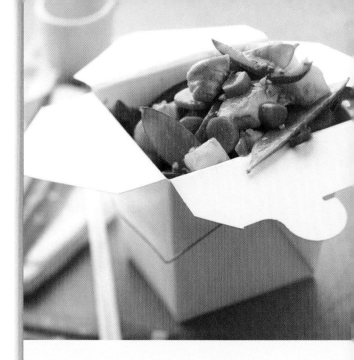

- ¾ cup reduced-sodium chicken broth
- 3 tablespoons red wine vinegar
- 2 tablespoons reduced-sodium soy sauce
- 4 teaspoons sugar
- 1 tablespoon cornstarch
- 1 clove garlic, minced
- 4 teaspoons canola oil
- 3 medium carrots, thinly sliced
- 1 large red sweet pepper, seeded and cut into bite-size strips
- 2 cups fresh pea pods, tips and stems removed
- 12 ounces skinless, boneless chicken breast halves, cut into 1-inch pieces
- 1 8-ounce can pineapple chunks (juice pack), drained
- 3 cups hot cooked brown rice

1 For sauce, in a small bowl stir together chicken broth, vinegar, soy sauce, sugar, cornstarch, and garlic; set aside.

2 In a large nonstick skillet heat 3 teaspoons oil over medium-high heat. Add carrot and sweet peppers; cook for 3 minutes. Add pea pods. Cook and stir about 1 minute more or until vegetables are crisp-tender. Remove from skillet; set aside.

3 Add remaining 1 teaspoon oil to skillet. Add chicken to skillet. Cook and stir for 3 to 4 minutes or until chicken is no longer pink. Push chicken from center of skillet. Stir sauce; add to center of skillet. Cook and stir until thickened and bubbly. Add vegetable mixture and pineapple chunks to skillet; heat through. Serve with hot cooked brown rice. Makes 6 servings.

Sweet-and-Sour Chicken

START TO FINISH: 30 minutes

NUTRITION FACTS per serving:

CALORIES 270
TOTAL FAT 5 g (1 g sat. fat)
CHOLESTEROL 33 mg
PROTEIN 18 g
CARBOHYDRATE 39 g
FIBER 4 g
SODIUM 321 mg

EXCHANGES 2 Starch, 1.5 Very Lean Meat, 1 Vegetable, 0.5 Fat

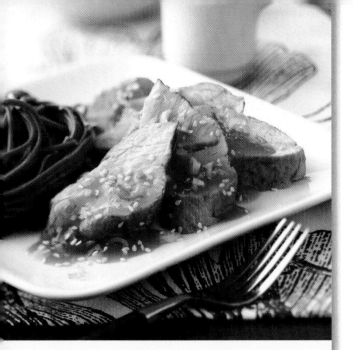

3 pounds turkey breast tenderloins
¼ teaspoon black pepper
⅛ teaspoon cayenne pepper
¼ cup reduced-sodium chicken broth
¼ cup soy sauce or reduced-sodium soy sauce
4 teaspoons grated fresh ginger
1 tablespoon lemon juice
1 tablespoon toasted sesame oil
2 cloves garlic, minced
2 tablespoons cornstarch
2 tablespoons cold water
2 tablespoons sliced green onion
1 tablespoon sesame seeds, toasted

Sesame Turkey

PREP: 20 minutes

COOK: 5 to 6 hours (low)

or 2½ to 3 hours (high)

NUTRITION FACTS per serving:

CALORIES 222
TOTAL FAT 3 g (1 g sat. fat)
CHOLESTEROL 112 mg
PROTEIN 42 g
CARBOHYDRATE 3 g
FIBER 0 g
SODIUM 373 mg

EXCHANGES 6 Very Lean Meat

1 Place turkey in a 3½- or 4-quart slow cooker. Sprinkle with black pepper and cayenne pepper. In a small bowl combine chicken broth, soy sauce, ginger, lemon juice, sesame oil, and garlic. Pour over turkey in cooker.

2 Cover and cook on low-heat setting for 5 to 6 hours or on high-heat setting for 2½ to 3 hours.

3 Transfer turkey to a serving platter, reserving cooking liquid. Cover turkey to keep warm.

4 For sauce, strain cooking liquid into a small saucepan. In a small bowl combine cornstarch and cold water. Stir into liquid in saucepan. Cook and stir over medium heat until thickened and bubbly. Cook and stir for 2 minutes more. If desired, slice turkey. Spoon sauce over turkey. Sprinkle with green onion and sesame seeds. Makes 8 servings.

COOK'S TIP

Sesame oil has a strong resistance to rancidity and when stored in a cool, dry place will keep for months.

Chapter 17

Holiday

On the opener: Herb Roast Turkey (see recipe, page 286)

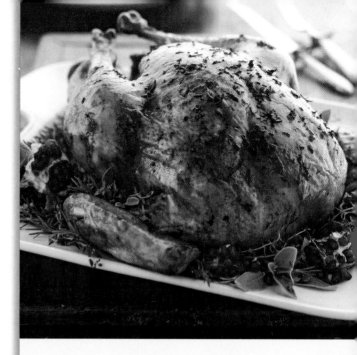

- 1   12- to 14-pound turkey
- 1   tablespoon snipped fresh rosemary or 1 teaspoon dried rosemary, crushed
- 1   tablespoon snipped fresh thyme or 1 teaspoon dried thyme, crushed
- 1   tablespoon snipped fresh sage or 1 teaspoon dried sage, crushed
- ½   teaspoon salt
- ½   teaspoon black pepper
- 1   tablespoon olive oil
     Fresh rosemary sprigs, fresh thyme sprigs, fresh sage leaves, and/or pomegranate pieces (optional)

Traditional Roast Turkey

PREP: 20 minutes   **ROAST:** 3 hours
STAND: 15 minutes   **OVEN:** 425°F/325°F

NUTRITION FACTS per serving:

CALORIES 229
TOTAL FAT 7 g (2 g sat. fat)
CHOLESTEROL 137 mg
PROTEIN 38 g
CARBOHYDRATE 0 g
FIBER 0 g
SODIUM 123 mg

EXCHANGES 5 Very Lean Meat, 1 Fat

1 Preheat oven to 425°F. Remove neck and giblets from turkey. Rinse the inside of the turkey; pat dry with paper towels. In a small bowl stir together snipped or dried rosemary, snipped or dried thyme, snipped or dried sage, salt, and pepper. Season inside of body cavity with half of the herb mixture. Pull neck skin to the back; fasten with a skewer. Tuck ends of the drumsticks under the band of skin across the tail. If there is no band of skin, tie the drumsticks securely to the tail with 100%-cotton kitchen string. Twist wing tips under the back.

2 Place turkey, breast side up, on a rack in a shallow roasting pan. Brush turkey with oil. Sprinkle turkey with remaining herb mixture. Insert an oven-going meat thermometer into the center of an inside thigh muscle. The thermometer should not touch bone. Cover turkey loosely with foil.

3 Roast for 30 minutes. Reduce oven temperature to 325°F. Roast for 2½ to 3 hours more or until the thermometer registers 180°F. About 45 minutes before end of roasting, remove foil and cut band of skin or string between drumsticks so thighs cook evenly. When turkey is done, juices should run clear and drumsticks should move easily in their sockets.

4 Remove turkey from oven. Transfer turkey to a serving platter. Cover; let stand for 15 to 20 minutes before carving. If desired, garnish platter with rosemary sprigs, thyme sprigs, sage leaves, and/or pomegranate pieces. Makes 24 (about 4-ounce) servings.

COOK'S TIP

Garnishing this dish with pomegranate seeds lends brilliant ruby color and a new flavor combination. And yes, the entire seed is edible.

1	2-pound boneless turkey breast, skinned
½	teaspoon salt
½	teaspoon black pepper
2	teaspoons finely shredded lemon peel
3	tablespoons lemon juice
2	tablespoons olive oil
1	tablespoon snipped fresh flat-leaf parsley
1	tablespoon snipped fresh rosemary
1	tablespoon snipped fresh sage
1	tablespoon snipped fresh thyme
6	cloves garlic, minced
1	cup chicken broth
¼	cup dry white wine or chicken broth
1	recipe Onion and Mushroom Gravy (see page 287) (optional)
1	tablespoon snipped fresh flat-leaf parsley

Herb Roast Turkey

PREP: 20 minutes   **ROAST:** 40 minutes
OVEN: 400°F/350°F

NUTRITION FACTS per serving:

CALORIES 170
TOTAL FAT 4 g (1 g sat. fat)
CHOLESTEROL 71 mg
PROTEIN 28 g
CARBOHYDRATE 2 g
FIBER 0 g
SODIUM 309 mg

EXCHANGES 4 Very Lean Meat, 1 Fat

1 Preheat oven to 400°F. Season turkey breast with salt and pepper. Place turkey in a shallow roasting pan. In a small bowl combine lemon peel, lemon juice, oil, 1 tablespoon parsley, rosemary, sage, thyme, and garlic. Sprinkle herb mixture evenly over turkey breast; rub in with your fingers.

2 Roast turkey for 15 minutes. Pour chicken broth and wine over turkey. Reduce oven temperature to 350°F. Roast turkey about 25 minutes more or until tender and no longer pink (170°F), spooning juices in pan over turkey every 10 minutes.

3 To serve, slice turkey. If desired, serve with Onion and Mushroom Gravy. Or spoon some of the cooking juices from the roasting pan over individual servings. Sprinkle with 1 tablespoon parsley. Makes 8 servings.

COOK'S TIP

Use a clean instant-read thermometer to check the temperature of cooked meat. Insert the thermometer into the thickest part of the meat and as close to the center as possible. Don't let the thermometer touch the pan or bone; doing so will produce an inaccurate reading.

Nonstick cooking spray

4 ounces shallots, peeled and coarsely chopped (about 1 cup)

1½ cups sliced fresh mushrooms (such as stemmed shiitake, cremini, and/or button)

1 14-ounce can reduced-sodium chicken broth

¼ cup all-purpose flour

2 teaspoons balsamic vinegar

1 tablespoon snipped fresh oregano or marjoram or ½ teaspoon dried oregano or marjoram, crushed

Dash black pepper

1 Lightly coat an unheated medium nonstick saucepan with nonstick cooking spray. Preheat saucepan over medium heat. Add shallots to hot saucepan; cook and stir about 6 minutes or until shallots are tender and golden brown. Add mushrooms; cook for 4 to 6 minutes more or until tender. Stir together ½ cup chicken broth and flour; add to saucepan. Add remaining broth, balsamic vinegar, and dried herbs (if using). Cook and stir until thickened and bubbly; cook and stir for 1 minute more. Stir in fresh herbs, if using. Season with pepper. Serve with turkey and/or potatoes. Makes about 2¼ cups (10 servings).

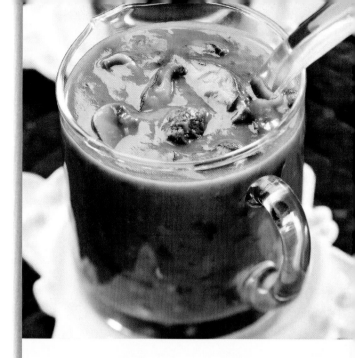

Onion and Mushroom Gravy

START TO FINISH: 25 minutes

NUTRITION FACTS per serving:

CALORIES 27
TOTAL FAT 0 g (0 g sat. fat)
CHOLESTEROL 0 mg
PROTEIN 1 g
CARBOHYDRATE 5 g
FIBER 0 g
SODIUM 97 mg

EXCHANGES Free

2 tablespoons canola oil

2 cups sliced fresh mushrooms

¾ cup coarsely chopped red and/or yellow sweet pepper

½ cup chopped onion

2 cloves garlic, minced

¼ cup all-purpose flour

¾ teaspoon salt

1½ teaspoons snipped fresh thyme or ½ teaspoon dried thyme, crushed

¼ teaspoon black pepper

2 cups fat-free milk

1 10-ounce package frozen chopped spinach, thawed and well drained

2 cups cooked brown or white rice

2 cups chopped cooked turkey or chicken (about 10 ounces)

½ cup finely shredded Parmesan cheese (2 ounces)

Turkey and Vegetable Bake

PREP: 35 minutes   **BAKE:** 30 minutes

STAND: 15 minutes   **OVEN:** 350°F

NUTRITION FACTS per serving:

CALORIES 302
TOTAL FAT 9 g (2 g sat. fat)
CHOLESTEROL 31 mg
PROTEIN 28 g
CARBOHYDRATE 34 g
FIBER 12 g
SODIUM 625 mg

EXCHANGES 2 Starch, 3 Very Lean Meat, 1 Vegetable, 0.5 Fat

1 Preheat oven to 350°F. In a 12-inch skillet heat oil over medium heat. Add mushrooms, sweet pepper, onion, and garlic; cook and stir until tender. Stir in flour, salt, thyme, and black pepper. Add milk all at once; cook and stir until thickened and bubbly. Stir in spinach, cooked rice, chopped cooked turkey, and ¼ cup Parmesan cheese.

2 Spoon mushroom mixture into a 2-quart rectangular baking dish. Sprinkle with remaining ¼ cup Parmesan cheese. Bake, covered, for 20 minutes. Uncover and bake about 10 minutes more or until heated through. Let stand for 15 minutes before serving. Makes 8 servings.

COOK'S TIP

Read labels on rice packages to determine how much dry rice will yield the amount of cooked rice needed. Usually for brown and wild rice, 1 cup dry will yield 3 to 4 cups cooked rice.

- 1 12-ounce package fresh cranberries
- 1 cup water
- ½ cup sugar
- 1 4-serving-size package sugar-free, low-calorie cranberry- or raspberry-flavored gelatin
- 1 15¼-ounce can crushed pineapple (juice pack), undrained
- ⅓ cup coarsely chopped pecans, toasted

1 In a large saucepan combine cranberries and water. Bring to boiling; reduce heat. Simmer, uncovered, about 3 minutes or until berries pop. Remove from heat.

2 Add sugar and gelatin to cranberries, stirring to dissolve. Stir in undrained pineapple. Transfer to a serving bowl. Cover and chill about 6 hours or until thickened.

3 To serve, sprinkle with pecans. Makes 10 servings.

Make-Ahead Directions: Prepare as above in step 2. Cover and chill for up to 1 week. Serve as above in step 3.

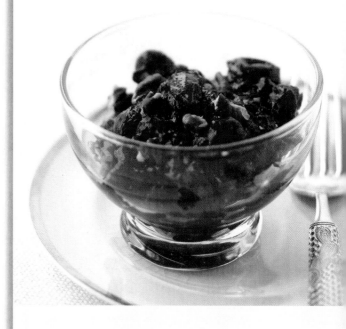

Cranberry-Pecan Salad

PREP: 15 minutes

CHILL: 6 hours

NUTRITION FACTS per serving:

CALORIES 106
TOTAL FAT 3 g (0 g sat. fat)
CHOLESTEROL 0 mg
PROTEIN 1 g
CARBOHYDRATE 20 g
FIBER 2 g
SODIUM 27 mg

EXCHANGES 1 Other Carbohydrates, 0.5 Fruit, 0.5 Fat

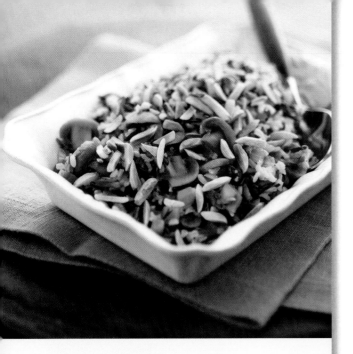

Wild Rice Stuffing

PREP: 15 minutes

COOK: 45 minutes

NUTRITION FACTS per serving:

CALORIES 97
TOTAL FAT 1 g (0 g sat. fat)
CHOLESTEROL 0 mg
PROTEIN 5 g
CARBOHYDRATE 19 g
FIBER 2 g
SODIUM 193 mg

EXCHANGES 1 Starch, 0.5 Vegetable

2½ cups reduced-sodium chicken broth

½ cup wild rice, rinsed

½ cup long grain brown rice

¼ teaspoon ground sage or dried thyme, crushed

3 cups sliced fresh mushrooms

1 cup chopped celery

6 green onions, sliced

½ cup slivered almonds, toasted (optional)

1 In a large saucepan combine chicken broth, wild rice, brown rice, and sage or thyme. Bring to boiling; reduce heat. Cover and simmer for 20 minutes.

2 Stir in mushrooms, celery, and green onions. Cover and cook over medium-low heat about 25 minutes or just until wild rice and vegetables are tender, stirring frequently. If desired, garnish with toasted almonds. Serve immediately. Makes 8 servings.

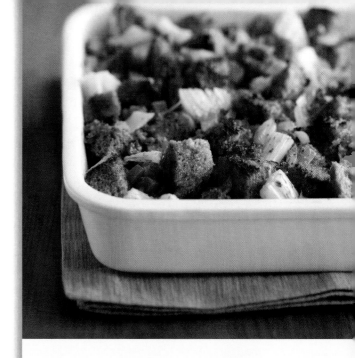

- 8 cups whole grain bread cubes (about 9 slices)
- 1 medium fennel bulb with tops
- 2 tablespoons olive oil
- 1 cup finely chopped carrots
- 1 cup chopped onion
- 2 cloves garlic, minced
- 1 teaspoon dried Italian seasoning, crushed
- ¼ teaspoon black pepper
- ⅛ teaspoon salt
- 1 to 1½ cups reduced-sodium chicken broth

1 Preheat oven to 300°F. Spread bread cubes in a large shallow roasting pan. Bake for 10 to 15 minutes or until bread cubes are dry, stirring twice. Cool. Increase oven temperature to 325°F.

2 Remove green leafy tops from fennel; snip enough of the tops to measure 1 to 2 tablespoons. Set aside. Cut off and discard upper stalks. Remove any wilted outer layers and cut a thin slice from the fennel base. Cut fennel bulb into wedges, removing the core. Coarsely chop fennel.

3 In a large skillet heat oil over medium heat. Add chopped fennel, carrot, onion, and garlic; cook until tender, stirring occasionally. Stir in snipped fennel tops, Italian seasoning, pepper, and salt. Place fennel mixture in a very large bowl. Stir in bread cubes. Drizzle with enough of the broth to moisten; toss gently to coat. Transfer mixture to a 2-quart casserole. Bake, covered, in 325°F oven for 20 minutes. Uncover; bake about 20 minutes more or until heated through. Makes 12 to 14 servings.

Fennel-Herb Bread Stuffing

PREP: 35 minutes   **BAKE:** 40 minutes
OVEN: 300°F/325°F

NUTRITION FACTS per serving:

CALORIES 98
TOTAL FAT 3 g (0 g sat. fat)
CHOLESTEROL 0 mg
PROTEIN 4 g
CARBOHYDRATE 17 g
FIBER 3 g
SODIUM 217 mg

EXCHANGES 1 Starch, 0.5 Fat

COOK'S TIP

Look for fennel bulbs that are clean and crisp with fresh green leaves and no browning. To store fennel, wrap it tightly in a plastic bag and refrigerate for up to five days.

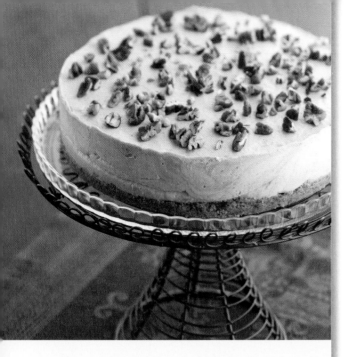

No-Bake Pumpkin Cheesecake

PREP: 35 minutes **BAKE:** 5 minutes
CHILL: 4 to 24 hours **OVEN:** 350°F

NUTRITION FACTS per serving:

CALORIES 150
TOTAL FAT 8 g (4 g sat. fat)
CHOLESTEROL 11 mg
PROTEIN 5 g
CARBOHYDRATE 14 g
FIBER 1 g
SODIUM 144 mg

EXCHANGES 1 Other Carbohydrates, 1.5 Fat

1	recipe Graham Cracker Crust
1	envelope unflavored gelatin
¼	cup water
1½	8-ounce tubs light cream cheese
1	15-ounce can pumpkin
2	tablespoons sugar or sugar substitute* equivalent to 2 tablespoons sugar
1	teaspoon ground cinnamon
¾	of an 8-ounce container frozen light whipped dessert topping, thawed
	Chopped pecans (optional)

1 Prepare Graham Cracker Crust; set aside. In a small saucepan stir together gelatin and water; let stand for 5 minutes to soften. Cook and stir over low heat until gelatin dissolves; set aside to cool slightly.

2 In a large bowl beat cream cheese with an electric mixer on medium speed until smooth. Add pumpkin, sugar, cinnamon, and gelatin mixture; beat until well mixed. Fold in dessert topping. Spread mixture into crust in springform pan. Cover and chill for 4 to 24 hours or until set.

3 Using a thin metal spatula or table knife, loosen cheesecake from the side of the springform pan. If desired, use a wide spatula to remove cheesecake from bottom of pan and place on a serving plate. Cut into wedges to serve. If desired, garnish with pecans. Makes 14 servings.

***Sugar Substitutes:** Choose from Splenda granular, Equal Spoonful or packets, or Sweet'N Low bulk or packets. Follow package directions to use product amount equivalent to 2 tablespoons sugar for both crust and filling.

Per serving with substitute: same as above, except 136 cal., 11 g carbo.

Graham Cracker Crust: Preheat oven to 350°F. In a small bowl combine ¾ cup finely crushed graham crackers, 3 tablespoons canola oil, and 2 tablespoons sugar or sugar substitute* equivalent to 2 tablespoons sugar. Mix well. Spread evenly in bottom of an 8- or 9-inch springform pan; press firmly onto bottom. Bake for 5 minutes. Cool on a wire rack.

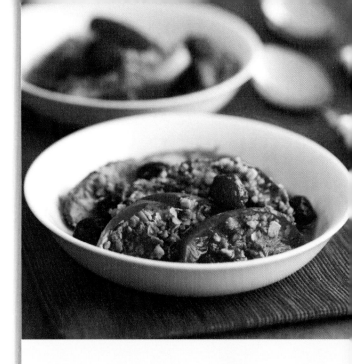

- 5 cups thinly sliced, cored cooking apple
- 1 cup cranberries
- 2 tablespoons granulated sugar
- ½ teaspoon apple pie spice or ground cinnamon
- ½ cup quick-cooking rolled oats
- 3 tablespoons packed brown sugar
- 2 tablespoons all-purpose flour
- ½ teaspoon apple pie spice or ground cinnamon
- 2 tablespoons butter

1 Preheat oven to 375°F. In a 2-quart baking dish combine sliced apple and cranberries. Stir together granulated sugar and ½ teaspoon apple pie spice. Sprinkle over fruit mixture in baking dish; toss to coat.

2 In a small bowl combine oats, brown sugar, flour, and ½ teaspoon apple pie spice. Using a pastry blender, cut in butter until crumbly. Sprinkle oat mixture evenly over apple mixture.

3 Bake for 30 to 35 minutes or until apples are tender. Serve warm. Makes 6 servings.

COOK'S TIP

Choose apples such as Jonathan, Rome Beauty, Granny Smith, and Gala for baking. These types hold up while cooking and retain good apple flavor.

Apple-Cranberry Crisp

PREP: 20 minutes   **BAKE:** 30 minutes
OVEN: 375°F

NUTRITION FACTS per serving:

CALORIES 168
TOTAL FAT 4 g (3 g sat. fat)
CHOLESTEROL 10 mg
PROTEIN 3 g
CARBOHYDRATE 33 g
FIBER 4 g
SODIUM 31 mg

EXCHANGES 1 Other Carbohydrates, 1 Fruit, 1 Fat

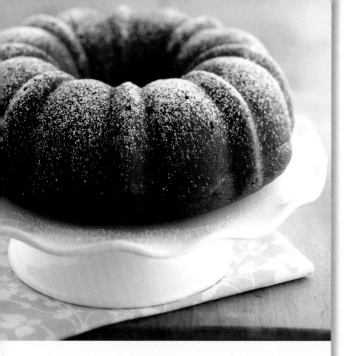

Pumpkin-Gingerbread Coffee Cake

PREP: 25 minutes   **BAKE:** 50 minutes
COOL: 40 minutes   **OVEN:** 350°F

NUTRITION FACTS per serving:

CALORIES 244
TOTAL FAT 6 g (1 g sat. fat)
CHOLESTEROL 40 mg
PROTEIN 6 g
CARBOHYDRATE 44 g
FIBER 2 g
SODIUM 189 mg

EXCHANGES 2 Starch, 1 Other
Carbohydrates, 1 Fat

NUTRITION NOTE

Pumpkin is a good source of vitamin A, which promotes eye health, growth, bone development, and immunity.

2¼	cups all-purpose flour
1¼	cups white whole wheat flour or whole wheat flour
1½	teaspoons baking powder
1½	teaspoons pumpkin pie spice
½	teaspoon ground ginger
½	teaspoon baking soda
½	teaspoon salt
1¼	cups buttermilk or sour fat-free milk*
1	cup canned pumpkin
¾	cup packed brown sugar
⅔	cup mild-flavor molasses
⅓	cup canola oil
3	eggs, lightly beaten
	Powdered sugar

1 Preheat oven to 350°F. Grease and lightly flour a 10-inch fluted tube pan; set aside. In a large bowl combine all-purpose flour, white whole wheat flour, baking powder, pumpkin pie spice, ginger, baking soda, and salt; set aside.

2 In a medium bowl whisk together buttermilk, pumpkin, brown sugar, molasses, oil, and eggs. Add to flour mixture and stir just until moistened (mixture will be thick). Spoon mixture evenly into prepared pan.

3 Bake for 50 to 55 minutes or until top springs back when lightly touched and cake sides pull away from the sides of the pan. Cool in the pan on a wire rack for 10 minutes. Invert cake onto a wire rack. Cool about 30 minutes. Sift powdered sugar over cake before serving. Serve warm. Makes 16 servings.

*To make 1¼ cups sour fat-free milk, place 1 tablespoon lemon juice or vinegar in a glass measuring cup. Add enough fat-free milk to equal 1¼ cups total liquid; stir. Let stand for 5 minutes before using.

- 1 cup whole bran cereal
- ¾ cup all-purpose flour
- ½ cup white whole wheat flour
- 1 teaspoon baking powder
- ¼ teaspoon baking soda
- ¼ teaspoon salt
- 1 cup fat-free milk
- ½ cup packed brown sugar
- 1 egg, lightly beaten
- 2 tablespoons canola oil
- ½ teaspoon almond extract
- ½ cup coarsely chopped dried cranberries
- ½ cup chopped almonds, toasted

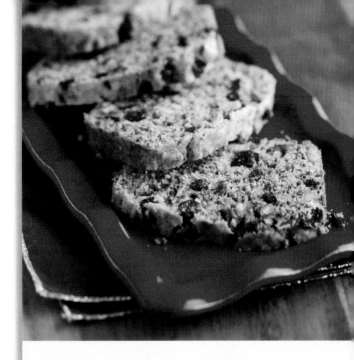

1 Preheat oven to 350°F. Grease the bottom and ½ inch up sides of an 8×4×2-inch loaf pan; set aside. In a large bowl stir together whole bran cereal, all-purpose flour, white whole wheat flour, baking powder, baking soda, and salt. Make a well in center of the flour mixture; set aside.

2 In a medium bowl combine milk, brown sugar, egg, oil, and almond extract. Add milk mixture all at once to flour mixture. Stir just until moistened (batter should be lumpy). Fold in dried cranberries and almonds. Spoon batter into prepared pan.

3 Bake for 45 to 50 minutes or until a wooden toothpick inserted near center comes out clean. Cool in pan on a wire rack for 10 minutes. Remove from pan. Cool completely on wire rack. Wrap and store overnight before slicing. Makes 12 servings.

Cranberry-Almond Bread

PREP: 25 minutes **BAKE:** 45 minutes
COOL: 2 hours **STAND:** overnight
OVEN: 350°F

NUTRITION FACTS per serving:
- -

CALORIES 165
TOTAL FAT 5 g (0 g sat. fat)
CHOLESTEROL 18 mg
PROTEIN 4 g
CARBOHYDRATE 28 g
FIBER 3 g
SODIUM 137 mg

EXCHANGES 1 Starch, 1 Other Carbohydrates, 0.5 Fat

6 cups sliced, cored cooking apple (such as Jonathan or Rome Beauty) (about 2 pounds)

3 tablespoons sugar

1 teaspoon ground cinnamon

1 tablespoon cornstarch

1 recipe Whole Wheat Pastry
Fat-free milk

1 In a 2-quart rectangular baking dish arrange apple slices; set aside. In a small bowl combine sugar and cinnamon; set aside 1 teaspoon of the mixture. Stir cornstarch into remaining sugar mixture. Sprinkle sugar-cornstarch mixture on apples; toss to combine.

2 Preheat oven to 375°F. On a lightly floured surface, flatten Whole Wheat Pastry dough. Roll dough from center to edges into a 10×5-inch rectangle. Cut pastry lengthwise into ten ½-inch-wide strips. Carefully place five pastry strips crosswise over apples. Fold alternate pastry strips back halfway. Place one of the remaining pastry strips in the center across the strips already in place. Unfold the folded strips; fold back remaining crosswise strips. Place another of the remaining pastry strips across the first set of strips parallel to the strip in the center. Repeat the weaving steps with remaining pastry strip. Trim pastry strips; tuck ends into dish. Brush pastry with milk; sprinkle with reserved sugar mixture.

3 Bake for 40 to 45 minutes or until apples are tender. Serve warm or cool. Makes 8 servings.

Whole Wheat Pastry: In a medium bowl stir together ½ cup all-purpose flour, ¼ cup whole wheat pastry flour or whole wheat flour, 2 tablespoons toasted wheat germ, and ⅛ teaspoon ground nutmeg. Using a pastry blender, cut in 3 tablespoons butter until mixture resembles coarse crumbs. Sprinkle 1 tablespoon cold water over part of the mixture; toss with a fork. Push moistened dough to side of bowl. Repeat, using 1 tablespoon cold water at a time, until moistened (2 to 3 tablespoons cold water total). Form dough into a ball.

Lattice-Topped Apple Pie

PREP: 30 minutes   **BAKE:** 40 minutes
OVEN: 375°F

NUTRITION FACTS per serving:

CALORIES 152
TOTAL FAT 5 g (2 g sat. fat)
CHOLESTEROL 12 mg
PROTEIN 2 g
CARBOHYDRATE 26 g
FIBER 3 g
SODIUM 48 mg

EXCHANGES 1 Other Carbohydrates, 1 Fruit, 0.5 Fat

- 1 recipe Oil Pastry
- 1 12.3-ounce package light firm silken-style tofu (fresh bean curd)
- 1 15-ounce can pumpkin
- ⅔ cup sugar or sugar substitute blend* equivalent to ⅔ cup sugar
- 1 teaspoon ground cinnamon
- ¼ teaspoon salt
- ¼ teaspoon ground ginger
- ⅛ teaspoon ground cloves
- Light frozen whipped dessert topping, thawed (optional)
- Ground cinnamon (optional)
- Chopped crystallized ginger (optional)

1 Preheat oven to 375°F. Prepare Oil Pastry. On a well-floured surface, use your hands to slightly flatten pastry dough. Roll dough from center to edge into a circle about 12 inches in diameter. To transfer pastry, wrap it around the rolling pin. Unroll pastry into a 9-inch pie plate. Ease pastry into pie plate, being careful not to stretch pastry. Trim pastry to ½ inch beyond edge of pie plate. Fold under extra pastry. Flute or crimp edge as desired. Do not prick.

2 Place tofu in a blender. Cover and blend until very smooth, stopping to scrape down side of container as necessary. Add pumpkin, sugar, 1 teaspoon cinnamon, salt, ginger, and cloves. Cover and blend until well mixed. Pour pumpkin mixture into pastry-lined pie plate, spreading to an even layer.

3 To prevent overbrowning, cover edge of the pie with foil. Bake for 25 minutes. Remove foil. Bake for 30 minutes more. Cool on a wire rack. Cover and refrigerate within 2 hours.

4 To serve, if desired, top with whipped topping, additional ground cinnamon, and crystallized ginger. Makes 10 servings.

*Sugar Substitute: Choose Equal Sugar Lite. Follow package directions to use product amount equivalent to ⅔ cup sugar.

Per serving with substitute: same as above, except 164 cal., 24 carbo.
Exchanges: 0.5 Other Carbohydrates.

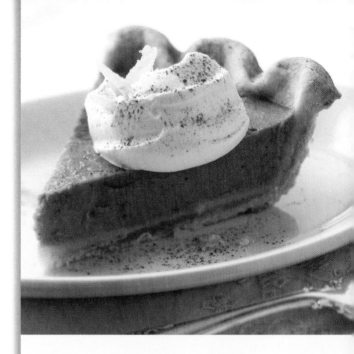

Light-Style Pumpkin Pie

PREP: 25 minutes   **BAKE:** 55 minutes
OVEN: 375°F

NUTRITION FACTS per serving:

CALORIES 190
TOTAL FAT 6 g (1 g sat. fat)
CHOLESTEROL 0 mg
PROTEIN 3 g
CARBOHYDRATE 31 g
FIBER 2 g
SODIUM 151 mg

EXCHANGES 1 Starch, 1 Other Carbohydrates, 1 Fat

Oil Pastry: In a medium bowl stir together 1⅓ cups all-purpose flour and ¼ teaspoon salt. Add ¼ cup cooking oil and ¼ cup fat-free milk all at once to flour mixture. Stir lightly with a fork until combined (dough will appear crumbly). Use your hands to gently work dough into a ball.

12 reduced-fat vanilla wafers

1½ 8-ounce packages reduced-fat cream cheese (Neufchâtel), softened

3 ounces white chocolate baking squares (with cocoa butter), melted and cooled

½ cup sugar

¼ cup fat-free milk

1½ teaspoons vanilla

1 egg white, lightly beaten

Chocolate curls, small whole or sliced strawberries, and/or sliced kiwifruit (optional)

White Chocolate Mini Cheesecakes

PREP: 20 minutes **BAKE:** 20 minutes

COOL: 1 hour 10 minutes **CHILL:** 3 to 24 hours

OVEN: 350°F

NUTRITION FACTS per serving:

CALORIES 169
TOTAL FAT 10 g (6 g sat. fat)
CHOLESTEROL 25 mg
PROTEIN 4 g
CARBOHYDRATE 17 g
FIBER 0 g
SODIUM 140 mg

EXCHANGES 1 Other Carbohydrates, 1 Medium-Fat Meat, 1 Fat

1 Preheat oven to 350°F. Line twelve 2½-inch muffin cups with foil or paper baking cups. Place one wafer in the bottom of each muffin cup. Set aside.

2 For filling, in a medium bowl beat cream cheese with an electric mixer on medium speed for 30 seconds. Beat in melted white chocolate, sugar, milk, and vanilla until well mixed. Stir in egg white. Spoon filling into prepared muffin cups, filling each about three-quarters full.

3 Bake about 20 minutes or until set. Cool in muffin cups on a wire rack for 10 minutes. (Centers may dip slightly as they cool.) Remove cheesecakes from pans. Cool on a wire rack for 1 hour. Cover and chill for 3 to 24 hours.

4 If desired, garnish with chocolate curls, strawberries, and/or kiwifruit before serving. Makes 12 mini cheesecakes.

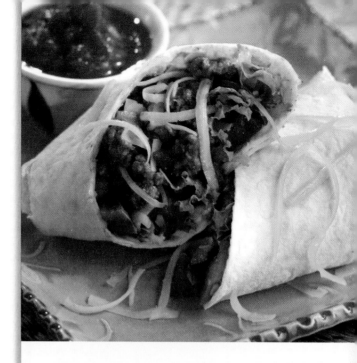

6	8-inch fat-free flour tortillas
12	ounces extra-lean ground beef
½	cup chopped onion (1 medium)
2	cloves garlic, minced
½	cup chopped green sweet pepper (1 small)
½	cup bottled salsa or picante sauce
2	teaspoons dried Mexican seasoning
1½	cups shredded lettuce
1	cup chopped tomatoes (2 medium)
½	cup shredded reduced-fat cheddar or Monterey Jack cheese (2 ounces)
	Shredded reduced-fat cheddar or Monterey Jack cheese
	Bottled salsa or picante sauce (optional)

1 Wrap tortillas in foil; bake in a 350°F oven about 10 minutes or until warmed.

2 Meanwhile, in a large skillet cook the ground beef, onion, and garlic over medium-high heat until meat is brown and onion is tender. Drain off fat. Stir in sweet pepper, the ½ cup salsa or picante sauce, and the Mexican seasoning. Bring to boiling; reduce heat. Simmer, covered, for 10 minutes.

3 Place tortillas on work surface. Top each tortilla with about ½ cup of the meat mixture and some of the lettuce and tomatoes. Sprinkle with the ½ cup cheese. Fold in sides; roll up. Cut in half to serve. If desired, sprinkle with additional cheese and pass additional salsa or picante sauce. Makes 6 servings.

Soft-Shell Burritos

PREP: 35 minutes
OVEN: 350°F

NUTRITION FACTS per serving:

CALORIES 252
TOTAL FAT 7 g (3 g sat. fat)
CHOLESTEROL 42 mg
PROTEIN 16 g
CARBOHYDRATE 29 g
FIBER 2 g
SODIUM 532 mg

EXCHANGES 1.5 Starch, 2 Lean Meat, 1 Vegetable

Chicken Fingers

PREP: 15 minutes
BAKE: 12 minutes
OVEN: 450°F

NUTRITION FACTS per serving:

CALORIES 212
TOTAL FAT 3 g (1 g sat. fat)
CHOLESTEROL 102 mg
PROTEIN 23 g
CARBOHYDRATE 23 g
FIBER 0 g
SODIUM 236 mg

EXCHANGES 1.5 Starch,
2.5 Very Lean Meat

12 ounces skinless, boneless chicken breasts
1 lightly beaten egg
1 tablespoon honey
1 teaspoon prepared mustard
1 cup packaged cornflake crumbs or 2 cups cornflakes, finely crushed
   Dash black pepper
   Purchased dipping sauce (optional)

1 Cut chicken into 3×¾-inch strips. In a shallow dish combine the egg, honey, and mustard. In another shallow dish stir together cornflake crumbs and pepper. Dip chicken strips into the egg mixture; roll in crumb mixture to coat.

2 Arrange chicken strips on an ungreased baking sheet. Bake in a 450°F oven about 12 minutes or until golden and chicken is tender and no longer pink. If desired, serve with your favorite dipping sauce. Makes 4 servings.

- ¼ cup low-fat mayonnaise dressing
- 1 teaspoon Dijon-style mustard
- ¼ cup finely snipped dried tart cherries or raisins
- 4 hamburger buns, split
- 4 ¾-ounce slices mozzarella cheese
- 6 ounces thinly sliced cooked turkey breast
- 1 medium tomato, thinly sliced

1 In a small bowl stir together the mayonnaise dressing, mustard, and cherries or raisins. Spread the bottoms of the buns with the dressing mixture. Top with cheese, turkey, and tomato. Add bun tops. Makes 4 sandwiches.

Make-Ahead Directions: Prepare as above. Wrap each sandwich in plastic wrap. Chill for up to 24 hours. To tote, place in insulated lunch bags with an ice pack.

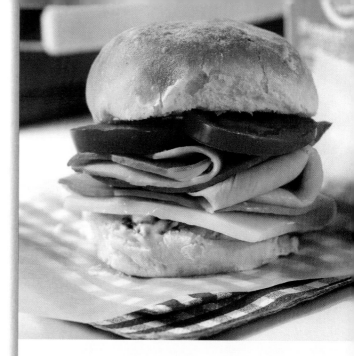

Lunch Box Sub Sandwiches

START TO FINISH: 15 minutes

NUTRITION FACTS per sandwich:

- -

CALORIES 301
TOTAL FAT 8 g (3 g sat. fat)
CHOLESTEROL 45 mg
PROTEIN 22 g
CARBOHYDRATE 34 g
FIBER 2 g
SODIUM 515 mg

EXCHANGES 2 Starch, 2.5 Medium-Fat Meat

2 14-ounce cans reduced-sodium chicken broth

2 cups water

¼ teaspoon black pepper

1 cup dried twisted spaghetti or broken fusilli

3 cups vegetable pieces (such as thinly sliced carrots, small broccoli florets, chopped green or red sweet pepper, and/or fresh or frozen whole kernel corn)

1½ cups cubed cooked chicken (about 8 ounces)

1 tablespoon snipped fresh basil

¼ cup finely shredded Parmesan cheese (1 ounce)

Choose-a-Vegetable Chicken and Pasta Soup

START TO FINISH: 40 minutes

NUTRITION FACTS per serving:

CALORIES 172
TOTAL FAT 4 g (2 g sat. fat)
CHOLESTEROL 35 mg
PROTEIN 16 g
CARBOHYDRATE 18 g
FIBER 2 g
SODIUM 447 mg

EXCHANGES 1 Starch, 1.5 Lean Meat, 1 Vegetable

1 In a Dutch oven combine the broth, the water, and black pepper; bring to boiling. Stir in the pasta. Return to boiling; reduce heat. Simmer, covered, for 5 minutes. Stir in vegetables. Return to boiling; reduce heat. Simmer, covered, for 5 to 8 minutes more or until vegetables and pasta are tender. Stir in chicken and basil; heat through. To serve, top with Parmesan cheese. Makes 6 main-dish serving.

- 2 cups elbow macaroni (8 ounces)
- 2 cups reduced-fat milk
- 2 tablespoons all-purpose flour
- ½ teaspoon dry mustard
- ¼ teaspoon salt
- ⅛ teaspoon black pepper
- ½ cup shredded cheddar cheese (2 ounces)
- 2 ounces American cheese, cubed (½ cup)
- ½ cup coarsely crushed purchased seasoned croutons
- 2 tablespoons finely shredded Parmesan cheese

Cheese shapes (optional)

1 Cook pasta according to package directions; drain and return to pan.

2 Meanwhile, in a large screw-top jar combine 1 cup of the milk, the flour, mustard, salt, and pepper; cover and shake until combined. Pour into a medium saucepan. Stir in the remaining 1 cup milk. Cook and stir over medium heat just until bubbly. Reduce heat to low. Add cheddar cheese and American cheese, stirring until melted. Pour sauce over pasta, stirring until combined. Spoon into a 1½-quart casserole.

3 Bake, covered, in a 350°F oven for 15 minutes. In a small bowl stir together the croutons and Parmesan cheese; sprinkle over casserole. Bake, uncovered, about 5 minutes more or until heated through. Let stand 5 minutes before serving. If desired, garnish each serving with a cheese shape. Makes 5 servings.

Macaroni and Cheese

PREP: 30 minutes **BAKE:** 20 minutes
STAND: 5 minutes **OVEN:** 350°F

NUTRITION FACTS per serving:

CALORIES 346
TOTAL FAT 11 g (7 g sat. fat)
CHOLESTEROL 33 mg
PROTEIN 16 g
CARBOHYDRATE 44g
FIBER 2 g
SODIUM 479 mg

EXCHANGES 3 Starch, 1 High-Fat Meat

Nonstick cooking spray

1¾	cups all-purpose flour
1	tablespoon sugar
1	tablespoon baking powder
¼	teaspoon salt
¼	teaspoon ground cinnamon
1½	cups fat-free milk
⅔	cup mashed ripe banana (2 medium)
1	slightly beaten egg
2	tablespoons cooking oil
2	cups bias-sliced banana
½	cup frozen light whipped dessert topping
8	maraschino cherries

Banana-Waffle Stacks

PREP: 15 minutes

BAKE: per waffle baker directions

NUTRITION FACTS per serving:

CALORIES 228
TOTAL FAT 5 g (1 g sat.fat)
CHOLESTEROL 27 mg
PROTEIN 6 g
CARBOHYDRATE 41 g
FIBER 2 g
SODIUM 257 mg

EXCHANGES 1.5 Starch, 1 Fruit, 1 Fat

1 Lightly coat the grids of a waffle baker with nonstick cooking spray. Preheat waffle baker according to manufacturer's directions. Meanwhile, in a large bowl stir together the flour, sugar, baking powder, salt, and cinnamon; set aside. In a medium bowl stir together the milk, mashed banana, egg, and oil. Add to flour mixture and stir until combined (batter should be slightly lumpy).

2 Spoon about 2 tablespoons of the batter onto each quarter of the waffle baker. Close lid quickly; do not open until golden brown. Bake according to manufacturer's directions. When done, use a fork to lift waffle off grids. Repeat with remaining batter.

3 For each serving, stack 3 of the waffles. Top with banana slices and a little dessert topping. Add a maraschino cherry. Serve waffles warm. Makes 8 servings (3 mini waffles per serving).

- 4   hard-cooked eggs, chopped
- ¼   cup shredded reduced-fat Colby Jack cheese (1 ounce)
- 2   tablespoons sweet or dill pickle relish
- 2   tablespoons finely chopped red sweet pepper
- ¼   cup low-fat mayonnaise dressing
- 1   tablespoon prepared mustard
- 10   slices whole wheat and/or white bread
- 5   small romaine leaves

     Halved cherry tomatoes and/or thin bite-size carrot strips

1 In a medium bowl stir together the eggs, cheese, relish, sweet pepper, mayonnaise dressing, and mustard.

2 If desired, use large cookie cutters to cut bread slices into shapes. Layer 5 slices of the bread with lettuce leaves. Spread on egg mixture. Top with remaining bread slices. If desired, garnish sandwiches with cherry tomatoes and/or carrots, using wooden toothpicks to secure. Makes 5 sandwiches.

Egg Salad Sandwiches

START TO FINISH: 20 minutes

NUTRITION FACTS per serving:

CALORIES 365
TOTAL FAT 11 g total fat (3 g sat. fat)
CHOLESTEROL 176 mg
PROTEIN 15 g
CARBOHYDRATE 54 g
FIBER 6 g
SODIUM 599 mg

EXCHANGES 3.5 Starch, 1 Medium-Fat Meat, 0.5 Fat

Sweet-and-Sour Pineapple Chicken

START TO FINISH: 25 minutes

NUTRITION FACTS per serving:
- -

CALORIES 337
TOTAL FAT 6 g (1 g sat. fat)
CHOLESTEROL 49 mg
PROTEIN 23 g
CARBOHYDRATE 46 g
FIBER 3 g
SODIUM 297 mg

EXCHANGES 1.5 Starch, 1 Fruit, 2.5 Very
Lean Meat, 1.5 Vegetable, 1 Fat

1 8-ounce can pineapple chunks (juice-pack)
½ cup bottled sweet-and-sour sauce
12 ounces skinless, boneless chicken breasts, cut into 1-inch pieces
1 tablespoon reduced-sodium soy sauce
1 medium red sweet pepper, cut into bite-size strips (1 cup)
½ cup thinly sliced carrot (1)
4 teaspoons cooking oil
1 cup fresh pea pods, tips and stems removed
2 cups hot cooked rice

1 Drain pineapple, reserving 2 tablespoons of the juice; set pineapple chunks aside. In a small bowl stir together the reserved pineapple juice and the sweet-and-sour sauce; set aside. In a medium bowl toss chicken with soy sauce; set aside.

2 In a large nonstick skillet cook and stir the sweet pepper and carrot in 3 teaspoons of the hot oil over medium-high heat for 3 minutes. Add pea pods. Cook and stir about 1 minute more or until vegetables are crisp-tender. Remove from skillet; set aside.

3 Add remaining 1 teaspoon oil to skillet. Using a slotted spoon, add chicken to skillet. Cook and stir for 3 to 4 minutes or until chicken is no longer pink. Add sweet-and-sour sauce mixture, vegetable mixture, and pineapple chunks; heat through. Serve chicken mixture with hot cooked rice. Makes 4 or 5 servings.

How Recipes Are Analyzed

The Better Homes and Gardens® Test Kitchen uses nutrition analysis software to determine the nutritional value of a single serving of a recipe. Here are some factors to keep in mind regarding each analysis:

- Analyses do not include optional ingredients.

- The first serving size listed is analyzed when a range is given. For example, if a recipe makes 4 to 6 servings, the Nutrition Facts are based on 4 servings.

- When ingredient choices (such as butter or margarine) appear in a recipe, the first one mentioned is used for analysis.

- When milk is a recipe ingredient, the analysis has been calculated using fat-free (skim) milk unless otherwise noted.

- The exchanges, listed for every recipe along with the Nutrition Facts, are based on the exchange list developed by the American Dietetic Association and the American Diabetes Association.

NUTRITION NOTE

Note on Sodium: For this cookbook, the goal was to keep the sodium levels at a reasonable level that would allow you to stay under the recommended limit of 2,400 mg a day. But for recipes that have high sodium ingredients, such as ham or other processed foods, the sodium levels are relatively high—1,000 mg or more. This only occurs in a small number of recipes but is something to watch for if you have hypertension and have been told to follow a low-sodium diet.

Nutrition Notes

Cook's tips

METRIC INFORMATION

The charts on this page provide a guide for converting measurements from the U.S. customary system, which is used throughout this book, to the metric system.

Product Differences

Most of the ingredients called for in the recipes in this book are available in most countries. However, some are known by different names. Here are some common American ingredients and their known counterparts:

- Sugar (white) is granulated, fine granulated, or castor sugar.
- Powdered sugar is icing sugar.
- All-purpose flour is enriched, bleached or unbleached white household flour. When self-rising flour is used in place of all-purpose flour in a recipe that calls for leavening, omit the leavening agent (baking soda or baking powder) and salt.
- Light-color corn syrup is golden syrup.
- Cornstarch is cornflour.
- Baking soda is bicarbonate of soda.
- Vanilla or vanilla extract is vanilla essence.
- Green, red, or yellow sweet peppers are capsicums or bell peppers.
- Golden raisins are sultanas.

Volume and Weight

The United States traditionally uses cup measures for liquid and solid ingredients. The chart below shows the approximate imperial and metric equivalents. If you are accustomed to weighing solid ingredients, the following approximate equivalents will be helpful.

- 1 cup butter, castor sugar, or rice = 8 ounces = ½ pound = 250 grams
- 1 cup flour = 4 ounces = ¼ pound = 125 grams
- 1 cup icing sugar = 5 ounces = 150 grams

Canadian and U.S. volume for a cup measure is 8 fluid ounces (237 ml); the standard metric equivalent is 250 ml.

1 British imperial cup is 10 fluid ounces.

In Australia, 1 tablespoon equals 20 ml, and 4 teaspoons equal 1 Australian tablespoon.

Spoon measures are used for smaller amounts of ingredients. Although the size of the tablespoon varies slightly in different countries, for practical purposes and for recipes in this book, a straight substitution is all that's necessary. Measurements made using cups or spoons should always be level unless stated otherwise.

Common Weight Range Replacements

IMPERIAL / U.S.	METRIC
½ ounce	15 g
1 ounce	25 g or 30 g
4 ounces (¼ pound)	115 g or 125 g
8 ounces (½ pound)	225 g or 250 g
16 ounces (1 pound)	450 g or 500 g
1¼ pounds	625 g
1½ pounds	750 g
2 pounds or 2¼ pounds	1,000 g or 1 Kg

Oven Temperature Equivalents

FAHRENHEIT SETTING	CELSIUS SETTING*	GAS SETTING
300°F	150°C	Gas Mark 2 (very low)
325°F	160°C	Gas Mark 3 (low)
350°F	180°C	Gas Mark 4 (moderate)
375°F	190°C	Gas Mark 5 (moderate)
400°F	200°C	Gas Mark 6 (hot)
425°F	220°C	Gas Mark 7 (hot)
450°F	230°C	Gas Mark 8 (very hot)
475°F	240°C	Gas Mark 9 (very hot)
500°F	260°C	Gas Mark 10 (extremely hot)
Broil	Broil	Grill

*Electric and gas ovens may be calibrated using celsius. However, for an electric oven, increase celsius setting 10 to 20 degrees when cooking above 160°C. For convection or forced air ovens (gas or electric), lower the temperature setting 25°F/10°C when cooking at all heat levels.

Baking Pan Sizes

IMPERIAL / U.S.	METRIC
9×1½-inch round cake pan	22- or 23×4-cm (1.5 L)
9×1½-inch pie plate	22- or 23×4-cm (1 L)
8×8×2-inch square cake pan	20×5-cm (2 L)
9×9×2-inch square cake pan	22- or 23×4.5-cm (2.5 L)
11×7×1½-inch baking pan	28×17×4-cm (2 L)
2-quart rectangular baking pan	30×19×4.5-cm (3 L)
13×9×2-inch baking pan	34×22×4.5-cm (3.5 L)
15×10×1-inch jelly roll pan	40×25×2-cm
9×5×3-inch loaf pan	23×13×8-cm (2 L)
2-quart casserole	2 L

U.S. / Standard Metric Equivalents

⅛ teaspoon = 0.5 ml	
¼ teaspoon = 1 ml	
½ teaspoon = 2 ml	
1 teaspoon = 5 ml	
1 tablespoon = 15 ml	
2 tablespoons = 25 ml	
¼ cup = 2 fluid ounces = 50 ml	
⅓ cup = 3 fluid ounces = 75 ml	
½ cup = 4 fluid ounces = 125 ml	
⅔ cup = 5 fluid ounces = 150 ml	
¾ cup = 6 fluid ounces = 175 ml	
1 cup = 8 fluid ounces = 250 ml	
2 cups = 1 pint = 500 ml	
1 quart = 1 litre	